W9-BPS-330

FEDERAL JUDGES
The Appointing Process

HAROLD W. CHASE

UNIVERSITY OF MINNESOTA PRESS Minneapolis

© Copyright 1972 by the University of Minnesota.
All rights reserved. Printed in the
United States of America at the University
of Minnesota Printing Department, Minneapolis.
Published in the United Kingdom and India
by the Oxford University Press, London
and Delhi, and in Canada by the Copp Clark
Publishing Co. Limited, Toronto

Library of Congress Catalog Card Number: 72-189381

ISBN 0-8166-0647-1

To GEORGE A. GRAHAM

Preface

THE IDEA for this study of how federal judges are appointed was George A. Graham's. He was at that time (1961) director of governmental studies at the Brookings Institution. He was impressed by the fact that, despite the importance of these posts in the American system of governance, little scholarly attention had been given to the matter of who gets the posts and how. Since that time, several scholars whose works are cited in the chapters to follow have done much to remedy that situation and it is hoped that this work added to theirs will provide a good and accurate picture and evaluation of the appointment process.

There is likely to be some confusion when one writes or speaks about "federal judges." Technically, every judge who operates in the federal system (as opposed to a state system) is a federal judge. But there are significant differences among the various federal courts and justices. One such difference is most helpful in categorizing them. Some of our federal courts are Article III courts, which means that they have been constituted by Congress in accordance with the provisions of Article III of the Constitution. Judges in these courts serve, in the words of Article III, "during good behavior," i.e., for life unless they choose to resign voluntarily. Other courts like the territorial

courts, certain courts in the District of Columbia, the Tax Court, and
the United States Court of Military Appeals have been set up by
Congress in consequence of Congress's power to do what is "necessary and proper" to execute its enumerated powers under Article I,
section 8, of the Constitution. Judges in these courts have fixed terms.
For example, judges in the territorial courts are appointed for eight
years except in Puerto Rico where by special provision judges hold
their offices "during good behavior."

In this study, George Graham and I decided in the beginning that
I would deal only with the judges who are appointed for life terms.
Specifically, this means the judges of the following courts:

The United States Courts of Appeals. These courts are the inter-
mediate appellate courts, created in 1891 to relieve the Supreme
Court from considering all appeals in cases originally decided by the
federal trial courts. Their decisions are subject to discretionary review
or appeal in the Supreme Court. There are eleven such courts of appeals, including one for the District of Columbia. Each state and ter-
ritory is assigned to a circuit. The judges on these courts receive a
salary of $42,500 a year.

The United States District Courts. These are the trial courts of
general federal jurisdiction. Each state has at least one such court, as
do the District of Columbia and the Commonwealth of Puerto Rico.
There are ninety-one district courts. (This figure does not include the
district courts for the Canal Zone, Guam, and the Virgin Islands which
are regarded as "legislative" courts and whose judges have only
an eight-year term.) District judges are paid $40,000 a year.

The United States Court of Claims. Basically, this court, established in 1855, has original jurisdiction to render judgment on any
claim against the United States based upon the Constitution, congressional acts, regulations of the executive agencies, or contracts
with the United States. The full panoply of its jurisdiction is set forth
in the U.S. Code Title 28, 1491–1506. The judges on this court receive $42,500 a year.

The United States Court of Customs and Patent Appeals. This
court, established in 1909, decides questions arising under the customs
laws. Since 1929, it has had jurisdiction to review certain patent and
trademark cases. It also reviews some of the decisions of the Customs

Court. The judges receive the same compensation as those on the Claims Court.

The United States Customs Court. This court, an outgrowth of the Board of United States Appraisers, and established as a court in 1926, has exclusive jurisdiction over civil actions under the tariff laws and internal revenue laws relating to imported merchandise, as well as other important functions. The judges on this court are paid $40,000 a year.

It is difficult to fix on the precise number of positions on the appeals and district courts at any time, for they are constantly being expanded. There were substantial increases in the number of judgeships on these courts in 1961, 1966, and 1970. Adding to the difficulty of giving precise figures is the practice Congress follows of establishing from time to time a new judgeship with the proviso that "the first vacancy occurring in the office of district judge in said district shall not be filled." The reason for doing this is to ease court congestion where a heavy case load does not appear to be a permanent problem or where a sitting judge is suffering a disability but will not retire, the thought being that there is not a long-range need for two posts—and that time will take care of the situation. In the judgeship bill of 1966, out of thirty-five new district judgeships, five were designated as judgeships which would terminate with the first vacancy; in 1970, three out of sixty-one new judgeships were so designated. In any event, as of this writing the number of federal judicial posts is as shown in the tabulation.

Court	No.
Courts of appeals	97
District courts	397
Court of Claims	7
Court of Customs and Patent Appeals	5
Customs Court	9
Total	515

It seemed clear to George Graham and me from the outset that to do a thorough study of the kind we envisioned it would be necessary to obtain Department of Justice cooperation. First, we wanted access to records pertaining to appointments. Second, we felt that, since we were starting at a time when a whole host of new appointments would be made, it would be most enlightening if I could be for a time a witness to the process as it took place, much as Theodore White was permitted to observe the process of presidential electioneering.

As luck would have it Nicholas Katzenbach was the deputy attorney general and Robert Kennedy the attorney general. Although I had not known Katzenbach well, we had been classmates as undergraduates and did know each other. Also, as a former professor, he understands and appreciates the scholarly enterprise. As we talked about the possibility of giving me access to records, it was clear that he did not regard the request as outrageous. He felt that a responsible scholarly job on the process as a whole was a good idea. He was sensitive about possible violations of confidences and about hurting particular individuals. We agreed that it should be possible to do such a study accurately and thoroughly without identifying individuals where this might unnecessarily hurt someone. I believe I have done that in this book. References to specific individuals which came from newspaper stories or other sources I feel do not constitute a breach of my agreement with Katzenbach. Before we could go ahead, we needed the approval of Robert Kennedy. His reaction was typical for him. Judicial selection was the people's business as well as his. He was willing for me to do the study and call the shots as I saw them but he wanted to be reassured (by Katzenbach) that I would do a responsible job. I have endeavored to keep the faith.

And so for a period of about two months in the fall of 1962, I was placed in the hands of Joseph Dolan, one of Katzenbach's assistant deputies and the man who did the leg work for the administration on judicial appointments. I was established in a conference room between the offices of Katzenbach and Dolan. The records I wanted were brought to me there. My location proved to be most fortuitous. Katzenbach would pass through the conference room several times during the day. As he walked through, he would occasionally ask how things were going and exchange pleasantries. I seized on these moments to ask questions about things I had read or observed. In this way, I had the benefit of hours upon hours of "interview" time that I would never have dared ask for on a formal basis. Also, after a few weeks in which we saw a great deal of each other and "established rapport," Dolan began the custom of inviting me in whenever there were discussions in his office on federal judgeships. I was impressed with how willing politicians are to talk before a complete stranger once he is vouched for. Dolan would introduce me as "a professor doing a study of the selection of federal judges." He would then usually be asked, "Is it all right to talk in front of him?" Upon being assured by Dolan that it was, the talk was most frank.

During my stint at the department, I had a unique opportunity to see and pick the minds of a few of the truly extraordinary team which Robert Kennedy had assembled, men like Burke Marshall, John Doar, William A. Geoghegan, and John W. Douglas. All of them were interested in what I was doing and all of them seemed to take special interest in seeing that I really understood what the selection process was all about.

After the period in the department, I did extensive interviewing around Capitol Hill to get a feel for how senators and other knowledgeable political leaders, staff men, and newsmen viewed the selection process. Following that, I went on the road. We had picked a sample of seven states in which I would interview lawyers and judges. The sample was designed to ensure that I would get a good and diverse group to interview. I went to California, Texas, New York, Georgia, Virginia, Minnesota, and Missouri. In all, I interviewed forty judges and a random sample in each state of thirty lawyers who practiced in the federal courts. As I moved about I checked in with other scholars who were interested and had a special knowledge with respect to federal judges. All of them were generous with time and ideas. In addition everywhere I went I endeavored to talk to people in the United States attorney's office and to knowledgeable politicians and newsmen.

Also, Bernard Segal, long-time chairman of the American Bar Association Committee on Federal Judiciary, whose activities are described in detail later in this book, was most generous with his time and his data. In view of some of my commentary, Mr. Segal may regret his generosity. But I wish to make clear that I truly appreciate his help and that my respect and admiration for him and his work are unbounded, even though I do not always agree with his ideas.

Beyond those already mentioned, there are others I would like at this time to single out for special mention. Many who helped asked that I not mention them by name. I will respect the requests, while asking them now once again to accept my thanks. The following people all helped enormously but must not be held responsible for my opinions and conclusions: Professor William M. Beaney, General Dwight D. Eisenhower, the Honorable Harry S. Truman, the Honorable William P. Rogers, the Honorable Lawrence E. Walsh, Ernest C. Friesen, Jr., Anna C. Denean, Marjorie Girth, Janet Porter, and Gene Anderson.

Last, but certainly not least, I must also acknowledge a great debt to my family. For several years, collecting data on judges was "family fun" in the Chase family. Sons Bryce and Eric, daughter-in-law Helen, and my wonderful mother-in-law, Vera M. Fadden, all contributed mightily to the efforts of my wife, Bernice, and me to assemble data on all the federal judges from 1789 to the present. It is hoped that these data can be further mined to provide additional insights into the federal judiciary and the judicial process.

Whatever accomplishment this book may represent, I must fully share it with Bernice. This work is truly as much hers as mine and only her modesty prevents her name from appearing on the title page. At every stage of the study she helped, encouraged, and provided inspiration.

Finally, I would like to say a word about the organization of the book. After a first chapter giving an overview of the appointment process, there are chapters on the Kennedy administration, the Eisenhower administration, the American Bar Association Committee on Federal Judiciary, and the Johnson administration in that order. The reader may wonder why I did not deal with the administrations chronologically and consecutively. I placed the Kennedy administration chapter first because it was based on the fullest exploration. It was the one administration I watched in operation close up for a substantial period of time. Based on what I learned from that exploration I was able to reconstruct from interviews with the chief participants in the Eisenhower administration how the appointment process worked while they were in office. In short, it seemed to me that the Eisenhower administration and the Johnson administration (in which I had less opportunity to observe systematically) could be better understood against the backdrop of a description of the process in the Kennedy administration. As to the positioning of the chapter on the American Bar Association committee, it appeared to me that the flow of events could be more interestingly described and better understood by placing that chapter before the chapter on the Johnson administration. It is my hope that the reader will find the book enjoyable as well as edifying to read. Toward that end, I confess that I sacrificed symmetry and simplicity. Whether I was wise in doing so, the reader will have to judge.

H. C.

July 1972

Contents

FEDERAL JUDGES
The Appointing Process

CHAPTER I

An Overview

ALL MAJOR LEAGUE baseball games are played under a well-defined set of rules and customs by teams of players manning prescribed positions, yet it is probably a safe bet that no two games in major league baseball history have been exactly alike. These generalizations about the national pastime provide a good analogy for the process of appointing federal judges. Such appointments are made pursuant to law and custom largely by a "lineup" of individuals who man prescribed positions. In making appointments, the "players" interact within the framework of law and custom differently each time. This is not to suggest that there are not established patterns. Rather, the point is made to stress that the "play" which is involved in each appointment is *sui generis*.

In one respect, the analogy breaks down. A major league baseball team fields nine men and has a roster of eligible players which is limited by statutory baseball law. In the appointing process, there are certain "players" who, of course, must participate in the game: the president; United States senators, some more than others; officials in the Department of Justice; the candidates for the judgeship; the Standing Committee on Federal Judiciary of the American Bar Association, particularly the chairman; and political party leaders. But

3

there is no statutory prescription limiting the game to only these participants. Others may be drawn into the process; still others, without limit in number, may inject themselves into the game.

As in baseball, how well the game is played, i.e., how good the appointments are, is determined in large part by the ability, drive, and experience of the players. But the appointing team has the capability of outperforming the greatest of the old New York Yankee teams. As a Department of Justice official observed, when the baseball analogy was mentioned to him, "Yes, but a baseball team can usually win a pennant by winning 70 percent of its games; we like to do better than that."

Law and Custom

Surprisingly enough, in view of the substantial opinion to the contrary, the Constitution is ambiguous concerning how federal judges, save Supreme Court justices, must be appointed. True, Article II, section 2, provides that the president "shall nominate, and by and with the Advice and Consent of the Senate, shall appoint Ambassadors, other public Ministers and Consuls, Judges of the supreme court and all other Officers of the United States, whose appointments are not herein otherwise provided for, and which shall be established by Law . . ." But that is not the end of the provision. It goes on to add "but the Congress may by Law vest the Appointment of such inferior Officers, as they think proper, in the President alone, in the Courts of Law or in the Heads of Departments." Are federal judges "other officers" or "inferior officers"? If they are "inferior officers," then Congress has the power to alter the mode of appointment within the prescribed limits without a constitutional amendment. It could, for example, grant to the Supreme Court the power to appoint judges to the lower federal courts.

For much of our history, it was simply assumed that federal judges were "other officers."[1] Early statutes dealing with federal judges stated only that they "be appointed" without indicating how, and the practice was from the beginning for the president to appoint with the advice and consent of the Senate. As Justice Story pointed out in a footnote in his celebrated *Commentaries on the Constitution of the United States*:

Whether the judges of the inferior courts of the United States are such inferior officers as the constitution contemplates to be within the power of congress to prescribe the mode of appointment of, so as to vest it in the president alone, or in the courts of law, or in the heads of departments, is a point upon which no solemn judgment has ever been had. The practical construction has uniformly been, that they are not such inferior officers. And no act of congress prescribes the mode of their appointment.[2]

But, in 1891, years after Story first wrote those words, Congress chose to provide specifically that "there shall be appointed by the President of the United States, by and with the advice and consent of the Senate, in each circuit an additional circuit judge."[3] In the recodification of the law in 1948, it was provided explicitly for the first time that all circuit and district judges be appointed with the advice and consent of the Senate.[4] This is in the law to this day.[5] Unfortunately, the legislative history of these provisions yields no clue to why Congress adopted them. No explanation was ever given nor were questions raised over them in the debates on the bills of which they were a part. It seems a fair conclusion that Congress did not consider that in these provisions it was making a significant change in constitutional interpretation.

As a part of three excellent articles published in the *Michigan Law Review* in 1930, Professor Burke Shartel argued persuasively that federal judges below the Supreme Court level are "inferior officers" in the constitutional sense. He suggested that although "inferior" is usually defined as "petty" or "unimportant," it "can also be understood in a relational sense," i.e., inferior to others.[6] This is precisely the view that had been taken by the United States Court of Claims in 1878 in a case not involving judges but other "inferior officers."[7] Thus, even very important officers could in that sense be inferior. As Shartel so well pointed out, the words of the Constitution support use of the relational connotation of inferior particularly with respect to federal judges, for the courts upon which they sit, when referred to in the Constitution, are styled as "inferior courts."[8]

Whatever the Framers intended regarding the appointment of federal judges, the Senate is deeply involved in the process, whether it be so required by the Constitution alone or by the Constitution and statutory law made in pursuance of it. We can only speculate on how the courts would react if Congress were to attempt to lodge the power to appoint the judges in the president alone, the courts of law, or the

5

attorney general (as head of a department) and the legislation were challenged.[9]

SENATORIAL COURTESY

What was the purpose of the Founding Fathers in granting the Senate the power to advise on and consent to appointments? In what manner did they expect the Senate to carry out these functions? Recall that formidable protagonists for two conflicting proposals regarding appointments battled to prevail at the Constitutional Convention. There were those, including Hamilton and Madison, who wanted the president alone to have the power to appoint; others, including Sherman and Franklin, wanted the Senate alone to have the power.[10] In *Federalist* 76, Hamilton, despite his own bias, preserved for us the flavor of the compromise which resulted and indicated in a general way what was expected of the Senate:

> The sole and undivided responsibility of one man will naturally beget a livelier sense of duty and a more exact regard to reputation. He will, on this account, feel himself under stronger obligations, and more interested to investigate with care the qualities requisite to the stations to be filled, and to prefer with impartiality the persons who may have the fairest pretensions to them. He will have *fewer* personal attachments to gratify, than a body of men who may each be supposed to have an equal number; and will be so much less liable to be misled by the sentiments of friendship and of affection. A single well-directed man, by a single understanding, cannot be distracted and warped by that diversity of views, feelings, and interests, which frequently distract and warp the resolutions of a collective body. . . .
>
> The truth of the principles here advanced seems to have been felt by the most intelligent of those who have found fault with the provision made, in this respect, by the convention. . . .
>
> To what purpose then require the cooperation of the Senate? I answer, that the necessity of their concurrence would have a powerful, though, in general, a silent operation. It would be an excellent check upon the spirit of favoritism in the President, and would tend greatly to prevent the appointment of unfit characters from State prejudice, from family connection, from personal attachment, or from a view to popularity. In addition to this, it would be an efficacious source of stability in the administration.

According to Hamilton, then, the Senate was expected to participate no further in the appointment process than to pass on presidential nominations and to do so *as a body*. In practice, however, from the earliest days, senators have not been willing to accept such a limited role, and for understandable reasons.

Senators, whether chosen by state legislatures, as they were at an earlier time, or by the voters of the state, must continuously nurture their political support back home; that is, if they hope for additional terms in office—and it is a rare senator who does not. In this connection, senators from the First Congress on have recognized that one or two senators have a much greater stake in a particular appointment than others. It is, of course, exceedingly helpful to a senator to be able to reward supporters with good posts in the federal government. Conversely, it is enormously damaging to a senator's prestige if a president of his own party ignores him when it comes to making an appointment from or to the senator's own state. What is even more damaging to a senator's prestige and political power is for the president to appoint to high federal office someone who is known back home as a political opponent of the senator. It was easy for senators to see that if they joined together against the president to protect their individual interests in appointments, they could to a large degree assure that the president could only make such appointments as would be palatable to them as individuals. Out of such considerations grew the custom of "senatorial courtesy."

For a good part of our history, "senatorial courtesy" could be defined accurately as a custom by which senators would support one of their number who objected to an appointment to a federal office in his state, provided the senator and the president were of the same party. It was only necessary for the senator to state that the nominee was "personally obnoxious" to him to invoke the courtesy.[11] That definition is too narrowly drawn and too absolutely stated to square with the practice that has prevailed from the 1930's to this day.

In our day, senatorial courtesy has come to mean that senators will give serious consideration to and be favorably disposed to support an individual senator of the president's party who opposes a nominee to an office in his state. But, as the chief clerk of the Senate Judiciary Committee has put it, "He just can't incant a few magic words like 'personally obnoxious' and get away with it. He must be prepared to fight, giving his reasons for opposing the nominee." If his reasons are not persuasive to other senators or if he is not a respected member of the Senate, he stands a chance of losing his fight.

7

That it is not enough for a senator to claim merely that a nominee is personally obnoxious to ensure Senate rejection was made clear in an obviously carefully prepared statement delivered to the Senate in 1947 by the chairman of the Judiciary Committee, Alexander Wiley. In the course of the debate over the confirmation of the nomination of Joe B. Dooley to be United States district judge for the northern district of Texas, Senator O'Daniel of Texas and of the president's party protested that Dooley was personally obnoxious. Although tending to credit senators with the best of motives and overstating the case for "adhering to the personal-obnoxiousness objection," Wiley's words constitute a candid assessment of the factors which most senaators will take into account when one of their number invokes the objection, and are worthy of quotation at length:

As my colleagues read through the Judiciary Committee's memorandum on the subject, they will note that the force of the personal-obnoxiousness objection is one that each individual Senator will have to determine for himself on the merits of the given case. Under the Constitution, the Senate is called upon to advise and consent, but each individual Senator, in turn, has the responsibility for interpreting that language.

I point out that there can be no absolutely inflexible rule with respect to adhering to or ignoring the personal-obnoxiousness objection. . . .

What, then, are the major factors which we must bear in mind in evaluating our actions along this line? I submit that those factors are:

(A) The United States Constitution itself giving the advice-and-consent power to the Senate.

(B) The *broken* practice of respecting personal obnoxiousness and senatorial courtesy.

(C) *The obligation which a Senator may feel to the objecting Senator to respect the latter's judgment.*

(D) Justice for the nominee himself. We must bear in mind, of course, that when a nominee is rejected by the United States Senate for whatever reason, forever after he lives, in a certain sense, under a cloud of official disapproval.

(E) Our obligations to the American public which means our obligation to secure the appointment of fit public servants.

(F) *The factor of whether or not a given nominee is to serve within the particular State of the objecting Senator.*

(G) Whether or not this is the first instance in which the objecting Senator has raised the personal obnoxiousness issue or whether it is a part of a long series of such objections.

(H) Whether or not circumstances permit open discussion of the reasons on which the objecting Senator bases his objection. We can all well understand that if a nominee had insulted a given Senator's wife in some manner, the Senator might not want to bring that to the open attention of the Senate. *Whether or not other Senators would be willing to accept the blanket statement of personal obnoxiousness from a particular Senator without specifying the reasons would depend on one of the preceding points which I stated, namely, the obligation which other Senators feel to the objecting Senator.*[12] [Italics added.]

True, there are precious few cases in our history where a senator of the president's party has lost a pitched battle to reject a nomination to a federal office *in his own state*. But there are a few.[13] Perhaps it was critical and not coincidental to confirmation in the few cases that the other senator from the state was also of the president's party and a sponsor of the nominee. Nonetheless, as indicated by Wiley's statement, most senators realize that there is no guarantee that they will be supported by their colleagues if they seek rejection of a nomination. The possibility of losing a battle, which might prove embarrassing to him, has the effect of making a senator careful about choosing to fight only those battles which he feels pretty sure of winning.

Imagine, for example, the considerations which a southern senator would have to take into account if he were to block the appointment to a federal district judgeship in his state explicitly or implicitly because the nominee was not a devout segregationist. He would have to bear in mind that many senators from other parts of the country could not afford politically to vote against confirmation, despite their realization that breaches in the custom lessen their own power. The fact that senatorial courtesy will not automatically prevail, that there might be a messy fight, and that he could conceivably lose prompts a senator to seek accommodation with the president or his agents rather than to engage them in combat. By the same token, the president and his men are eager for an accommodation because, from their vantage point, a senator's opposition seems generally too formidable to challenge. They tend to feel as Deputy Attorney General Walsh did while he was one of the appointment-makers, ". . . it is virtually impossible to have a person confirmed for a federal judgeship if one of the Senators from his state is either openly or secretly opposed to the nomination."[14]

To be fully appreciated, it must be understood that senatorial courtesy extends beyond a senator of the president's party who objects to an appointment to office in his own state. Senators will sympathetically hear objections of a senator of the state who is not of the president's party.[15] Also, they will give special consideration to the protest of a senator, particularly if he is of the president's party, on an appointment to a national or circuit post when the nominee comes from the senator's state.[16]

Because the Senate has the power to confirm, senators are *legally* free to make whatever conventions they wish, and can agree upon, about how they shall exercise that power. If they chose, they could, legally, go so far as to provide for an automatic veto for any senator to any presidential appointment. To a degree, then, current practice with regard to senatorial courtesy bears the marks of self-restraint. This is not to imply that the president would be powerless in the face of Senate opposition for, as we shall see shortly, he has impressive weapons in his arsenal which he can employ in a contest with the Senate on an appointment.

As a corollary of the development of senatorial courtesy there grew a custom by which senators, when of the president's party, nominated to the president candidates for federal offices in their respective states and, if these candidates passed the president's muster, he appointed them. The basis for this custom was laid early, as a matter of fact in George Washington's administration. One of his nominees to a federal post in Georgia was rejected by the Senate out of courtesy to the Georgia senators (there were not yet distinct political parties). Washington yielded with a mild protest and appointed the nominee of the Georgia senators.[17] Had Washington, with his tremendous prestige, held his ground, he might well have established a precedent which would have stunted the growth of senatorial courtesy. Be that as it may, when later presidents like Theodore Roosevelt and Woodrow Wilson sought to reassert for the presidency the leading role in making appointments to federal offices within specific state boundaries, they met with only limited success.[18] Although some presidents, and indeed some senators, have tried to bully the Senate into giving up the custom of senatorial courtesy, the custom at least in modified form retains vitality.[19] Senate devotion to the custom can readily be understood in terms of self-interest. Nonetheless, all of us tend to rationalize what we do to put the best complexion on our actions. Senator proponents of senatorial courtesy have over the years rationalized it on much the same basis as Senator Douglas did in blocking two appointments by President Truman to a district court in Illinois:

". . . great as the knowledge of a President may be, he cannot, in the nature of things, in the vast majority of instances, know the qualifications of the lawyers and local judges within a given state as well as do the senators from that state. However excellent his general knowledge, the President does not have the detailed knowledge of the qualifications, background, and record of judges in a particular State. . . . "[20] The fact of the matter is that neither a president nor a senator is normally in a position to know from his own knowledge whether or not a particular individual is a good nominee for a judicial post. The question really is who has the better resources for finding out. The resources available to a president dwarf those available to a senator. This is not to imply that a president would always make better appointments than a senator if each were a free agent, because the question of personal standards is pertinent. And in the Douglas-Truman controversy, it would appear that Douglas's candidates were superior to those of the president.[21]

It has become common to exaggerate the role and power of individual senators in the matter of district court appointments. For example, Evan Haynes wrote in his fine book, *Selection and Tenure of Judges,* in 1944 that "with respect to District Court judges . . . the Senate has expropriated the President's power of nomination so far as concerns appointments of interest to senators of the party in power; and the President has virtually surrendered his power directly to local party politics as to appointments in states where the senators are of the opposition."[22] Professor Joseph Harris, writing nine years later, suggested that "the custom of senatorial courtesy . . . has in effect transferred from the President to the senators of his party the selection of district judges in their own state."[23] But as Harris himself so well demonstrated in the facts he marshaled to arrive at a contrary conclusion, when a president chooses to inject himself into the appointment of district judges, he can at times do so effectively as Presidents Theodore Roosevelt, Wilson, and Hoover did.[24] Note the interesting comments in excerpts from a letter Herbert Hoover wrote me shortly before his death:

I suppose that every President leans heavily on his Attorney General for guidance in appointments of Judges, and thus the quality of Judges reflects the goodness of the Attorney General. I appointed the former Solicitor General, William D. Mitchell, a Democrat, and I think you will

11

find him of a high level among Attorney Generals. One of the reasons for my choice was the fact that the Solicitor General had a number of cases before the Supreme Court, and continuity of Government Counsel was desirable.

At the time I began my term as President, the Senators were practically choosing the Federal Judges. Since they controlled confirmation of the President's appointment, the practice had grown up for the President to accept their nominees unless there was substantial opposition. The Senators, by control of appointments of Judges, were able to secure from them appointments to judicial staffs and to influence such jobs as receiverships to their own law firms or their friends. The result was that the standards needed for Judges were far below the level which the then Attorney General and I could wish.

I devised the following method of selection: to meet the needs of Senators and at the same time secure good Judges, the Attorney General was usually advised in advance of approaching retirement of a Judge because of ill health, age, or otherwise. We then selected five or six good appointees and offered the Senators the choice of them. This resulted in a great improvement over the previous method of practically accepting Senators' selections.

And Dean Acheson has provided an interesting insight on how Franklin D. Roosevelt asserted himself with senators. He tells us that when FDR phoned him to urge him to accept nomination to the Court of Appeals for the District of Columbia this was the argument the president used:

The President then explained to me that he was in a row with the Senate about a judicial nomination in Virginia which he had submitted without prior consultation with the Virginia senators. To make his point he wanted to submit three nominations without consultations which the Senate would have to confirm. They were to be: Robert Patterson, afterward Under Secretary and Secretary of War, for the United States Court of Appeals in New York; Francis Biddle, afterward Attorney General and Judge of the Nuremberg Court, for the Court in Philadelphia; and myself for the one in Washington. I could not, he urged, break the symmetry of this plan.[25]

But even granting that senators of the party in power may have "owned" district judgeships at an earlier time in our history, they have not during the incumbency of the presidents since Truman. Appointments to the district bench are not made by the senators alone. There are other parties of interest who are deeply involved in the process. And just as the legal power to confirm, with its corollary, the custom of courtesy, provides a senator with a formidable practical power which he can employ in behalf of a particular nomination, other parties of interest have special powers which can be used as counters. It does not necessarily follow that because individual senators may well be in a position to exercise a veto power in the appointment of judges they must do the appointing. Close examination of the appointment process suggests otherwise.

THE PRESIDENT: EXPECTATIONS AND POWERS

Curiously, at a time when knowledgeable people have been apt to see it as a fact of life that senators appoint district court judges, other (and perhaps some of the same) knowledgeable people have been quick to hold the president or his agents responsible for the quality and character of judicial appointments, giving him or them credit or blame, whichever seemed more appropriate. Editorial writers wise in the ways of government have written:

The heavy responsibility that thus necessarily falls on the President to choose wise judges has been largely delegated during this Administration [Eisenhower] to the Attorney General, and in practice to the Deputy Attorney General. Their performance on the whole has been excellent. [*New York Times,* January 2, 1961.]

It seems to us extremely unfortunate that the Kennedy administration has not made more headway toward freeing the federal courts from the bondage to political patronage. The fact is there has been no headway. [*Christian Science Monitor,* October 6, 1961.]

The nomination of Frank M. Coffin to the United States Court of Appeals, First Circuit, affords a good occasion on which to note the generally high qualifications of President Johnson's appointments to the Federal bench. [*Washington Post,* September 19, 1965.]

Even the American Bar Association's Standing Committee on Federal Judiciary, well versed in the ways of judicial appointments, publicly observed in 1962:

Great and deserved credit will adhere to the Administration if it finally breaks the bonds of partisanship and elevates the judiciary to the level where mere patronage does not play so major a role in appointments to the Bench. The time is especially auspicious for the Administration to forego substantially unbalancing the judiciary any further, and to announce publicly and unequivocally that a policy of bipartisanship has been adopted and will be further effectuated in the years ahead. [They also acknowledged the role played by senators.][26]

These quotations are offered not to suggest that the president and his agents alone are responsible for appointments to the federal bench

13

but rather to demonstrate that, like it or not, the president would be hard put to escape all responsibility for appointments made in his name. Consequently, a number of our presidents have been very concerned that the quality of appointments made during their incumbency be high. And where a president wants to ensure a high level of appointments, he has legal powers which afford him considerable coin with which to bargain with the senators individually and collectively.

First, it is the president who must submit the nomination for formal consideration of the Senate. He is under no legal compulsion to make nominations within a prescribed time limit. He can, therefore, stall or refuse to fill a vacancy. Doing so may be very effective in forcing some concessions from a senator. Our courts are generally and normally overburdened and run well behind in their work. To leave a judgeship unfilled creates difficulties for the sitting judges and lawyers who can usually be counted upon to bring pressure to bear on their recalcitrant senator to seek some kind of rapprochement with the administration. How annoying delay can be to a senator is manifested in this communication from a senator to the deputy attorney general:

> You have had my recommendation of L_____ for a Judgeship since February 3. I am amazed to learn from your letter that you hadn't even begun the FBI check until July 7. There is no legitimate basis for failing to move rapidly on L_____.
>
> I am as aware as you are of the difficulties of the Court Calendar in the District, but I think I am entitled to insist that your Department give fair and expeditious consideration to the names I have pending before you ask for any others.
>
> When action has been taken with reference to those matters presently pending, I will be glad to discuss with you further recommendations.

Refusal to nominate can be particularly effective when coupled with a suggestion "leaked" to the press that a distinguished lawyer or state judge is the president's choice. For then the senator is put in the position of publicly opposing the president's distinguished candidate, which may have a much different impact in legal circles and on public opinion than a situation in which the only apparent candidate is the senator's. The pressure on a senator may even be greater if both the senator's and the president's candidates are known and if there is a feeling among bar and press that the president's candidate is superior.

A second relevant important power of the president is his constitutional mandate "to fill up all Vacancies that may happen during the Recess of the Senate, by granting Commissions which shall expire at the End of their next Session." There has been vigorous argument throughout our history about what the word "happen" means in that context. Some have argued that the president could fill any vacancy which happened to exist during the recess; others have urged that he could only fill those which happened to occur during the recess.[27] The practice has been for presidents to take the broader view of their powers and to fill both kinds of vacancies. This practice has received judicial sanction from the United States Court of Appeals of the Second Circuit. Judge Irving Kaufman, speaking for that court, pointed out the practical difficulties in doing otherwise:

> If petitioner is correct that the President's recess power is limited to vacancies which arise while the Senate is away, all . . . preparation [to screen candidates] must be telescoped into whatever time remains in a session if the vacancy arises while the Senate is in session. If a resignation or retirement is received late in the session, as in the present case, the President must either forego the opportunity of utilizing all available sources of information and help, or leave the office unfilled for months until the Senate reconvenes. Even if this problem could be alleviated by suggesting to judges that they notify the President considerably in advance of anticipated resignations or retirements, we could hardly expect the President and Attorney General to possess prescience so that they may predict when vacancies caused by death or unexpected illness will occur.[28]

Congress as early as 1863 sought to discourage presidents from making too easy and too frequent use of the recess appointment. In that year, Congress passed into law a provision reading: "nor shall any money be paid out of the Treasury of the United States to any person appointed during the recess of the Senate, to fill a vacancy in any existing office . . . until such appointee is confirmed by the Senate."[29] Current law on the subject is more carefully drawn to withhold salary payment, with some exceptions, from a recess appointee who was picked to fill a vacancy which "existed while the Senate was in session and was by law required to be filled by and with the advice and consent of the Senate, until the appointee has been confirmed by the Senate. . . ."[30]

Despite the fact that a recess appointment must still be confirmed by the Senate and despite the financial risk which the appointee may run, in some situations a president may find such an appointment advantageous: he may be able to obtain confirmation for a "sitting"

15

judge which might have been impossible had the Senate acted before the appointee filled the post on a temporary basis. For example, in 1961, when the nomination of Judge Irving Ben Cooper to be United States district judge for the southern district of New York ran into a stormy controversy before the Senate Judiciary Committee, the fact that he had been serving on an interim appointment was very helpful, if not critical, to his cause.[31] Significantly, the controversy did not involve senatorial courtesy, for neither of the two New York senators opposed the nomination. Nor had they taken any initiative in proposing other candidates, since they were not of the president's party.[32] The chief opposition came from the organized bar. Such serious charges were leveled at Cooper by such formidable people as presidents of various bar associations, including former Attorney General Herbert Brownell, that, had they not been countered, the Judiciary Committee might have felt compelled to urge Senate rejection. It was charged that Cooper lacked judicial temperament, proper experience, and qualifications.[33] In preparation for the open hearings before a subcommittee of the Judiciary Committee, the deputy attorney general sought and received a highly commendatory letter from Sylvester J. Ryan, the chief judge of the court to which Cooper had been nominated and on which he had been serving on an interim basis.[34] In the hearings, counsel for and supporters of Cooper laid great emphasis on the fact that Chief Judge Ryan and other judges who had served with Cooper in the interim period as well as lawyers who had appeared before him agreed that he was performing in an exemplary way. It would seem a fair estimate of events to say that Cooper's on-the-job record helped enormously in securing the committee's approval in the face of stout opposition. And this settled the matter, for the Senate accepted the committee's recommendation without debate. But, even if one were to argue that, since there was no opposition from the senators of New York, approval by the Judiciary Committee was foreordained, it is noteworthy that parties in interest felt that it was critical to make a good defense of the Cooper nomination, at least as a face-saving device for all concerned, and that the best way to do it was to establish that he had been performing well in the post.

Because of the prestige of his office and his access to the mass media, the president is able to exert a powerful influence upon public expectations concerning judicial appointments which may, in turn, affect the negotiation leading to appointment. If the public is conditioned to expect high-level appointments, it may become poor politics for a senator or state party leader to seek to place on the bench men who do not measure up to the expectation. A president himself may find it poor politics to make a particular appointment which he may desire if that appointment does not measure up to the level of expectation he has helped to create. For example, when it was rumored that "President Kennedy wants to name Boston Municipal Judge Francis X. Morrissey, his former secretary and a life-long friend of the Kennedy family, to the single new federal judgeship now available in Massachusetts," members of the Boston and Massachusetts bar associations and the press were outraged because Morrissey seemed poorly qualified for the post.[35] Influential elements of the press were quick to point out the irony of a president considering the nomination of a man who did not meet the standards for the office that the president himself had set.[36]

THE DEPUTY ATTORNEY GENERAL

Where George Washington could be personally acquainted with virtually all the outstanding people of his day and appoint to judgeships men who were known quantities to him, no modern president can hope to do the same. If a president takes seriously his legal responsibility for nominating and appointing federal judges, the search for and screening of candidates requires more time than he can personally give to it. But even if he eschews a major responsibility and is willing for senators to name appointees, he will at the least want to assure himself that appointments will not reflect adversely upon him, and to obtain such assurance requires investigation which he is too busy to undertake himself. Consequently, it has become customary for the president to assign to his attorney general the responsibility for advising him about judicial appointments. In turn, it has become customary, at least since the Eisenhower administration, for the attorney general to make recommendations for such appointments the primary duty and responsibility of the deputy attorney general. In the Kennedy and Johnson administrations, where there were an unusually large number of judicial appointments to be made, the day-to-day leg work of acquiring data on prospective nominees and negotiating with senators was assigned by the deputy to an assistant.

Because the relationship between the attorney general and the deputy must be and is close in an organizational and personal sense, the attorney general is kept apprised of important developments as the deputy seeks to fashion a recommendation. At any time the attorney general may indicate that he would like the deputy to proceed in a specific way and, of course, the deputy will. The attorney general may even make the initial suggestion of a possible nominee, asking the deputy to check him out. Whatever word the attorney general receives from senators and others will be passed on to the deputy with or without comment.

To a lesser extent, the attorney general will keep the president informed of developments. If it appears that a particular recommendation may cause difficulty with a senator or party leaders, there will very likely be some discussion. Conversely, if the president himself has had conversations with or communications from a senator or party leaders, he will relay the information to the attorney general with some comment. The president can, of course, at any time indicate specifically whom he wants nominated and that settles the matter for the attorney general and his deputy. But presidents do so rarely. Rather, they generally are willing for the attorney general to make the recommendation, even though they might make occasional suggestions and comments. In the end, the president will take one good, hard look at the nomination recommended to him and, at that point, he may seek assurance from the attorney general that the nomination will stand up when it goes to the Senate or that he has been made aware of any difficulties which can be anticipated and the reasons for going ahead with the nomination in spite of them. President Eisenhower frequently took the added precaution of talking with the recommended candidate before submitting the nomination.[37]

Although the president or the attorney general may at any time direct the deputy attorney general to follow a prescribed course of action or refuse to accept his recommendations, the deputy, as a practical matter, plays the leading role in exercising the president's power with respect to making appointments to the federal bench. This fact has an important bearing on the selection process. First, the office of deputy attorney general has attracted in recent years men of extraordinary ability like William P. Rogers, Lawrence E. Walsh, Byron P. White, Nicholas deB. Katzenbach, Ramsey Clark, and

Richard G. Kleindienst. Such men, proud and ambitious as well as able, are not going to be content with mediocre performance in one of their important assigned tasks. Consequently, it is to be expected that they will take more than a passive role in the selection process and, in fact, they do. They are not content to sit back and screen recommendations offered by senators. Wherever they can, they take the initiative in seeking out and proposing candidates. As an assistant to one of these deputies put it: "We take all the ground the senators let us take." True, the deputy has no *legal* power in his own right to make nominations. But to the extent he can influence the attorney general and the president, he can invoke the president's power. This is known and understood by other principals in the appointment process and makes possible effective direct negotiations between them and the deputy.

THE WHITE HOUSE STAFF

During the Kennedy administration, the contact between the attorney general and the president was very close and direct. No member of the White House staff participated actively in the process of judicial selection. Of course, members of the staff who dealt with senators liked to be informed about the progress of nominations. Shortly after Robert Kennedy's resignation, however, President Johnson asked John Macy, the president's special assistant on personnel matters and chairman of the Civil Service Commission, to review nominations suggested by the Department of Justice. As Macy saw it, his function was to maintain a kind of quality control. To this end, he endeavored to have his office make an independent investigation and evaluation of each suggested nominee. One could speculate that the president's original purpose in imposing a White House screening was merely to protect his own political interests at a time when he could not be sure about the political loyalties of the team at the Department of Justice.[38] But Macy felt that his search for men and women to fill important vacancies in government had to include those being considered for judgeships, since a person might well be considered a good prospect for both a seat on the bench and a high administrative post at the same time. Whatever the reasons, Macy and his small staff took a hard independent look at all recommendations made by the department.

THE AMERICAN BAR ASSOCIATION

In 1946 the American Bar Association established the Special Committee on Federal Judiciary; it later grew into the Standing Committee on Federal Judiciary.[39] A later chapter will deal extensively with the operation of the ABA committee. Suffice it to say here that the committee passes on the qualifications of nominees to the federal bench. Since 1945 it has become customary for the Senate Judiciary Committee to receive reports from the ABA committee. It has also become customary for the ABA committee upon request to give an "informal" report to the Department of Justice on any person the department is seriously considering for appointment. The committee will indicate, after investigation, whether a particular person is "exceptionally well qualified," "well qualified," "qualified," or "not qualified" for a judicial post. Needless to say, the committee has a profound impact on the selection process. As experience attests, a rating of "not qualified" will not necessarily mean that a particular man will be withdrawn from consideration. But no administration is eager to have very many of its appointments so classified. For this reason, the ABA committee, by obtaining and reporting ratings in accordance with newly developed customs, is significantly involved in the selection process.

THE SENATE JUDICIARY COMMITTEE

Senate rules require that the Judiciary Committee pass on all nominations to the federal bench and make recommendations to the Senate. It has become customary for a subcommittee to hold hearings on all such nominations. In most cases, the hearing is perfunctory. The committee members do not regard it as their function to help select judges actively. Rather, they look on themselves as watchdogs, safeguarding the interests of senators individually and collectively and the public interest.

To safeguard the interests of individual senators, the committee automatically checks with the senators of the state where the nominee will hold his post, in the case of a district judge, or the state where the nominee is from, if he is to serve on a circuit, special, or District of Columbia court. As indicated earlier, with rare exception, the committee will support an individual senator who objects to a nominee. To safeguard the nation and the Senate's prestige against confirmation of a poor appointment, the committee receives a report from the ABA Committee on Federal Judiciary on the qualifications of a nominee and the chairman is apprised of the contents of the file put together by the FBI as a result of its investigation of the nominee on behalf of the Department of Justice. Also, the committee provides an opportunity in its open hearings for anyone to come forward and object to a nomination, offering whatever "evidence" he may have that the nominee is not fit for the post. Some effort is made to keep such testimony relevant and responsible but the committee will bend over backwards to allow people to be heard.

The committee can affect the selection process markedly in three ways. First, it can delay Senate action on confirmation in the hope of embarrassing the president or to test his determination to make a particular appointment. Is he determined enough, for example, to make his nominee a recess appointment if the committee takes no action? If he is not, perhaps he will be willing to back down and submit another nomination in due course. Delay may be used to afford the committee or individual members the opportunity to seek Senate support in opposing the nomination. President Kennedy's nomination of Judge Thurgood Marshall, a Negro who had served many years as special counsel for the NAACP Legal Defense Fund, and the events which followed provide a good example of the use of delay by some committee members. Marshall was originally nominated September 23, 1961. A few weeks later, October 6, 1961, he was made a recess appointment. As was to be expected, Senator Eastland of Mississippi was not happy about the nomination of a man whose name had become synonymous with the NAACP. Nothing was done by the committee about the appointment until May of 1962. Then, hearings were held before a subcommittee selected by Eastland. Two of the three subcommittee members were southerners: Johnston of South Carolina and McClellan of Arkansas (the other member was Hruska of Nebraska). When the subcommittee failed to report, the full committee under tremendous political pressure bypassed the subcommittee and voted to recommend confirmation, 11–4, on September 7, 1962. A few days later the Senate confirmed the appointment. Perhaps the chairman and other southern members only hoped to demonstrate to the folks back home that they were opposed to the nomination, for the odds seemed poor from the start that in this particular case they would be able to embarrass or discourage the president or pick up enough Senate support to reject the nomination. Thus, although delay can be effective at times, it is not effective against a determined president who can expect support from a majority of the senators. For even if the Judiciary Committee as a whole refuses to act, a majority of the Senate can take the matter out of the committee's hands by a discharge petition.

Another observation worth making on the Marshall case is that, although it could be argued that it was one of those rare instances where committee members were using the committee to serve their own personal interest, the southerners, by their lights, may have felt that they were trying to prevent a poor appointment in the public interest.

A second way in which the committee can affect the selection process strongly is, of course, to recommend against confirmation. But, actually, the hearings that the committee holds afford the group individually and collectively their best means for influencing judicial selection. For it is through this medium that the Senate as a whole, the press, and the public can best be attuned to the objections that are raised against a nominee, an objective which the committee members are in a position to overcome or support by their arranging for and questioning of witnesses. Appointment-makers view with foreboding the prospect of a public hearing in which their candidate may be denounced by the official representative of the ABA committee in such terms as the following: "I was given substantial evidence of unjudicial conduct on the special sessions bench, involving tantrums, excoriation of counsel, and general lack of poise on the part of Judge Cooper. While I do not mean that every one of my informants gave me this testimony, an overwhelming majority did, and their testimony was to the effect that Judge Cooper lacked judicial temperament."[40] Or in which a man like Herbert Brownell, president of the Association of the Bar of the City of New York and a former attorney general of the United States, may testify: "I conclude, if ever a clear case of lack of judicial temperament existed, this is it. If ever a candidacy for judgeship called for refusal of confirmation, I respectfully submit this is the case."[41] To have the City Bar Association and the American Bar Association submit a biting brief in opposition to confirmation, a brief which carried the signatures of Brownell, Samuel I.

Rosenman, former special counsel to President Franklin D. Roosevelt and at this time chairman of the Judiciary Committee of the Association of the Bar of the City of New York, John C. Satterfield, president of the ABA, Whitney North Seymour, immediate past president, and Bernard Segal, chairman of the Committee on Federal Judiciary, was embarrassing to the president and his agents to say the least.[42] It is true that Cooper was confirmed in spite of this cannonade, but it is safe to assume that those who were instrumental in securing the nomination for Judge Cooper were chary about getting involved soon in another such donnybrook. In the sense, then, that the Senate Judiciary Committee's hearings provide an opportunity to expose real or alleged weaknesses of nominees, they can exert a powerful influence on the conduct of parties to the nomination process.

In the same fashion, Senate debate over confirmation affords still another opportunity for senators to seek to embarrass the administration by questioning the wisdom of a particular appointment. The Morrissey case offers a particularly dramatic example of such debate and will be discussed at length in a later chapter. Here, individual members of the Senate Judiciary Committee who have dissented from the majority's recommendation can be expected to play a leading role, for they will as a result of the committee's work have a familiarity with the nominee's record. A senator who is not in a position to or who does not desire to invoke senatorial courtesy can still throw some telling punches. Such action will rarely defeat a nomination, but the prospect of denunciation on the Senate floor may weigh heavily in the deliberations of appointing principals.

THE FBI REPORTS

As a matter of course, the Department of Justice runs an FBI investigation on serious contenders for nomination to federal judicial posts. In addition to seeking information on the character of the person, FBI investigators interview lawyers and judges to get an indication of the professional standing of the possible nominee. The merits of such a custom are obvious. Federal judges should be men of unassailable integrity. FBI agents are in a position to interview a wide variety of people who may be able to provide information about a man's character, information which would not come to light in the investigation conducted by the ABA's Committee on Federal Judiciary. Investigating lawyers could, for example, thoroughly investigate a man's professional activities without uncovering the fact that he has a clandestine relationship with some racketeers. But, at the same time, there is also a real possibility that an FBI report could be used unfairly in the tugging and hauling over candidates.

A report from the FBI which is considered to be "adverse" is lethal to a candidacy. But what is an adverse report? What are the criteria? In this connection, it is well to bear in mind that FBI agents collect and report whatever information is given them by the people they interview. They attempt to verify important allegations made against the person being investigated but they will not take it upon themselves to delete such allegations from their report even if they do not seem very substantial. This, at first thought, may seem a dubious practice, but its virtues become manifest when one examines the reason for it which J. Edgar Hoover articulated to a Senate subcommittee years ago: "I think that when the time comes that the Bureau must decide what shall go into a report and what shall not go into a report, then we are functioning as a Gestapo. I think we must report accurately and in detail what any person tells us. . . . In the reports we submit to other agencies, we do report on the reliability of the source of information, if we know it."[43] Also, it is important to note that the FBI does not evaluate its own reports. As J. Edgar Hoover explained: "While the FBI's jurisdiction has progressively increased, its role as an impartial investigative agency has remained unchanged. Now, as in the past, the FBI is strictly a fact-gathering and fact-reporting branch of the Department of Justice. It does not draw conclusions concerning the guilt or innocence of persons investigated, makes no recommendations as to prosecutive action, never issues 'clearances' or makes charges. . . ."[44] Consequently, the evaluation of the FBI report on a candidate for the judiciary is made by Department of Justice officials. The questions of what kinds of information make a report "adverse" and what kinds of criteria are employed are matters for them to decide, at least initially. Solid evidence of personal dishonesty or meaningful association with racketeers or subversives will, without question, be regarded as adverse. But beyond that, department officials have never established clear-cut criteria. Each report is evaluated on an *ad hoc* basis. What it boils down to is this: to borrow a felicitous phrase from a former Supreme Court justice, Felix Frankfurter, whatever "shocks the conscience" of the officials in the Department of Justice or, perhaps, whatever they feel would shock senators, the press, or the public will be defined as conduct unbecoming a prospective judge. To some, an illicit romance of any kind might be enough to eliminate a contender from consideration. To others, it might not, if the principals were discreet. One situation which sometime ago caused consternation among officials in Justice involved a contender who, as a lawyer, had helped trap a wife for a divorce proceeding. Significantly, despite misgivings, department officials did not feel that they could oppose the nomination on that ground alone, for in every other respect the candidate checked out well.

Despite its virtues, the FBI investigation raises some specters. J. Edgar Hoover has consistently and for good reasons taken the position that FBI files must be confidential.[45] Aside from appropriate officers in the appropriate agencies, no one is allowed to see the FBI files, not even senators except under very special circumstances. In this connection, the Department of Justice has worked out a procedure for transmitting file information to the chairman of the Senate Judiciary Committee. An officer of the department, normally the executive assistant to the deputy attorney general but sometimes the assistant deputy attorney general, calls on the chairman of the Senate Judiciary Committee with the FBI file of the nominee the committee is to consider. The officer gives an oral résumé of anything in the file which might possibly be considered derogatory and answers any question the chairman may ask by way of clarification. If the chairman wishes to look at the file, he will do so but only in the presence of the officer. In some rare instances, another member of the committee who has been serving on the subcommittee dealing with a particular nomination has been allowed to see the file, but only in the presence of the Department of Justice officer. Under no circumstances is the file ever left with the chairman or other committeeman. As a practical matter, therefore, the members of the Judiciary Committee only know what the Department of Justice or the chairman of the Judiciary Committee wishes to tell them. (This, of course, does not prevent persons outside the government who oppose the nomination from supplying committee members with derogatory information which may be identical with that in the file.)

It would be possible for department officials, in jockeying for

25

position with a senator over a particular nomination, to indicate that the senator's man had been knocked out of contention by an adverse FBI report. In our times, the suggestion of an adverse FBI report carries overtones of incontrovertibility and finality which might well make a senator feel that he should drop the matter without pursuing it further. In fairness, Justice Department officials assert this could never happen, that senators will persist in finding out in general "what you have on my man," that in many cases they are already familiar with the facts which constitute the "derogatory" information and do not feel that it is critical. Be that as it may, it would appear possible for those who have access to the FBI report to allude to it in such a way as to discourage some senators from pushing a particular candidacy. Such allusions could be groundless, part of a daring maneuver to head off a nomination to which the real objection was lack of competence and where a senator could be expected to counter effectively such an objection—apparently, it is always possible to produce witnesses and statements from members of the bar and judiciary to support any candidate for a judicial post. It is also possible that those who have access to the FBI reports may be more prissy about human peccadilloes than most. Suppose a candidate had been tardy in paying income taxes or had received unusually high contingency fees when serving as counsel in personal liability cases. Some may feel that such actions show a lack of character, others may not. It is important to bear in mind, in connection with the use of FBI reports, that because of the requirement of confidentialty, it is not usually possible to confront a possible nominee in an open hearing before the Senate Judiciary Committee with "derogatory" information and allow him to defend himself. In short, the only check on an "adverse" report is a senator's zeal and persistence, and, by the nature of things, these are only brought into play when a senator is interested in a candidacy.

Pressures at Work

Every candidate for major political office, however great his own resources are, needs help from others in his campaigns. People, in large numbers, jump into the fray expecting no personal favors. They may feel ideologically that it is important for a particular candidate or party to win. They may need the kind of stimulation and fulfillment they obtain by participation in the rough and tumble of a campaign.

Or they may become involved out of a sense of duty, the idea that a good citizen should participate. Others, however, give of their time and money with the full expectation that should their candidate win, they will have a good claim to favors. The favors sought frequently are public offices. It is axiomatic that one way to obtain appointive office is to ingratiate oneself with those who hold the appointing power. Baldly stated, the axiom has disturbing overtones. It implies that appointments are obtained as a *quid pro quo* for service rendered without regard for qualifications. But look at it another way. A person working in a campaign has a unique opportunity to demonstrate his ability to a candidate. If the candidate wins and then has the responsibility of appointing or helping appoint to high office, he has a coterie of people well known to him who have demonstrated that they are like-minded in political philosophy and that they are able. What is more natural in such a situation than to seek to place such people in high governmental posts? This phenomenon, in a sense, is not unique to politics. In business, academic, or other endeavors, it is common for someone upon attaining high office to seek to find places in his organization for people with whom he has worked before and for whom he has a high regard. To the degree that an appointment is made on qualifications and ability, it is inaccurate to describe it as a "purely political" appointment. But political considerations exert enormous pressures on the appointment-makers. Here, "political" is used in its grossest sense to describe considerations which enable, or are thought to enable, a party or candidates to win elections.

At one time, fresh from his experience of steering the presidential campaign of Franklin D. Roosevelt to victory, James A. Farley had the temerity to suggest that he could keep a party together and working effectively without patronage: "I am convinced that with the help of a few simple ingredients like time, patience, and hard work, I could construct a major political party in the United States without the aid of a single job to hand out to deserving partisans."[46] Not many professional politicians believe it would be possible to do so. Rather, they believe it is imperative to use appointments to high office to encourage future political participation. Or to put it another way, they believe that, if there were no expectation of reward, a good many very able people would no longer take part in campaigns and other party work. Consequently, the party professionals will pressure appointment-makers to reward the faithful. Rewarding the faithful has become so much a part of our system that it would be fair to say that it has the significance of custom. Although an appointment-maker might want to make his selection on merit alone, he cannot, without risk of sparking great discontent among the professionals in his party, ignore custom. Appointment-makers are not unaware of the limitations set for them, however much they might desire to mitigate them. A kind of practical compromise is often effected by an approach suggested by an appointment-maker in this way: "We feel that we owe certain people jobs but we do not feel that we owe them *specific* jobs." In elaboration, he explained that no one is promised a judgeship for services rendered nor will anyone be appointed to a judgeship if he does not have the qualifications for the post. But there is a frank recognition that it is incumbent upon the appointment-makers to "take care" of those who contributed heavily to the efforts of the past campaign and that somewhere in the vast spectrum of posts available they can find a spot becoming to the talents of those who have a substantial claim to consideration.

The essence of the observations just made boils down to this. Appointment-makers are under constraint to appoint to judgeships those who have rendered service to the president or to the senator(s) from their state, if of the president's party, or to the president's party generally. There is freedom to pick and choose among the faithful for specific jobs. Byron White's forthright statements (when he was deputy attorney general) are very much to the point. He told the American Bar Association House of Delegates that "there is nothing odious about the preference for Democrats," that the selection of judges is "a political process in the best sense of those words," and that "the central question in choosing them [the judges] was ability, not politics."[47]

Unfortunately, there is no quick litmus-paper test to divine who is the most deserving of the deserving. People active in the party and campaigns all have their own notions about who has done most for the cause. There is a further complication in the fact that in our system it is possible for someone to perform Herculean tasks in behalf of the candidacy of a president without doing much or anything for a senator's candidacy or vice versa. Thus, the chief appointment-makers, the appropriate senator(s) and those who represent the presidency, may feel a strong obligation to and admiration for two different men, both of whom have labored hard in party vineyards. But neither the senator(s) nor the president's men can safely take into account only their own estimates of a potential appointee's contributions to the party's efforts if they want to ensure future support for themselves and to keep the party sinews strong. They must consult with party leaders in the state and make it clear that they have given consideration to their views. The extent to which a party leader's views will receive consideration depends in large part upon his real or apparent power in party circles. For example, a Justice Department official in a Democratic administration was emphatic that in making judicial appointments to the district courts in Illinois, "Mayor Daley of Chicago must have a seat at the conference table." In the reckoning of senators and of the president's men, the views of governors and congressmen of their own party normally must be taken into account and special consideration will normally be given to the views of the vice-president and cabinet officers with regard to appointments in their respective states, if they retain a lively interest in state politics. Consideration will also be given to the views of mayors of large cities and party national committeemen. These people will in turn be importuned by lesser lights in the party who feel that their efforts in the party's behalf entitle them to some consideration from party leaders.

PRESSURE FROM CANDIDATES

It is often said in respect to honorific posts of all kinds, in government and out, that "the post should seek the man." Perhaps this is the ideal. It certainly does not describe what happens when it comes to judicial appointments. Rarely is it the case that a person who has not actively sought the appointment receives it. On the contrary, some of the most distinguished jurists have fought like tigers for their nominations.

For lawyers and state judges in virtually all jurisdictions, a federal judgeship is a highly sought-after prize. The pay is, by most people's standards, substantial. When it is coupled with life tenure and a most favorable retirement arrangement, it is very attractive.

To lawyers, there are special attractions which transcend the financial benefits. For them, it is hard to conceive of more important or prestigious positions. As far as lawyers are concerned, the judges are kings in their courtrooms and they are treated accordingly inside and outside the courtroom. To get some feel for a judge's standing among lawyers it is recommended to the non-lawyer that he attend a bar association meeting or a law school alumni banquet and observe the respect, and in some cases the obsequiousness, lawyers manifest for the judges present. Illustrative of how much the importance and prestige of being a judge can mean is the answer I received when I respectfully asked a distinguished and elderly appeals court judge, "Why, in view of the favorable retirement plan, don't more judges retire at age seventy?" His answer was as simple as it was profound: "When you are an active judge, you are somebody. When you are a retired judge, you are nobody."

In the subculture of lawyers, with rare exception, federal judgeships are so highly regarded that almost to a man both the lawyers and the appointment-makers who have been interviewed asserted that "you can take it as a matter of fact that 99 percent of the lawyers would like to be federal judges." Unfortunately, the 1 percent frequently includes some of the very finest lawyers who, by objective standards, have the best qualifications for service on the bench.

In order to be in serious contention for a judgeship, an aspirant must usually make it clear that he wants the post. He can do this in a variety of ways, ranging from very active campaigning in his own behalf to having others do it for him. Efforts will be made by the candidate or those working for him to bring pressure to bear on the appointment-makers through political leaders. Obviously, it is to a candidate's advantage to have a record of active support in the campaigns of the president or the appropriate senator or for the party generally. In such a situation, a good case can be made that the candidate is owed special consideration. This point was well made by Judge Samuel Perry in a humorous and candid speech in which he told the Chicago Bar Association in 1951 how he became a federal judge: "Since we are talking confidentially I will be perfectly frank with you folks in admitting that I tried to obtain the appointment seven years ago and learned then that it requires not one but two senators. At that time I was out of politics and they did not need me. Therefore, I decided that this time if I wanted that appointment I had better get back into politics—which I did. . . ."[48]

When a candidate has not made such a record, he must rely more heavily on the backing of those in the party who seek support of his candidacy on the basis of consideration due them. If he is not a member of the president's party, it becomes necessary to convince party leaders that in this particular situation it is good politics to appoint someone of the other party. Sitting federal judges will be frequently drawn into the campaign in spite of the myth that judges must and do refrain from involvement in political processes. This involvement will be discussed more fully shortly.

Aspirants invariably seek to enlist the aid of local and state bar association groups to help pressure the appointment-makers. The Committee on Federal Judiciary of the American Bar Association does not solicit the views of the local and state bar associations as such. Therefore, it is quite possible and is frequently the case that someone who has received the endorsement of those groups will not be rated as qualified by the ABA committee. Presumably, state political leaders and senators cannot afford to ignore the advice of local and state bar associations. Wherever and in whatever manner possible, candidates will, of course, endeavor to marshal support from the press.

The following letter from a former distinguished district judge to his senator, written at a time when he was seeking nomination, is illustrative of how hard candidates normally campaign for the office, even if they try to convey the impression, as this particular letter writer did, that they "have hardly moved a muscle." In reading the letter bear in mind that neither the candidate nor the senators of the state were of the president's party and take note of the involvement of federal judges.

Dear Senator J——:

As you suggested at my pleasant visit at your home Sunday, I give you herewith a confirmatory memorandum.

In the first place, the matter was a great surprise to me. In fact, when Chief Judge P—— of the Federal Circuit spoke to me many months ago, I gratefully declined.

But, when he and Chief Judge L—— of the District Court again talked with me, in September, during the course of the Conference of Chief Justices, and when I found that our good friend Judge X—— [the chief justice of the state supreme court] was in accord, I reconsidered. For, after all is said and done, the Federal judiciary have far and away the most interesting judicial jurisdiction in the entire country, which to my mind outweighs the salary loss.

From then on they have taken the matter in hand, while I, whether wisely or not, have hardly moved a muscle, save to talk to you and Senator Z—— [the other senator from the state], who has been an intimate friend for years.

31

Judge L—— has, however, kept me advised. Immediately after we talked at the above conference, he and Judge P—— went to see Chief Justice M—— [of the United States Supreme Court], who expressed unusual interest, and indicated he might, perchance, contact the highest quarters. Thereupon, Judge L—— visited the Deputy Attorney General A——, in charge of such matters for the Attorney General, and a long-time friend. He told L—— he felt a Republican appointment to one, at least, of the two vacancies in the state would be good Democratic politics, since there are now but two active Republican federal judges in the entire circuit. In this view I think you told me the Attorney General himself concurred.

Then Judge L—— got Judge M—— of [another] Federal Court of Appeals, and my predecessor as Chairman of the . . . committee of the American Bar Association, to write Assistant Attorney General H——, and Judge P——, in turn, wrote the Attorney General. For your information, I enclose copies of the above-mentioned letters and my "Who's Who."

Furthermore, Judge L—— communicated with Judge C——, of the Court of Appeals, who is such a long-time friend of the President that he always stays at the White House when he visits Washington. Judge C—— came to know me as my successor as Chairman of the ABA Committee, and he promptly wrote L—— that he would take the matter up with the President personally, and "present it in the most favorable manner that I know." Unfortunately, Judge C—— is a very sick man unable to leave his home, and as yet has, therefore, been unable to talk to the President face to face as he hoped. Doubtless, however, he will shortly take the matter up personally otherwise, if he has not done so already. I hope to have word on this shortly, and will immediately advise you, since I would think it desirable, though perhaps not necessary, for this to precede even a follow-up news article on a Republican appointment, as to which I gathered you thought you might appropriately contact Mr. D—— [newspaper publisher].

Meanwhile—and altogether—I have talked with but two close personal friends; (1) F——, because of his letter to you, who will help on the Democratic angle; (2) W——, President of the X.Y. Bank, who serves with me on the board of a foundation, both of them being very glad to help. W—— has already spoken with N—— [president of a university in the state] and I—— [president of a large bank in the state]. Both will be glad to write the President.

Judge X—— [chief justice of the state supreme court] thinks it would be a good idea to have the State Bar Association at their meeting Friday, December 8th, go on record favoring a Republican appointment to at least one of the two vacancies. Do you concur in this?

. . . .

PRESSURE OF STATE TRADITION

Frequently, state tradition makes for political pressures which appointment-makers can ignore only at peril to themselves and the party. It is sometimes traditional for judgeships to be divided up on a geographical basis or to be spread among the constituent nationality groups in the state. To upset the usual balance may create the impression among a minority group that the appointment-makers are hostile to them. If it has become customary for an American of Italian ancestry to be on a particular court, Americans of Italian descent, sensitive as are all minority groups, might interpret the failure to select one of their own as a deliberate slight.

Consequently, appointment-makers are sometimes in the position where failure to make a particular appointment may be misinterpreted to their political disadvantage. For example, in one district it had become customary to elevate the United States attorney to the district bench when a vacancy occurred. At the time of one such vacancy, the United States attorney was of the Jewish faith. When there was speculation that someone else might be appointed, the senators from the state and the Department of Justice were deluged with communications pointing out that the considerable Jewish community in the state would regard it as a deliberate affront to them if the custom were broken when a Jew happened to be the United States attorney. To the appointment-makers, it became apparent that, practically, they had little choice but to elevate the United States attorney, who fortunately achieved an outstanding record of service.

THE PRESSURE OF "GOOD POLITICS"

Running counter to the pressures described above is the pressure that is sometimes generated by the idea that it is "good politics" to avoid the usual political considerations in selecting judges. For example, there is no doubt that a Democratic president will be hailed in many quarters for nominating outstanding Republicans to the bench. It is sometimes "good politics" to appoint an extraordinary lawyer or state judge to the bench regardless of political considerations. Consequently, the appointment-makers occasionally bow to such considerations in making a particular appointment even in the face of anguished wails from party regulars. This can be done more easily in situations where "package deals" can be made. Thus, if there are three openings in a particular state, the president's men may propose a slate including two nominations which the senator(s) and/or state party leaders are eager to see named and a nonpartisan or opposing party member for the third. It will then be suggested that agreement be reached on the slate as a whole. To wring a concession in those circumstances is easier, at least relatively so, than it would be if there were only one post available.

On the whole, in any administration of modern times, selections made as a consequence of the pressure of "good politics" have been few in number, the exceptions and not the rule.

PRESSURE FROM SITTING JUDGES

Although pressure from sitting judges is rarely a decisive factor in the appointment of judges, it is worthy of attention.[49] It is generally supposed that sitting judges with meticulous regard for the separation of powers would not actively seek to influence the appointment-makers. The fact is that they do. As pointed out earlier, they are consulted by officials in the Justice Department and by the ABA committee in regard to prospective nominees and to them they give their opinions freely. What is perhaps more surprising is that frequently judges will take it upon themselves to urge a candidacy without waiting to be consulted, as indicated so well in the letter previously quoted. Often, a judge will manifest an uneasiness or self-consciousness which undoubtedly reflects feelings of guilt about becoming involved in promoting a candidacy.

If the judge is a Learned Hand or a prestigious member of the Supreme Court a strong letter may have a profound impact on the appointment-makers, particularly where the field has been narrowed to a few choices. Imagine the impact of a letter from a Learned Hand which states in part:

I think there have been not more than two occasions during the long period that I have served as a judge when I felt it permissible to write a letter in favor of anyone for a judicial appointment. However, I feel so strongly that the Second Circuit would be greatly benefited by the appointment of Mr. X—— that I cannot refrain from writing you to express my hope that you may see fit to fill the vacancy now existing in the Circuit by selecting him. . . .

Or the impact of a letter from an outstanding member of the Supreme Court, a letter which elaborates in great detail on his general estimate of a candidate:

In view of my close concern during practically the whole of my professional life with the quality of the federal bench, I venture to commend to your favorable consideration Mr. Y——. Y—— is one of those rare creatures whose talents and capabilities so far exceed those of even able men that in talking of him one must indulge in conscious understatement in order to avoid disbelief on the part of those who have not had intimate experience with his capacities. . . .

The Interplay of Forces in the Appointment Process

DISTRICT COURTS

The appointment process cannot be described adequately as a series of formal and automatic steps. An appointment grows out of the interaction of a number of people with varying and, to some extent, countervailing powers attempting to influence each other within a framework imposed on them by law, custom, and tradition. Metaphorically speaking, this is the process under the microscope.

Once it is known that there is or will be a vacancy on the federal bench, the jockeying for position begins in earnest. Some groundwork undoubtedly will have been laid far in advance. Provident aspirants may have built well by their political activity for the day when the opportunity would surely arise. The president, at the beginning of his administration, will have indicated implicitly or explicitly what he wishes done with respect to appointments. His men in the Department of Justice will have been actively or passively collecting names and information about "good prospects." The appropriate senator(s) will have been importuned from time to time with suggestions for future judicial appointments. If there has been a recent appointment to a post in a particular state, all parties to the nomination process have in mind the also-rans, some of whom must be contenders for the next vacancy. A large percentage of nominees have been considered one or more times before actually being designated.

While the contenders contend by firing up or having others fire up as much steam as they can for their candidacy, the president's men in the Justice Department are canvassing people whom they know, in and outside the department, about first-rate candidates. Strategic in this situation are members of the department who have or are thought to have special knowledge about lawyers in their native states. They may recite the virtues of particular individuals from memory or they may get in touch with people back home and relay the information so garnered. Others who have worked in the political hustings with the

35

crucial department officials will also be queried. Or, as is frequently the case, they will not wait to be queried but will offer gratuitous advice.

At the same time, the senator(s), if of the president's party, will be actively or passively collecting information on candidates. In regard to district judgeships, there are several courses of action available to a senator. Some few senators like former Senators Lausche and Byrd (Virginia) do not like to play an active role in judicial selection. By their lights, appointment of judges is the president's constitutional job and they feel that for them to ask the president to appoint their candidates would be akin to asking favors for themselves. They do not want to feel beholden to the president. They do, of course, feel that they have the right to oppose a presidential nomination if they do not like it. Consequently, in such situations, the initiative lies with the officials in the Department of Justice. But they will still be sure to clear with the senator a prospective nominee before formally proposing him, for they do not want to run into trouble in confirmation.

A much larger number of senators will submit a list of candidates and suggest to the department that any one of those named on the list will be acceptable to them, inviting the department to make the selection. The reason for such an approach can be readily understood. As the old saw goes, "In making an appointment, you make fifty enemies and one ingrate." By drawing up a list and placing the onus for decision on the department, a senator can satisfy more and disappoint fewer candidates. As indicated earlier, the team at Justice is happy to move into the breach and make the selection. But senators who submit lists do not always do so for the purpose of letting the president's men pick and choose. Some use the list as camouflage. For while they send a letter with the list to the department with copies for all interested parties, they call upon or phone officials there to indicate who their real choice is.

Most senators feel that if they are of the president's party they should designate the nominee subject to the approval of the Department of Justice. Some even take a proprietary view, that they own the job. For example, one senator wrote to the attorney general in a letter in which he submitted five names, "On the basis of your investigation and survey, I shall make my final choice of the nominee. . . ." The president's men bristle at the suggestion that they only investigate and check on candidates for a senator. In this connection, it is amusing and illustrative to note that in the margin beside the quotation above, a department official had placed two large exclamation points which in the context appear to be marks of indignation. But a good measure of how some senators feel is this excerpt from a letter to me from Senator Dirksen: "I have never submitted a panel of names to the Attorney General for processing and submission to the President. I have always felt that if I had the capacity to discharge the obligations of a senator I should certainly be able to select a proper person for the Federal Bench. . . ."

When a senator feels strongly about what he considers to be his prerogative, the president's men may have considerable difficulty thwarting his attempt to impose on them a nominee with whom they are unhappy. It is understandable, then, why there is a ready disposition in the department to accept without much question what they consider a good suggestion for nominee from a senator. If there are two senators of the president's party from a particular state, department arithmetic has it that the effect of two senators wanting a particular man for a district judgeship in their state is more than one plus one. The sum is more like infinity, for it would only be with great trepidation that the president's men would attempt to counter the will of both senators.

Interestingly enough, the fact that two senators are involved may give the president's men a wedge for taking more ground in the appointment process. If the senators are not agreed on a candidate, as is frequently the case, the president's men can try to find a nominee who is their choice primarily but acceptable to both senators. In such situations, it is important for the president's men not to convey the impression to either senator that he has favored the candidate of the other. But senators are not unaware of the effectiveness of "divide and conquer" tactics and many of them will seek to work out an arrangement with the other senator from their state so that they will always appear to make common cause on appointments. The easiest device for doing so is to split up appointments, including nonjudicial appointments.

Despite the efficacy of presenting a united front, some senators are so estranged politically from the other senator of the state that they just cannot work out a satisfactory arrangement. The American elec-

torate apparently has no overpowering allegiance to either party or
political ideology. The state of Illinois, for example, can send to the
Senate concurrently a Paul Douglas and an Everett Dirksen. And even
where the senators are nominally of the same party, it is possible for
them to be as far apart politically as were Senators Ralph W. Yar-
borough and Lyndon B. Johnson of Texas, who had great difficulty
in maintaining rapport.

As indicated previously, when a senator or two senators of the
state has or have settled on a candidate, the president's men are pre-
disposed to accept him, unless they feel he does not meet their standard for character and competence. But this does not mean that they
have played a passive role. Operating on the basis that "you can't
beat someone with no one," the president's men frequently take the
initiative in proposing candidates to the senator(s). It may turn out
that all interested parties have had the same person in mind all along.
But such initiative on the part of department officers may put the
senator in a position in which along with presenting his own candidate he must actively oppose the man suggested by the department.
This can become embarrassing for the senator if word is leaked to
the press who it is the department is "considering" and the state press
finds the department's choice worth lauding. The senator is then
placed on the defensive locally, for he must now not only press the
claims for his choice but explain why he opposes the "choice" of the
department. His position may be untenable if the department has
fixed on a prestigious lawyer or state judge who has considerable
support in his own right among party and bar leaders in the state.

The senators have a counter-strategy available to them. If a senator
beats the department to the punch and issues a press release stating
that a particular person will be the next federal district judge, he has
placed his own prestige on the line. For the president's men, at that
point, to contest the senator's choice involves the politically important
issue of face-saving. It is a daring maneuver, for should the department oppose his choice and it turns out that they have good grounds
for doing so, the senator will have difficulty saving face. On the other
hand, the president's men may prefer to swallow hard and take the
senator's man without contest in preference to embarrassing him.
This is particularly true if the senator is regarded as powerful.

Senatorial strategy in the use of the premature press release in a particular case was described and decried by the *St. Louis Post-Dispatch*. That newspaper editorialized, after Senator Stuart Symington announced he would recommend James H. Meredith, his former campaign manager, for nomination to a district judgeship:

> By announcing his choice, and Senator Long's concurrence, when he did, Senator Symington made it difficult for Attorney General Robert Kennedy to exercise independent judgment in the matter. Although the Kennedy Administration owes nothing to Mr. Symington, who for a time was a candidate for the Democratic presidential nomination, it would be naturally reluctant to embarrass or humiliate any Senator by rejecting his nominee. Yet the Attorney General is not bound to accept Mr. Meredith.[50]

A few days later, in a news story, the paper reported:

> Obviously realizing there is a good deal of opposition to Mr. Meredith because of his lack of judicial background, Senators Symington and Long decided this week to recommend him for the post left vacant by the death of United States District Judge Randolph Weber, rather than Judge Moore's seat. This would enable Mr. Meredith to be appointed quickly on a temporary basis by President Kennedy, and to serve on this basis until confirmed by the Senate. Such an appointment would tend to prevent opposition forming.[51]

When several appointments are to be made to the bench in a particular state, the department and the senator(s) may be able to work out a compromise plan, whereby each gives a little and takes a little. For example, in the Kennedy administration, it was easier, as was pointed out earlier, to get senators to accept a Republican appointment for one of several appointments to be made than it was where only one vacancy was to be filled.

By and large, the president's men and the senators, when they are of the same party, want to avoid open conflict. There is good understanding that each has weapons with which to inflict heavy damage on the other. Negotiations, therefore, begin in a spirit of accommodation. The principals want to avoid a fight but most of them are prepared to take all the ground they can.

Depending upon personality, the principals may be frank and direct in their approach or they may play it close to the vest, trying to gauge the true feelings of the others without giving up the same information on themselves. Frequently, pointed banter in face-to-face situations is a useful device for drawing out information. How does the senator react when the deputy attorney general or his assistant says to him, with a smile, "Oh, you can't be serious about putting Joe Smith on the bench"? Conversely, the senator may watch closely for a reaction when he tells the attorney general in what appears to be a joking manner, "If Jack Jones doesn't get that judgeship, I'm going to be MIGHTY unhappy."

If it turns out that the senator has a candidate who pleases the president's men the negotiations are swiftly closed, provided the reports of the FBI and the ABA Committee on Federal Judiciary are in the candidate's favor. Where the candidate of the senator does not please department officials or where the president's men are pressing a candidacy which is not to the liking of the senator or where both are happening at the same time, the jockeying for position becomes a serious business. The best strategy for the president's men at this point is to sit tight and not move forward in the formal process of appointment. This will cause immediate concern for the senator. If the senator had not been very strong on his proffered candidate, he may quickly back down and seek agreement on another choice. On the other hand, the senator may try to force the issue by dragging his feet in some endeavor which means a great deal to the president.

Despite frequent allegations to the contrary, appointment-makers do not like to be put in a position in which votes in the Senate on the president's program depend upon a particular judicial appointment. Few senators want to bargain away their independence to vote as they see fit on major issues. In many cases, it is more important to them politically to vote against the president on a particular issue than to have a specific individual named judge. The president's men may at times feel that going along with a senator on a judgeship in return for a key vote would be in the public interest. Suppose one vote were needed on a foreign aid bill the president regarded as essential to the security of the nation. Would it be folly to compromise principle on one judgeship if such compromise would secure the needed vote? Yet there is good reason for avoiding such trading. As one Justice Department official saw it, "Once you give ground even for momentous reasons, you are in the position of the young lady who was asked if she would spend the night with a man for a million dollars and, upon replying 'yes,' was asked, 'well, how about for five dollars?' To her outraged 'what do you think I am?' came the answer, 'we've already established that, we're just bargaining on price now.' " Undoubtedly, there have been occasions when there has been an unspoken *quid pro quo,* presidential acquiescence to a senator's wishes with respect to a judicial appointment in return for a vote, but it has been rarer than is generally believed. And it must be remembered that when a president does attempt to bargain with judgeships he is limited in what he can do. For reasons which we have already explored, the president cannot just go ahead and name someone whom the senator from the state and of his party will oppose, and expect to have him confirmed. His best currency for purchasing compliance is delay and favoring one senator in the state over the other senator.

The idea that judgeships are wantonly bargained away by presidents seems to have gained currency as a consequence of a quotation attributed to Franklin D. Roosevelt in a *Collier's* article written by James A. Farley. But notice that President Roosevelt was aware of the limitations, for, according to Farley, he said: " 'First off, we must hold up judicial appointments in States where the delegation is not going along. We must make appointments promptly where the delegation is with us. Where there is a division we must give posts to those supporting us. Second, this must apply to other appointments as well as judicial appointment. I'll keep in close contact with the leaders.' "[52] Note, too, that Roosevelt was not suggesting that his powers be used to secure votes on specific legislation but rather on general support. This puts a different complexion on the matter. It is a much higher order of politics for the party leader to insist upon general support from party members in the Senate in return for his support than it is for a president to trade acquiescence on a judgeship for a vote on one particular issue before the Senate. After all, the notion that a president should give special consideration to senators from his own party should logically call for the same senators to give special consideration to the president. If they fail to do so, then by what logic can they insist upon preferred treatment for themselves?

But whatever one makes of the Roosevelt record, in recent times judgeships have not been used to pressure senators to vote "right" on specific issues. Myths die slowly, however, and in a city where rumor and gossip are like meat and drink, it is not surprising that from time to time a newsman will report as Joseph Alsop did that "getting the foreign aid bill off the cliff where it was so desperately dangling also required judgeships and public works and much other pork and patronage."[53]

White House aides who are involved in liaison work with Congress like to be kept informed on the status of appointments so that they will know what to say if queried about an appointment when they are talking to a senator about the president's legislative program. At times they may ask that an announcement of a particular appointment be held up pending a vote in the Senate, not to bargain, but rather to prevent a senator from reacting to a legislative proposal in a moment of personal pique. In recent years, there has been one situation, but probably not more than that, in which a senator made it clear that unless the president's men accepted his nominee he would refuse to go along with the administration in any matter. Interestingly enough, he did carry out his threat.

When the president's men employ Fabian tactics and the senator chooses not to succumb, a ready and available strategy is to try and outwait them. They normally like to fill vacancies quickly so that the work of the judiciary will keep apace with the demands on it. This gives the senator an opportunity to test the resolve of the president's men. But the senator is at a disadvantage at this point, for the political pressure to fill the vacancy comes from within the state and means more to the senator than to national officers. Also, as indicated earlier, the president might make a recess appointment with the risks involved and this might make the situation more difficult for the senator. When things reach such an impasse, there will generally be more effort to seek accommodation rather than resort to open warfare. For the president's men are not eager to go the route of the recess appointment which will, under the circumstances described, not avoid but only forestall an open fight with the Senate which they stand a good chance of losing.

When the president's men and a senator are at odds, the president's men may in their efforts to dissuade the senator from backing a particular candidate receive a big assist from an adverse report from the FBI or the ABA Committee on Federal Judiciary or both. Not many senators will want to bear such a cross, particularly if the grounds for the unfavorable reports are the kind which will engender public opprobrium if aired. And aired they will be in Judiciary Committee hearings. As explained earlier, the FBI file is confidential, but the chairman is free to indicate the nature of the facts which are regarded as adverse. The ABA committee is under no wraps when it reports formally to the Judiciary Committee as evidenced by the earlier quotations from its report on Judge Cooper.

When accommodation cannot be reached, one of three possible results occur: (1) the president's men make no effort to fill the vacancy; (2) the president formally designates a nominee unacceptable to the senator and invariably loses the contest for confirmation, if the senator fights to the bitter end; (3) the president makes a recess appointment and at the next session of Congress sends the same name in nomination and loses the contest for confirmation. As suggested earlier, when a president risks courses of action 2 and 3, the pressure may be too great for the senator to persist in opposition. But the outcomes indicated are based on the assumption that the senator will go the limit in opposition. It is important to stress, also, that in the end, when an impasse has been reached, the senator is not in a position to initiate the action which constitutes a throwing down of the gauntlet. In a very real sense, the president's constitutional power to make the formal nomination provides him with the advantage that is inherent in taking offensive action, whereas the senator in the moment of truth has only defensive weapons.

CIRCUIT COURTS

When it comes to making appointments to circuit courts, the balance of power shifts markedly to favor decision-making by the president's men.[54] Bear in mind that the power of an individual senator in respect to appointments to the district bench is derived from the custom of senatorial courtesy. By the nature of things, the custom cannot be invoked effectively in the same way where circuit court judgeships are involved. Each circuit covers at least three states. No one senator or pair of senators can claim that they are the only members of the Senate with a vital interest in appointments to the court. As a matter of fact, senators from the states covered by the circuit must vie with each other to obtain consideration for their choices. Since there is no legal prescription for distributing circuit judgeships so many to a state, no senator can claim that as a matter of legal right a particular nomination should go to a person from his state. (Conceivably, senators from states in a circuit could combine and work out a plan for distributing circuit judgeships among the states and present a united front against the president's men if they fail to accept the plan. But this has never been done.) In such a context, a senator from one state objecting to an appointment to the circuit court approved by the senator(s) of the state from which the appointment is made cannot hope for support from his colleagues in the face of conflicting claims for support. In short, senatorial courtesy cannot be invoked in that situation. But, as suggested earlier, senatorial courtesy can be invoked effectively by a senator of the state *from* which the nominee of the president's men comes.

What this all boils down to in practice is that the president's men may pick and choose among candidates urged upon them by the senators of the president's party from all the states in the circuit but more importantly it gives them more latitude for selecting their own candidates. Suppose they have in mind a first-rate man from the state of Missouri for a vacancy in the Court of Appeals for the Eighth Circuit. Suppose also that the senator from Missouri, of the president's party, has been pushing a candidacy which is not acceptable to the president's men. The president's men are in position to say to the Missouri senator, "We cannot appoint your candidate. If you persist in pushing him, we'll just have to appoint Smith [who is the choice of the Minnesota senators of the president's party]. However, if you can see your way clear to accepting Jones of Missouri [the person they really want], we will be happy to appoint him." Most senators in such situations feel that it is important to have the appointment made from their state even if they have to give way on the precise choice. Obviously, it is important to a senator's political prestige to appear to be able to obtain a larger share of patronage than others.

Just as in the case of district judgeships, some senators eschew responsibility for designating and pushing candidates for circuit judgeships, reserving the right to oppose a nominee from their own state who is distasteful to them. But most senators will strive to have a judgeship go to someone from his state. In this connection, a senator will endeavor to show why his candidate deserves more consideration on the grounds that either his state rates the post on the court or his candidate is superior to others or both. The following is a typical presentation made by a senator in a letter to the attorney general: "For many years New Jersey has had only one of the seven judgeships in the Court of Appeals for the Third Circuit. Considering all factors including, importantly, the relative volume of the Court's business originating in New Jersey, we feel very strongly that an increase in New Jersey's representation on the Court would be most appropriate assuming, of course, that the right man can be found. Judge Q——— is indisputably the right man."

In making their selection, the president's men are not exactly free agents. They must take into account the FBI report, the informal report of the ABA committee (which indicates the ultimate position the committee will take on the qualifications of the nominee), the reaction of the senator(s) from the state from which their candidate comes, and the political power of the senators who have manifested a great interest in particular candidacies. In that connection, a candidate of the Senate majority leader, or the whip, or a particularly prestigious senator will rate more serious consideration than the candidate of a senator who has been regarded as a party maverick.

None of these factors has a precise value in the equation which adds up to appointment. Each appointment is the result of an interplay of forces which is *sui generis*. But the fact remains that the president's men and the forces which pressure them play a more important role in the selection of circuit judges than of district judges.

THE OTHER FEDERAL COURTS

In appointing judges to the District Court of the District of Columbia, the Court of Appeals for the District of Columbia, the United States Court of Customs and Patent Appeals, the United States Court of Claims, and the United States Customs Court, the power of the individual senator is further diminished in favor of the president's men. Since the selection for these posts can be made from any state in the union, any one senator's claim to an appointment cannot be very strong. This does not mean, however, that senators will not endeavor to press candidacies for these posts. On the contrary, there is in them a special attraction for a senator. Frequently, a senator desires to see in a judicial post someone whose qualifications do not impress him. If that someone were to be appointed to the district court in the senator's state or the court of appeals in the circuit, a poor performance on the judge's part would be a constant reminder of the senator's poor judgment. Discontent with a particular judge may help contribute to disenchantment with the senator who urged his appointment among constituents, particularly among lawyers who as a group are articulate and politically powerful. Consequently, the best solution in such cases is for the senator to secure for his man an appointment to the federal bench which will remove the man from home base.

When it comes to the District Court and the Appeals Court for the District of Columbia, there is a powerful countervailing force to the senators' desire to unload on them judicial appointments they would not accept for courts operating back home. Because the District of Columbia is the situs of the federal government, a large share of important court actions involving government agencies and officials is brought to those courts. The president's men, therefore, are not about to put second-raters on the bench of courts which are so important and to which they must bring much of their own considerable legal business.

For the special courts, there is no such countervailing force. There is a tendency for the president's men to regard these courts as relatively unimportant. It is not considered a great compromise of principle to oblige a senator or to meet the president's own political obligations by appointing to those courts persons who would not meet standards they set for district and appeals courts. Bear in mind, however, that the number of these posts is limited and senators in making claims on them must compete with all other senators of the president's party as well as with those individuals who want the posts and who have legitimate claim to special consideration from the president. Senators who hold powerful positions in the Senate formal and informal hierarchies and senators who have been exceptionally loyal to the president will normally be able to do more to secure the nominations for their candidates. It is unlikely, however, that any one senator will obtain more than one such nomination from any administration.

Again, it is important to emphasize that a senator of the president's party may effectively forestall the nomination of a person from his own state to a national office if that person is not acceptable to him. That this generalization applies to nominations for the special courts is illustrated by Senator Harry F. Byrd's effective opposition to the confirmation of J. Lindsay Almond for a post on the Court of Customs and Patent Appeals.[55] For this reason, the president's men will normally clear such appointments with the senators of the state from which their desired appointee comes before making the designation official. In this connection, it is pertinent to recall President Kennedy's answer in a press conference to a question regarding the difficulty in securing confirmation for Almond: "Well, I don't quite understand why the Senate is failing to act. Almond's the distinguished governor of Virginia. It was my understanding when his name was sent up here there was no objection by the Senators that were involved." [56] The president's words suggest that no effort was initially made to by-pass Senator Byrd but rather that signals were crossed.

In conclusion, the time has come to set aside the simplistic explanation that senators alone determine the appointments to the federal bench. For better or worse, the process is much more complicated and, indeed, much more interesting.

CHAPTER **II**

The Kennedy Administration

THE KENNEDY ADMINISTRATION was confronted by a unique situation in its first two years. Because legislation in 1961 provided for a host of new judgeships, the president and his aides had in relative terms an enormous number of judgeships to fill quickly. The magnitude of the task was described by Bernard Segal, then the chairman of the American Bar Association Standing Committee on Federal Judiciary, in his statement to the ABA House of Delegates on August 7, 1962:

In the matter of judicial appointments, the year which has elapsed since this House last met is without precedent in American history. . . . there have been 147 judicial vacancies in the Kennedy Administration thus far— almost 40% of all the judgeships in the Federal system at the time President Kennedy came into office. Except for Presidents Truman and Eisenhower, this is more vacancies than any President of the United States has had to fill in two entire terms of office.[1]

In October of 1962, the Justice Department supplied a further and more detailed breakdown of the figures used by Segal which are summarized in Table 1.

The large number of vacancies which required immediate attention was bound to give to judicial selection an unusual aura of importance and urgency. Consequently, the way the Kennedy administration han-

Table 1. Judicial Appointments from January 21, 1961,
through October 13, 1962

Kind of Judgeship	Nominations Confirmed	Total Vacancies during Period
New district judgeships (created by new law)	57	62*
Old district judgeships	36	43
New circuit judgeships (created by new law)	10	10
Old circuit judgeships	7	11
Other judgeships (includes two for Supreme Court)	4	6
Term judgeships	11	12
Tax Court judgeships (where recommendations are made to the president by Treasury and not Justice)	3	3
Total	128	147

SOURCE: U.S. Department of Justice, *Judicial Appointments, January 21, 1961 through October 13, 1962* (undated; mimeographed).

* The Justice Department explained that the figure of 62 new district judges conflicted with the total of 63 such judgeships created by Congress but that the sixty-third judgeship, for a specified term rather than for life, was created for Puerto Rico, and is accounted for in the term-judge category.

dled appointments to judgeships during its first two years in office may well have been atypical, not only as compared with other administrations but as compared with the manner in which it would have performed in more normal circumstances. For one thing, the time and attention given to appointments by the leading decision-makers in the Department of Justice were inordinately high.

The large number of appointments affected the process markedly in another way. The administration was in a position to press for "packages"—to form slates which would be acceptable to the appropriate senator(s), who might balk at some appointments if they were proposed one at a time. The opportunities for slate-making are suggested by Table 2, which lists states with multiple vacancies in the federal district courts and with some claim to consideration for a vacancy on the appropriate circuit court.

The situation was unique in yet another way. Never in American history has an attorney general been so close to and so trusted by a president. This is not merely to observe that the Kennedys were broth-

Table 2. Distribution of Judicial Vacancies by State during the
First Two Years of the Kennedy Administration

State	District Court Vacancies	Circuit	Circuit Court Vacancies
California	7	IX	2
Connecticut	2	II	3
Florida	4	V	2
Georgia	2	V	2
Illinois	4	VII	2
Indiana	3	VII	2
Iowa	2	VIII	2
Kansas	2	X	2
Louisiana	4	V	2
Maryland	2	IV	2
Massachusetts	2	I	0
Michigan	5	VI	1
Missouri	5	VIII	2
New Jersey	4	III	3
New York	10	II	3
North Carolina	3	IV	2
Ohio	3	VI	1
Oklahoma	3	X	2
Pennsylvania	10	III	3
South Carolina	3	IV	2
Tennessee	4	VI	1
Texas	5	V	2
Virginia	2	IV	2
Washington	2	IX	2

ers. The feeling of friendship and admiration that each manifested for the other transcended by far the usual brother relationship. Consequently, they saw each other much more frequently as friends and brothers than they did as government officials transacting government business.[2] These unofficial and social meetings gave the attorney general unusual opportunities to keep the president informed about departmental business and problems, to discuss matters like judicial appointments informally, and to learn about the president's wishes and intentions. In addition, the president had inordinate confidence in the judgment of his attorney general concerning governmental problems not generally within the ambit of the Department of Justice. For these reasons the Kennedys acted and reacted to each other in the process of judicial selection as no other president and attorney general have.

The President's Role in Judicial Selection

Aside from the appointments to the Supreme Court, President Kennedy did not involve himself deeply in the selection of nominees to the federal bench. This is not to suggest that he regarded these appointments as unimportant. His statement at the time he signed the new judgeship bill suggests otherwise, and also set the standard by which he would measure recommendations made by the Department of Justice:

I want to take this opportunity to say that for our federal courts, I shall choose men and women of unquestioned ability.

I want for our courts individuals with respected professional skill, incorruptible character, firm judicial temperament, the rare inner quality to know when to temper justice with mercy, and the intellectual capacity to protect and illuminate the Constitution and our historic values. . . .[3]

But the president was content to allow Justice officials wide discretion to act for him in negotiations with other interested parties and to rely heavily on their judgments concerning who the nominees should be. This approach was understandable for three reasons. First, President Kennedy, like our other recent presidents, carried the fate of the free world on his shoulders as well as the burden of a host of perplexing domestic problems. No wonder then that, despite its importance, the selection of particular judges rated a low priority in bidding for the president's valuable and limited time. Second, by President Kennedy's reckoning, he could be sure that his attorney general would make the best possible selection in the circumstances surrounding a particular choice. Third, aside from ensuring that the caliber of judges be high in general, the president did not have the same burning interest in the judiciary that he had in policy-making and new programs. He was action-oriented and he naturally gave a higher priority and more personal attention to the selection of those who were to head or assist in important programs than he did to the selection of judges below the Supreme Court level. When the president personally sought to recruit a lawyer for government service, he recruited him for the executive branch, not the judiciary. The penchant for action, which he and the attorney general shared, led to a belief that the more vigorous of the able lawyers must prefer positions in the administration to places on the bench. For example, neither of them was sure that Byron White would be willing to move from his important post in the Justice Department to the Supreme Court. At the last moment before the nomination was announced, the attorney general took the pains to ask

White's assistant and friend Joseph Dolan, "Do you think Byron really wants to go on the court?"

However, the president's inclination to prize administrative posts more highly than places on the bench did not as a practical matter affect judicial selection adversely. To say he prized administrative posts more is not to say that he regarded judgeships less. Rather, in his view, as important as judgeships were, top administrative posts were even more important. Also, there are a very limited number of top administrative posts and, even assuming that some potential judicial candidates will succumb to the siren songs sung in behalf of them, the number is small. In addition, the Kennedy bias was partly offset by the bias of most lawyers that there is no post like a judicial post.

In sum, the president personally played a permissive role, keeping informed but delegating much of the responsibility. He was kept informed by the attorney general on an informal basis and he transmitted direct communications from senators, party leaders, and other interested people as well as his own ideas in the same fashion. When the president was confronted by an anxious senator, he would not hesitate to call the deputy or the assistant deputy directly to find out the status of a particular judgeship. The president knew personally and well his first deputy attorney general, Byron White, and the assistant deputy, Joseph Dolan. Both White and Dolan had played important roles in his campaign for the presidency. Dolan had also acted briefly as an aide to the president when he was a senator. Nicholas deB. Katzenbach, who became deputy in May of 1962, came to that post from service as assistant attorney general in charge of the Office of Legal Counsel, where he served as the president's lawyer and, of course, had to be consulted frequently. Consequently, communication was easy and informal between the president and those in the Department of Justice who shared the major responsibility for selecting nominees.

The White House Staff

No one on the White House staff tried to project himself into the judicial selection process, even though there were several with a large and legitimate interest in it. For example, Lawrence O'Brien, who had a major responsibility for marshaling the president's program through Congress, and Ralph Dungan, who made recommendations for top administrative appointments, could have been expected to have some strong convictions about who should receive nominations to judgeships in the over-all interests of the president. In other circumstances, they might have been tempted to pressure for particular appointments. But whatever leverage a presidential aide could usually derive from the assumption of other administrative officials that the aide spoke for the president, a member of Kennedy's staff would have had difficulty wearing the president's rank on his collar in dealing with the Department of Justice. Who would have had the temerity to suggest or imply that he knew the president's mind and heart better than the attorney general? There was also a general recognition among White House aides who worked with the attorney general closely in the campaign—and who knew, liked, and respected him—that he was not one to take kindly to poaching on his domain. Whatever the reasons, O'Brien, Dungan, and the others did not try to exert pressure on the selection of judges.

White House aides and Justice officials did, however, exchange information. Aides who were closely in touch with senators in the course of their own duties passed on to Justice information regarding senators' views on prospective nominees. Such observations were a factor which Justice officials had to take into account in their negotiations over a particular candidacy. At the same time, it was essential that those in the White House who had to maintain good relations with senators be kept informed about what was happening on judicial candidacies. For senators are prone to see the administration as monolithic and when a presidential aide comes to them or calls to discuss the president's legislative program, it is natural for them to raise questions with him about any matter in which the administration has a hand, even though the hand is not the aide's.

Of the White House staff, the one most frequently in contact with officials at Justice was Mike N. Manatos, O'Brien's assistant with special responsibility for Senate relations. But O'Brien himself and Kenneth O'Donnell, who had the job of coordinating work in the presidential office, also kept in close touch with Justice. Although these men seldom made suggestions about appointments, they did have an opportunity to affect the timing of an appointment. As pointed out earlier, when appointment papers went to the White

House for signature, a decision sometimes was made there by the president on his own initiative but usually on the advice of staff aides that it would be wise to hold off announcement of an appointment which would displease a particular senator until a Senate vote on an important bill was taken, the purpose being to prevent a senator from voting against the president's wishes out of momentary pique rather than well-considered judgment.

Frequently, it was helpful for those considering candidates for judicial posts to confer with Dungan as it was for Dungan to confer with them about his work. As was indicated in the last chapter, while there is frank recognition in all administrations that certain people deserve special consideration for a post in government, if they want one, this does not mean that they will necessarily be considered for the post they would like to have. One who may aspire to be a judge may be better fitted for an administrative post and vice versa. Naturally it is helpful in turning someone down for the job he wants to be able to offer him an attractive alternative. In the search for the proper holes for particular pegs, conversations between officials in Justice and Dungan were desirable and fruitful. For example, in the course of screening possible nominees for a judicial post, department officials felt that one of the people being considered was a man of high ability but "just not ready" for the bench. After conversations with Dungan, he was offered and accepted a position as commissioner of an independent regulatory commission where he established himself in an exemplary way and was later appointed a federal judge.

The personal relationships between the White House staffers with an interest in judicial selection and the key officials in the Justice Department were close and in most cases had roots which antedated their taking office. Dolan and Dungan had worked together for a time on Capitol Hill. During the campaign, they, along with the attorney general, O'Brien, O'Donnell, and White, played key roles, even before the Wisconsin primary, the date which, for the faithful, separated the in-group from the Johnny-come-latelies. O'Donnell and Robert Kennedy had been college roommates and had worked together as staff members on a congressional committee. Although Katzenbach had not served with the president before being appointed assistant attorney general, in that position he came in close contact not only with the president but also with his staff. By the time he moved up to the post of deputy and became involved in judicial selection, he had already established close personal ties with the others. As a consequence of these relationships, there was little resort to formalities and written memoranda. Consultation about judgeships between White House and Justice officials took place over the phone, at lunch, or during quick office visits and was frequently just one item of business sandwiched among many others, some of which were deemed more important by the principals. For example, during a meeting primarily to discuss events at the University of Mississippi, a moment was spared to discuss a particular judgeship. These discussions were characterized by a candor which comes easily to men who know, like, and trust each other. Despite the banter, these men were all intensely earnest about their work. Each had a fierce devotion to the president personally which apparently transcended his own immediate ambitions. This kind of adulation which President Kennedy inspired in those who worked closely with him was awesome and perhaps to some degree unhealthy, but it did provide them with a common purpose in their consultations, to do what was good for the president. Although there was room for disagreement about what was good, to have such a frame of reference simplified many problems and issues.

The Team at Justice

President Kennedy's hand in judicial selection was played by three officials, the attorney general, the deputy attorney general, and the assistant deputy. Since there were two deputies in the Kennedy administration, White and Katzenbach, this involved a total of four people. It would be superfluous to add to the vast newspaper and periodical literature describing the personality and character of the late Robert Kennedy and the fabled Byron "Whizzer" White. The deputy, Nicholas deB. Katzenbach, and the assistant deputy, Joseph F. Dolan, whom I had the privilege of observing at close hand, are not so well known, however, and it would contribute to an understanding of how they worked to know something of them personally.

Nicholas deBellevue Katzenbach was born in 1922, the son of a remarkable pair of parents. His father, now deceased, was virtually blind from the time he graduated from law school. Despite that handicap, he became a successful lawyer and an admirable attorney general of New Jersey. His mother was for many years extraordinarily active and effective in New Jersey politics. She was vice-president of the convention which framed the widely acclaimed Constitution of 1947 and played a leading role in obtaining its adoption. Despite the fact that she did not have a college education, she became a recognized authority in the field of education and was the president of the New Jersey Board of Education in the early sixties. Katzenbach has a brother, Edward, several years older, whose interest in governmental affairs is attested to by the fact that he was deputy assistant secretary of defense (Education and Manpower Resources) in the Kennedy administration. His uncle was for many years a member of the Supreme Court of New Jersey. Patently, in such a family a drive for achievement and an interest in government and politics came naturally. Katzenbach revealed such interest early, when he chose to major in public and international affairs as a Princeton undergraduate.

As a young man, Katzenbach was an unusually good student. At Phillips Exeter, Princeton, and the Yale Law School, he garnered a host of academic honors. He was tied for first man in his class academically at the Yale Law School, editor in chief of the *Yale Law Review,* and a Rhodes scholar.

Later, as a professor of law at both Yale and the University of Chicago, Katzenbach quickly gained the reputation of being one of the country's top scholars in the field of international law. With Professor Morton Kaplan of the University of Chicago he wrote an important book, *The Political Foundations of International Law.*[4] One reviewer referred to it as "an exciting application of systems theory to international law just because it has opened new and relatively unexplored approaches to the discipline." [5] Professor Richard A. Falk called it an "extraordinary" book which "strikes me as almost certain to exercise a helpful influence upon serious thinking about international law in the generation ahead. Not many books give occasion for such a prediction." [6]

Although his forte was international law, Katzenbach had broader interests, too. He taught courses in contracts and conflicts of law. Previous to embarking on his academic career, he served in the Truman administration as attorney-adviser and consultant to the secretary of the air force and for a short time practiced law privately in Trenton, New Jersey.

Katzenbach is far from being the stereotype of the effete intellectual that his academic achievements might suggest. He is a big, rugged man who was as adept at athletics in school and college as he was in the classroom; the kind of man who, as an army air force officer, chose to be in a combat crew in preference to any other post. To understand Katzenbach, it is important to know that he was a very fine hockey goalie at Exeter and Princeton in a day when Ivy League hockey generally, and Exeter and Princeton hockey particularly, compared with the best played in American schools and colleges. At first thought, this observation may seem superficial, but think on this question: what manner of man will choose to be a goalie and be good at it? To stand in the nets alone to face the forward line, streaking down to project a stone-hard rubber puck with such breathtaking speed that it can break bones or teeth should it elude the gloves and pads of the defender, must require a love for competing under pressure and cool courage. Above all, it requires an ability to take enormous pressure without losing one's composure. Katzenbach has all of these qualities in abundance. And they stood him in good stead in his days in the post of deputy as the performance of his official duties at the University of Mississippi in the face of angry Mississippians suggested. During the crisis which developed over the admission of James Meredith to the university, Katzenbach was the department's senior officer present on the scene at the most critical times, and as such acquitted himself in an impressive way.[7] Those who worked with him in obtaining the release of the Bay of Pigs prisoners marveled at his ability to take in stride constant changes and disappointments and to make good decisions quickly.

In the process of judicial selection, such a man is hardly likely to be intimidated by senators, the American Bar Association, or political leaders. This is not to suggest that Katzenbach is rigid, hardheaded, or stubborn, although some of his critics in his later role of undersecretary of state thought he was. On the contrary, the amalgam of qualities which make up his character and personality includes generous portions of tolerance, patience, and genuine humility, warmth, and compassion, qualities which enable him to be a good listener. It is tempting to conjecture that these qualities were enhanced by Katzenbach's experience in a German prisoner of war camp where he was incarcerated for more than a year as a captured army air force officer. But those who knew him best as a younger man feel that it was precisely because he had these qualities that he was able to take the ordeal without damage to his spirit. At best, prison camp life with the monotony of routine leads to debilitating ennui which makes it difficult for those who have suffered it to survive in good mental condition. Because of his nature, Katzenbach was able to salvage something from even this dismal experience. Since he had left Princeton before completing his work for a bachelor's degree, he resolved to use his time as a POW to prepare for early completion of that work. His family was permitted to send him reading material, and he read 432 books, about one a day for the period of incarceration.

The personality and character of Katzenbach were reflected in the performance of his duties in connection with judicial selection. He had his own ideas on standards and candidates, yet he listened to others. He was not afraid to make a decision and he was smart enough to make good ones. He was not afraid to face up to pressures and speak his piece candidly and forthrightly to powerful elements who disagreed with him. This he demonstrated by appearing before the House of Delegates of the American Bar Association to explain why he disagreed with them on the role they should play in judicial selection, a matter which will be discussed more fully shortly.

Undoubtedly, the years and the impact of the assassinations of both Kennedys for whom he worked and to whom he was devoted have left their mark on Joseph F. Dolan. It is the Dolan of the early sixties whom I describe. Dolan is richly blessed with endowments which make him a natural for politics. He is tall, trim, and handsome, as if cut from the same mold as the Kennedy brothers. He has a youthful, clean-cut, athletic appearance, yet there are enough lines in his face to suggest experience, character, and seriousness of purpose. Bright, articulate, engaging, and informal in manner, he establishes rapport with others quickly and easily. When he chooses to, he can exude that special kind of charm so often associated with the Irish. In particular, he has a delicious sense of humor which combined with his ability to think quickly enables him to make a suggestion, sum up a situation, or convey an idea with a deft and humorous (sometimes wry) turn of phrase. There were a host of aficionados in Washington who regaled each other with Dolanisms such as this one.

At an interdepartmental committee meeting, in the days when

Dolan was at Justice, there was agreement in the committee that an official should be dispatched for a special and important assignment at a certain place. Other members of the committee agreed that the official should be given two weeks to get ready to go. Dolan could not contain himself. He asked, "Why can't he go tomorrow?" He then went on to add, "You know what department I come from; I'd be ashamed to go back and admit that I had even *been* at a meeting where we decided to send someone to do a job two weeks from now instead of tomorrow."

With such qualities of personality, Dolan's meteoric rise in Colorado politics, despite his short residence there, is not surprising.

Dolan was born in New York City in 1921, and was brought up there. During his three and one-half years of war service, he had occasion to be stationed in Colorado and came to like the area. One of its special appeals is its superb facilities for skiing, an activity which Dolan indulges with great enthusiasm as frequently as possible. He returned to New York briefly after the war to complete his law work at St. John's University, where he finished in the top 5 percent of his class. In his earlier years at the same institution, Dolan achieved outstanding grades while working outside as well. His family was of comfortable means but not affluent and he was able to lighten the burden of the cost of his education by earning part of it. After law school, Dolan became an attorney in the United States Department of Justice and later counsel for the House Select Committee on Lobbying Activities. In 1953 he was offered an opportunity to join a law firm in Denver, which he was happy to accept. Until 1960, he was an attorney in the private practice of law in Denver, with time out in 1956 and 1957 to serve as assistant counsel to the United States Senate Special Committee Investigating Lobbying and Campaign Finance and as an assistant to the then Senator John F. Kennedy. Consequently, he had not lived in Colorado very long before he successfully ran for a seat in the Colorado House of Representatives in 1958 to which he was reelected in 1960.

There is another dimension to the Dolan character and personality. He is ambitious and an extraordinarily hard worker. Engrossed in a problem or assignment, he will strike others as being preoccupied or taciturn rather than engaging. He pushes himself brutally, blithely ignoring regular meals and the eight-hour day as if they had somehow gone out of style. He strives hard for excellence in his work and is meticulous about details. From anyone working for him on a project, he expects the same attention to duty and standard of performance to which he holds himself. Woe be unto him who does not give it, for he may feel the heat of the Dolan temper which is as much a part of Dolan as his charm. Anger hones his sense of humor to a sharp cutting edge.

When it came to the Democratic party and President Kennedy, Dolan was fiercely partisan with no apologies. He, along with Byron White, was zealously pushing the Kennedy candidacy in Colorado before that candidacy looked very promising. In private conversation, he would frequently say of another New Frontiersman "and he would lay down his life for the president" as if those words were the highest accolade he could bestow on anyone. From another, such an expression might have seemed meaningless, good hyperbole at best, but, when Dolan said it, he conveyed the impression that this was precisely the way he felt about the president.

Dolan was admirably suited for the role which his superiors set for him in the process of judicial selection. It was Dolan who did the detail work in securing the names of possible nominees and screening them. This was more important, more difficult, and more time-consuming than it sounds. For what it boiled down to was that Dolan became in addition to the chief gatherer and evaluator of information the department's chief contact and negotiator with others involved in the selection process. As pointed out in the first chapter, once the name and information gathering begins, the appointment-makers and other parties in interest begin to interact in earnest. Shrewdly, those with candidates or causes to push tend to converge on the one who is feeding information into the departmental decision-making apparatus. In the tasks of information collection and negotiation, Dolan put to good use all of his charm and wit as well as his considerable intelligence. For it is important in the jockeying for position to learn as much from others as one can without tipping his own hand. It was a thing of beauty to witness Dolan in action as he charmed a caller, appearing to give in good fellowship more information than he actually did while extracting information from his caller with the deftness of a skilled pickpocket taking a wallet. To an unusual degree, in connection with his duties in judicial selection,

Dolan carried as a conscience the conviction that he was working for the president personally as well as for his superiors in the department. For him, a failure to protect the president's best interests would have been more than a mistake, it would have been Dolan letting President Kennedy down in a very personal way.

The Decision-Making Process

Developing a departmental decision with respect to judicial selection was a highly informal process in which it is difficult to assess with any precision the impact of each or any of the participants. There were no prescribed steps and precious little routine except for the broad division of labor which left to Dolan the detail work. Attorney General Robert Kennedy's interest ranged over the wide gamut of departmental responsibilities including such matters of great moment as civil rights and antitrust activity. In addition, he was from time to time given special responsibilities by the president such as over-seeing the effort to release the Bay of Pigs prisoners. In matters of great interest to him, the attorney general generally involved his deputy (the word "deputy" is used in these paragraphs to mean both White and Katzenbach) and the deputy his assistant. This meant that all three officers were engaged in a host of activities simultaneously, only one of which was judicial selection. And for proper perspective, it must be recognized that most of the time other activities required more, and more immediate, attention than judicial selection. These men were in constant contact with each other face to face and over the "squawk boxes" discussing aspects of a host of items on their mutual agenda. Since they were in the same age bracket, knew each other well, liked and admired one another, they spoke openly, candidly, and on a first-name basis. Despite the easiness of the relationship, there was no ambiguity about who was in charge. Once a superior made a decision or expressed a wish, that was it for the subordinate.

In the process of formulating a decision, no one was inhibited in what he said. Final decisions were preceded by a great deal of ad hoc discussion as information came in. Since Dolan was assigned to gather data, which included finding out how other parties in interest stood on particular appointments, most information came to him first and he conducted most of the preliminary negotiations with others out-side the department. He relayed important information to the deputy, acquainting him with any difficulties he had encountered, and obtained instructions on how to proceed. In some situations the deputy checked with the attorney general or suggested that Dolan do so. Important decisions were made by the deputy subject to review by the attorney general. But the deputy did not wait until he was ready to make his final recommendation to call the attorney general's attention to prob-lems and to seek his views and advice.

Nor would it be realistic to discount Dolan's influence on the deputy's decision. For Dolan, judicial selection was a labor of love and he was intensely interested in it. His superiors had made it policy to take all the initiative they could in judicial selection. Nothing pleased Dolan more than to lay a departmental claim to a good judi-cial appointment. He viewed all judges nominated in the Kennedy administration as either "ours" or "theirs." By "ours," Dolan meant a judge who was the first choice of the department and in whose nomination the department was able to achieve the acquiescence of other decision-makers. "Theirs" were those judges who would not have been the department's first choice but on whom the department had to give some ground and do some acquiescing. Consequently, Dolan did much more than transmit information; he was quick to make suggestions and recommendations forcefully. The deputy ap-preciated his zeal and good judgment, weighing Dolan's views heav-ily in making his decisions, as did the attorney general, when called upon to do so.

Although departmental decision-makers preferred that Dolan serve as the funnel for information and as negotiator, there was no prac-tical way that they could prevent other interested parties from making special appeals directly to the attorney general or deputy. After all, if a senator or party leader insisted upon communicating with them, it would not have been politic to refer them to Dolan. Conversely, if it seemed strategically wise to have the attorney general or deputy conduct negotiations with people outside the department, he would do so. This was determined by (1) special personal relationships, like the attorney general's close relationship with Senator McClellan for whom he once worked and who looked upon him with a kind of paternal interest which suggested that it was appropriate for the attorney general to make the contact; (2) the fact that these officers may have been sought out by others in the first instance, making it wise for them "to report back," so to speak; (3) the need at times to invoke all the prestige possible for bargaining purposes and, of course, prestige is roughly in proportion to the importance of office. In such cases, all information was relayed to Dolan who pieced it with other information and evaluated the total situation for his superiors.

Decision-making was, in short, a continuing and informal process. By the time the nomination papers had to be drawn up for the president's signature, the deputy, his assistant, and in many cases the attorney general had arrived at a consensus which resulted from a number of ad hoc discussions and interim decisions collegially arrived at, which made the final decision a foregone conclusion. In some cases, there was a final review by the three officials to make sure that they understood each other and had considered all alternatives and contingencies. Then they made a final decision.

Identifying Candidates: The Dolan Variation

In casting for names of candidates Dolan used all the conventional sources used by his predecessors in earlier administrations. He sometimes solicited and sometimes received gratuitously suggestions of names from the chairman of the ABA Committee on Federal Judiciary, the party's national committee, party leaders, and other officials in the department. He, in accordance with well-established practice, sought informal ABA committee reports on prospects as well as an FBI report. In addition, he developed the systematic practice of personally seeking advice and information from two special kinds of sources.

Dolan made it a practice to canvas a sprinkling of sitting judges both for assessments of those under consideration and for the names of possible nominees. This is not to suggest that sitting judges had never before played a role in the selection of judges. As pointed out in the previous chapter, not all sitting judges have been averse to making gratuitous suggestions to the department. Always in gathering data for its reports both informal and formal, the ABA committee has interviewed sitting judges. But for an official of the department to consult with them directly on his own initiative was a new approach.

In a fashion resembling the scouting systems of major league football and baseball teams, Dolan also established a network of state "spotters." These men, no more than one to a state, were lawyers who had extensive contacts in their respective states. All of them were men in the same general age bracket as the president, Katzenbach, and Dolan and who had established their interest in and loyalty to the president by service in his campaign for the office, usually before the Wisconsin primary. Dolan sought their advice in several ways. When there was a vacancy, he asked them to scout around for good prospects. When candidates were suggested by senators or others, he asked his "spotters" to check out both their fitness for the post and their posture with the party. As in all administrations, it was of prime concern to departmental officials that the administration should not appear to be rewarding men in the party who had been opponents of the president unless there were other overriding considerations. Dolan's use of the "spotters" ensured that there were fewer mistakes of this sort. For these were men who knew the state situation well and whose first allegiance was to the president and his interests. In the contest for choice positions, the men at Justice were often confronted by claims and counterclaims in behalf of favorites, claims which they were in no position to evaluate accurately on the basis of personal knowledge. But the "spotters," active in their respective states in the president's behalf, knew where people stood politically.

In some cases, these men played another important role. Once a "spotter" came up with a suggestion on a possible nominee, he was sometimes asked to try to sell his candidate to the state's senator(s). Frequently, where his relationship with a senator was good, he was successful in doing so. At times this worked so well that a senator little knew that the candidate he was presenting to the department as his own was the very man the department wanted from the start. Short of that, the "spotter" at times was able to persuade a senator not to object if the department took the initiative in putting its man forth as the nominee. Instead of approaching a senator directly, a "spotter" frequently built up support for his man within the state so that others put pressure on the senator.

In their field activity, the "spotters" never purported to be acting as agents for Dolan and Dolan took great pains to keep their identity secret. He explained that, like CIA men at work in the field, they would be rendered ineffective if their tie to the department was known. If known, they would be immediately besieged by candidates and their promoters. One might wonder how they could have been effective in promoting candidacies with senators and others without the base of power which their affiliation with the department, if known, would have given them. The answer lies in the fact that each of these men had considerable standing of his own in the state party and had been recruited precisely because he also was exceptionally able, personable, and persuasive.

Until he became ambassador to Australia, William Battle (born 1920) was the "spotter" for Virginia. Battle, able and energetic with a magnetic personality, is the son of a former governor of the state and as such came to know early in his life Virginia politics and politicians. As he grew older, he became very active in his own right. He had endeared himself to the Kennedy loyalists by participating early in the promotion of John F. Kennedy's candidacy at a time when there was reason to believe that in doing so he put his own budding political career in Virginia in jeopardy. But, despite his efforts in Kennedy's behalf, he managed to maintain good relations with the state's political leaders, including the senators. Having attended the University of Virginia Law School and practiced law as well as having been active in city, county, and state bar associations for fourteen years, he was well acquainted with the leading lawyers and state judges. Officials in the department felt that he contributed mightily toward securing appointments to federal judgeships in his state which they regarded as excellent.

William H. Orrick (born 1915) did the spotting for California from his position as assistant attorney general, Civil Division. He had been in law practice in San Francisco for twenty years before coming to Washington. He, too, had the intelligence and the personality required of the "spotters" and had served in the Kennedy campaign. His knowledge of California politics and his contacts among practicing lawyers there were extensive. Most of his work as "spotter" had to be done by telephone, but this did not curtail his effectiveness. He knew whom to call and could make good judgments on the reports he obtained, for his knowledge of the California situation was still fresh in his mind. When Orrick went on to the Department of State where he was deputy undersecretary of state for administration he ceased playing a key role in judicial selection.

The White-Katzenbach Standards for Selection

EXPLICIT CRITERIA

There is a general belief that appointment-makers should, in the public interest, set as their goal the naming of "the very best" persons available. However laudable such a goal may be in principle, setting it may create some practical difficulties which will inhibit the selection of top-quality people. First, as Katzenbach liked to ask, "How do you determine who is 'the very best'?" If the department unequivocally commits itself to selecting or accepting only "the very best," it complicates the process of negotiating a consensus. Such an absolute standard which is also a will-o'-the-wisp would encourage controversy among and intransigence in the participants. Relatively, it is much easier to gain agreement that a potential nominee is good as compared to agreement on who is the best. Not only that, but stressing the need to find the very best strengthens the hand of the American Bar Association in judicial selection at the expense of the department. It is one thing to have the ABA Committee on Federal Judiciary pass on the qualifications of a possible nominee; it is quite another for it to determine if he is the best possible. To do the latter would enable the committee to virtually oppose all candidates save one for a particular vacancy. In a real sense, the committee would once again be in the business of officially proposing candidates with a kind of sanction from the department.[8] Aggrandizement of the role of the committee might encourage local and state bar associations to demand a strong voice in judicial selection, for they could plausibly contend that if the organized bar is to help determine which candidates are best, they, rather than the national committee, are the proper agencies for doing so. In this connection, two sentences in the committee's Annual Report for 1960 are very illuminating. They read: "Your Committee eschews the role of judgemaker. The Committee does not suggest nominees; it urges that only qualified candidates be nominated; *and where more than one name is submitted, it strives to have the better or best qualified person selected*" (emphasis supplied).[9] Whether this would net better results is an arguable

66

proposition which will be explored later. Suffice it to say here, White and Katzenbach did not think that it would. To avoid the difficulties described, the position taken was, in Katzenbach's words, "to make good appointments, appointments we can be proud of, without making any claims that they are the very best."

For an impression of the magnitude of the difficulty avoided by such an approach, note the figures given below showing the ABA committee's rating of President Kennedy's appointments (they include six nominees who were confirmed during Johnson's incumbency). Obviously, by definition only 19 of the 130 could have been acceptable to the committee by a "very best" standard, unless an area was so bereft of legal talent that there was no one in the whole area "exceptionally qualified."

Rating	No.
Exceptionally qualified	19
Well qualified	63
Qualified	40
Not qualified	8
Total	130

So far in the discussion "good" has been used in almost a derogatory way to emphasize that it means less than "the very best." But "good" as White and Katzenbach used it meant a very high standard. Important criteria for what constituted a good appointment had been laid down in the president's statement quoted earlier. It was initially drafted by White and Dolan and changed very little by the president and his White House aides. To recapitulate, these criteria were as follows: (1) "unquestioned ability"; (2) "respected professional skill"; (3) "incorruptible character"; (4) "firm judicial temperament"; (5) "the rare inner quality to know when to temper justice with mercy"; (6) "intellectual capacity to protect and illuminate the Constitution and our historic values." It is instructive to compare these criteria with those which Eisenhower's second attorney general, William P. Rogers, felt prevailed during Eisenhower's tenure of office. While he was still deputy attorney general, Rogers explained that departmental officials operated "under standards which President Eisenhower has affirmed and reaffirmed at his press conferences":

First, and most important, the candidate must be an outstanding lawyer

67

and leader in the community from which he comes. Both his personal and professional reputation must be beyond reproach.

Second, the age and health of the candidate must be considered. This policy is designed to provide the bench with men of vigor who are physically capable of carrying the heavy burdens now imposed on federal judges.

Third, whenever a vacancy occurs in a Circuit Court or in the Supreme Court, the President has expressed his desire that outstanding judges should be carefully considered. . . .

Finally, President Eisenhower has stated that in connection with judicial appointments he places considerable weight on "the recognition of the American Bar Association."[10]

There are some interesting differences in emphasis in these statements of standards. The Kennedy administration stressed the qualities of mind and character desired in judges. The Eisenhower administration made more of age, health, and the rating of the Bar Association. Both administrations also applied some of the same standards. The Eisenhower men sought in a judge the same qualities of mind and character that the Kennedy men sought. The Kennedy men took into account the factors of age, health, experience, and Bar Association ratings, but not as rigidly as their predecessors. The difference in approach lies in the respective weights accorded the standards and ratings of the ABA Committee on Federal Judiciary in the two administrations. The extent to which the Eisenhower administration came to be guided by the ABA committee can be gathered from these words of the committee chairman, Bernard Segal, delivered in March of 1961 before he had much experience with the Kennedy administration:

. . . It is only three years since it has become *firmly established* that no lawyer 60 years or over should be appointed to a lifetime judgeship for the first time, unless he is regarded by professional opinion as "Well Qualified" or "Exceptionally Well Qualified," and is in excellent health. . . .

One other qualification—really disqualification—has aroused even more dispute. This is the question whether a lawyer should be required to have trial experience before he is considered qualified for appointment to the Federal Bench. . . . we have taken the position, *from which we have refused to recede,* that in the case of a vacancy in a United States *District Court* . . . a lawyer to be considered must have a reasonable amount of trial experience, preferably at least some of it in the Federal courts. *We have stood firm in this position,* even though it has resulted in delaying appointments of needed judges for a year and a half in two cases and for more than a year in a third. . . . *Nevertheless, the President [Eisenhower] and the Attorney General supported the Committee's position and the appointments were not made.* [Emphasis supplied.][11]

Although the Kennedy men accepted in principle the committee's position on age, they were flexible about its application. Two of the eight Kennedy appointments which were rated unqualified by the committee involved considerations of age. Judge Louis Rosenberg of the western district of Pennsylvania was over sixty when appointed but not yet sixty-four. The committee did not feel that his qualifications were exceptional enough to warrant his appointment in view of his age. Judge Sarah T. Hughes of the northern district of Texas was appointed after her sixty-fourth birthday. The committee flatly opposed the appointment of anyone who had reached the age of sixty-four. But the administration went ahead anyway. Kennedy and his aides felt that Judge Hughes was an extraordinary woman and judge and were proud of the appointment. Amusingly enough, when the committee and departmental officials were locked in controversy over her appointment, it was seriously argued in her behalf that the greater longevity of women generally should be taken into account to equate age sixty-four for a woman with sixty-three for a man.

Again as to physical health, the Kennedy men placed a high premium on good health but were willing to allow more leeway than their predecessors. One of the judges rated unqualified by the ABA committee by reason of poor health was deemed acceptable to them after an investigation convinced them that the reports of poor health were exaggerated and that the judge would not have to stint on performance.

On the question of experience, White and Katzenbach had a profound difference with the committee and did not succumb to the committee's view. From the beginning of the Kennedy incumbency, there was a running argument between Justice officials and Segal. Segal insisted that a nominee for a district court should have, as he liked to phrase it in conversation, "an easy familiarity with the courtroom." White and Katzenbach insisted that qualities of mind and character were more important, that if a choice lay between an outstanding man who had no or little courtroom experience and someone not so outstanding but who had extensive courtroom experience, they preferred the former. They refused automatically to rule out of contention a candidate who did not have "an easy familiarity with the courtroom," although they considered it a real plus factor. This difference of opinion accounted for the appointment by the administration of another of the committee's "unqualifieds." A fifth "unqualified" appointment touched on experience in another way. Although the committee did not insist on courtroom experience for all *appellate* judges, it did insist on considerable legal experience. The committee felt that James R. Browning, appointed to the Ninth Circuit Court at the age of forty-three, did not have adequate over-all legal experience.

As to the weight accorded to committee ratings of professional ability and character aside from any considerations of age, health, and experience, there was an important difference between the two administrations. During the Eisenhower administration, the committee had a virtual veto. If the committee found a person unqualified in ability and character the department officials might try to dissuade it, but, if they failed to do so, they would accept the committee's decision and not make the appointment. White and Katzenbach took the position that they would give great weight to committee evaluations, but, if on consideration of all the information, they felt a particular nomination was sound, they would rely on their own judgment. As Katzenbach told the committee, publicly and directly in an extemporaneous speech he delivered in 1962 to the ABA House of Delegates, as much as he respected it, he did not regard the committee as infallible.[12] He also made it clear in the same speech that he felt it was unhealthy for the committee to exercise a veto power. The *American Bar Association Journal* reported that part of his speech as follows: "As a member of the Association, he said he shared the Committee's disappointment that eight 'not qualified' persons were appointed. But 'as a member of the Administration,' he continued, 'I would remind all of you gentlemen that the responsibility is the President's and the Senate's, and this Association does not have and would not wish a veto over the appointments to be made.' "[13] In private conversation, Katzenbach made the point that he felt it was fortunate that there were some differences of opinion between Justice and the committee, so that it could be clearly established that the administration was not prepared to grant a veto power to the committee.

Differences of opinion over professional ability and character accounted for two appointments of men deemed unqualified by the committee. One involved a question of the professional ethics of the appointee when he was a young lawyer; the other involved the ability and judicial temperament of Judge Irving B. Cooper, discussed earlier.

IMPLICIT CRITERIA

Considerations of Party Affiliation. In public statements regarding criteria for judicial selection, it is rare for officials in any administration to state on their own initiative the obvious truth that the political party affiliation and the party standing of a prospective nominee are weighted heavily. Perhaps the truth is so obvious that it goes without the saying. More probably, however, political leaders feel that the public does not take kindly to emphasis on partisanship in the selection of judges. To mention it in a public statement on standards would be to accentuate the negative, so it is better left unsaid. Our political leaders when queried or when speaking or writing to a politically sophisticated audience never deny that party is important. But they do tend to minimize its importance. When President Kennedy was importuned by the president of the American Bar Association to indicate during the campaign for the presidency in 1960 whether or not he subscribed to the Bar Association's proposal to divide judgeships between the parties, his careful and studied answer was: "I would hope that the *paramount* consideration in the appointment of a judge would not be his political party but his qualifications . . ." (emphasis supplied).[14] William P. Rogers in addressing lawyers, while serving as President Eisenhower's deputy attorney general, said: "Historically, and I suppose it will be true prospectively, each administration appoints principally from its own party. That, in practice, has not proven to be a serious weakness in the system of selection of federal judges."[15] He then went on to add that it would seem desirable national policy "to prevent a gross imbalance from occurring" and that the two major parties should give consideration to finding "some appropriate safeguard" to prevent it. Although Rogers indicated that in his opinion "no fixed formula is practicable," he maintained that "an 80–20 ratio is at least an undesirable imbalance."

Strangely, our political leaders have been apologetic in defending the consideration given to party affiliation and have been unwilling to make the case for it offered in the conclusions of this study. When a defense is articulated, it is usually on the grounds that the particular administration is only doing what has been done traditionally. In this connection, the importance of party in judicial selection is writ large on the record provided by American history, which is set forth in capsule form in Table 3 taken from the *Congressional Quarterly*. Considering the fact that we have had states in which there has been virtually one party, the importance of party is even greater than suggested by

Table 3. Party Affiliation of Judicial Appointments from
Harding to Eisenhower*

President	Number		Percentage from Own Party
	Democrats	Republicans	
Harding	3	57	95.0
Coolidge	8	92	92.0
Hoover	14	67	87.2
F. D. Roosevelt	229	12	95.0
Truman	143	14	91.0
Eisenhower	15	186	92.5

SOURCE: 20 *Congressional Quarterly* 1175 (1962).
    * My calculations for the Truman and Eisenhower administrations give Eisenhower 95 percent and Truman 90 percent. I suspect the *Quarterly*'s figures include some term federal judges.

these percentages. At times a Republican president has been hard put to find a Republican to place on a district court in Mississippi and Alabama, just as Democrats have had difficulty in finding a Democrat in Maine and Vermont.

In the main and in principle, White and Katzenbach felt that judgeships should go to Democrats—if possible, Democrats who had been faithful supporters of the president. They held that it is important to the maintenance of party strength and presidential leadership in the party to reward supporters. This does not mean that they disregarded the explicit criteria. They contended that either major party can meet these criteria in making selections from its own ranks; accordingly, to do so did not mean compromising the explicit criteria.

Occasionally, in order to close ranks in the party, it has been helpful in a particular situation to appoint or accept men who opposed the president at an earlier time. Consequently, some Kennedy appointments went to those who had supported Hubert Humphrey and Adlai Stevenson for the presidency, just as the Eisenhower men had felt it would be wise to appoint some Taft supporters. At other times, an insistent senator has made discretion appear the better part of valor and Justice officials have acquiesced in appointment of a judge who was not regarded as a supporter of the president.

Given their druthers, the Kennedy men would have preferred that judges be appointed from the ranks of the Democratic party exclusively. But as Table 3 demonstrates, it had become customary for at least some of the judges to be nominally of the opposing party. Furthermore, for several years before the Kennedy administration took office, the American Bar Association, prodded by the persuasive and influential Bernard Segal, among others, had accepted and advocated the gospel of bipartisanship preached by Segal. The best statement of that gospel is found in the 1961 Annual Report of the Committee on Federal Judiciary:

> But we cannot hope to achieve full citizen respect for our courts, so long as members of the public have their present cynicism concerning judicial appointments and politics, so long as they continue to regard judicial appointments as matters of political patronage just as they do appointments of local postmasters. . . . the American Bar Association has long contended for the objective that only the best qualified lawyers or judges available should be appointed federal judges without regard to their political affiliation. . . .
>
> In the meantime, your Committee believes that bipartisanship in appointments is an intermediate step. Bipartisanship would serve to differentiate judicial appointments from the predominately political aspects of executive appointments. It would create a wholesome atmosphere around judicial appointments. . . .[16]

In 1959, the ABA House of Delegates resolved (1) "to urge the adoption by the President of the United States of the principle that the number of judges in our federal courts from each of the two major political parties should be approximately equal," (2) "that the Special Committee on Non-Partisan Selection of the Federal Judiciary and the Standing Committee on Federal Judiciary be authorized and directed to endeavor to secure the adoption of such plank at the 1960 National Convention," (3) "that the President of this Association in 1960, after the nominations of the candidates for President . . . by the two major parties, be requested to seek a pledge from each candidate that he will support . . . [bipartisan selection]."[17] As a result of the efforts of Bar Association members, the Republican party included a plank in its platform calling for appointments "on the basis of the highest qualifications and without limitation to a single political party."[18] Although the plank could be interpreted to mean little more than the acceptance of customary standards, the ABA Committee on Federal Judiciary hailed it as "a great step forward."[19] (Note that the words read "without limitation to a single political party" and *not* "without regard to party.")

In any case, Republican candidate Richard M. Nixon, in contrast to candidate Kennedy's more guarded response, answered the inquiry of the ABA president by writing, ". . . I believe it is essential . . . that the best qualified lawyers and judges available be appointed to judicial office, and . . . that the number of judges in Federal courts from each of the major political parties be approximately equal. . . ."[20]

The idea of bipartisanship had received substantial and additional impetus when, in seeking to have the Democratic-controlled Congress pass a pending bill creating new and needed judgeships, Attorney General Rogers announced that the president (Eisenhower) had authorized him "to tell Congressional leaders that he would fill the posts on a 50–50 basis from the two parties."[21] And Deputy Attorney General Walsh later reassured the House Judiciary Committee that the Democrats they would pick would be satisfactory Democrats, not just Democrats acceptable to the Republican administration.[22]

In the course of these events, bipartisanship picked up considerable support from the nation's press.[23]

Under the circumstances, the Kennedy men decided that it would be politically wise to make some concessions even though they regarded Republican exhortations for bipartisanship with great skepticism. As they saw it, the Eisenhower administration had been just like all the others in allowing appointments to be made overwhelmingly from the Republican party before making the offer to split new judgeships, if created. If the Republicans had truly wanted a bipartisan judiciary, they could have led the way from the start by appointing half from each party, setting a precedent that a succeeding administration would have been under great constraint to follow, and in a relatively short time, owing to deaths and retirements, the judiciary would have been balanced. Also, as to what a Nixon administration would have done had he won, the Kennedy men could point out that there was a significant difference that required the Republicans to be conciliatory. There was no doubt going into the 1960 election that the Democrats would control the Congress. This meant that no new judgeship bill could be enacted without a rapprochement, and for the Kennedy men this explained the motives behind the offer to split the appointments. The Democratic leaders in Congress felt that they would rather wait, gambling that a Democrat would be elected. As Emanuel Celler, chairman of the House Judiciary Committee, explained: "Very frankly I believe they [congressional leaders] contemplated a change in the Executive and the leadership gambled as it were—and won—that a new administration will make the appointments. That is nothing new in our political history. . . ."[24] Had they lost, they were still in position to make an arrangement. Not only could they prevent or delay the establishment of new judgeships, but, as a consequence of controlling the Senate, they could prevent confirmation of appointments to old ones. No wonder then, thought the Kennedy men, that the Republicans were prepared to accept bipartisanship; they had no choice.

To keep the issue of bipartisanship in perspective, it is important to bear in mind the point made by the ABA committee quoted earlier: bipartisanship is not the same as nonpartisanship. Making bipartisan appointments would still require taking party into account as a criterion for selection.

But having decided to make some concessions, the Kennedy men had to determine how far they should go. After much thought, it was decided that they should seek to have enough Republicans named to the federal bench to ensure that the percentage of opposing party members would exceed the percentages which had generally prevailed in recent American history. This meant setting a goal of roughly 20 Republican appointments out of the first 140.

Obtaining a consensus on Republican appointments proved a troublesome task. Although Democratic senators and party leaders could see the wisdom of making some appointments from the ranks of the Republicans, none of them were eager to see a post in their own state go to their opponents. In anticipation of difficulty, Justice officials decided that it would be wise (1) to appoint a Republican in Massachusetts, home base for both the president and attorney general; (2) to try to win confirmation for the three Republican judges to whom President Eisenhower had given recess appointments in the last days of his second term; and (3) to attempt to obtain appointments for Republicans in states where there was more than one vacancy. It was felt that it might be more difficult to persuade others to accept Republicans if the president and attorney general seemed unwilling to do so for their own state. Also, Justice officials thought that it would be difficult to explain why, if they wanted some Republican appointments, it was better to make new appointments rather than allowing the three Republicans already on the bench to stay there. Finally, they were convinced that, the more posts there were available in a state, the easier it would be for Democratic senators and party leaders to acquiesce in a Republican appointment.

Following this general strategy, Andrew A. Caffrey, C. Nils Tavares, and John Feikens, the Eisenhower recess appointments, were nominated by President Kennedy for the district courts in Massachusetts, Hawaii, and Eastern Michigan at the end of July 1961. Caffrey and Tavares were confirmed within two months but Feikens was not. The only Democratic senator in Massachusetts was the president's college roommate Benjamin Smith, who had been the president's choice to fill the Senate seat he left vacant. He offered no protest to Caffrey's nomination. Senator Oren E. Long, the only Democratic senator from Hawaii, was not delighted with the idea of a Republican appointment to the bench there, but he chose not to make an issue of it. Michigan's two Democratic senators flatly refused to accept Feikens. He had been highly rated by the ABA committee and officials in Justice regarded him as a first-rate choice, but they were not prepared to carry the fight further in the face of the intransigence of the senators. If they had chosen to prolong the controversy, the next step would have been to give Feikens another recess appointment and await developments.

The next Republican appointments came only after great difficulty. Eighty-six appointments were made before the first new Republican was nominated in March of 1962. In all, nine more Republicans were added to the district courts and none to the circuit courts. One of the nine, Stanley A. Wiegel of California, was a Republican who had been active in Republicans for Democratic candidates groups. There was a real question whether he should be counted as a Republican. Of the remaining eight, four, William C. Hansen, George Templar, Harold R. Tyler, and Edward C. McLean, came from Iowa, Kansas, New York, and New York respectively, states which had two Republican senators at the time of appointment. Since only ten states (20 percent) had two Republican senators at the time, it is clear that such states were overrepresented. Patently, it was easier for the administration to win confirmation for a Republican where there was no Democratic senator to contend with. But this is not to imply that the administration did not have to consider the wishes of the party leaders in those states where there was no Democratic senator. For party leaders did their utmost to dissuade the administration from making a Republican nomination in these states on the grounds that it would undercut the party. In this connection, there is an amusing and instructive illustration. Kansas Democrats told department officials that they were aware that the administration desired to name some Republicans to the bench. They suggested that if Judge Delmas C. Hill was moved up to the Tenth Circuit Court from Kansas, they would have no objection to a Republican being named in their state. Just as soon as Hill, a very fine judge who would have been nominated anyway, was promoted, these same people began to agitate against the selection of a Republican saying that it would be one of the greatest disasters ever to strike the party in Kansas.

Senator Vance Hartke of Indiana, the only Democratic senator from his state at the time, was not happy about a Republican appointment, but he was willing to go along if that appointment went to Republican Jesse Eschbach, and it did. Senators Harrison A. Williams of New Jersey, Clair Engle of California, and Paul A. Douglas of Illinois accepted Republican appointments to the bench in their states but without enthusiasm. The appointment of Bernard Decker in Illinois is of particular interest. The Justice Department was eager to obtain a Republican appointment in that state. Department officials felt, however, that it was necessary to wait until after the election of 1962 to press for it. To nominate a Republican in Illinois before the election might have given substance to a rumor which was being bruited about that the president really wanted Senate Minority Leader Everett M. Dirksen reelected because he had been helpful to the president in obtaining passage of important parts of his program. At the same time, the fact that the vacancy was not being filled gave rise to another rumor—that the judgeship was being saved for Dirksen's opponent, Sidney R. Yates, in the event that he lost the race. That there was no substance to the rumor became apparent when the post went to Decker, even though Yates lost the election.

All in all, the Kennedy administration nominated 11 Republicans out of the 130 federal judges it successfully nominated. (This includes

6 judges who were nominated while Kennedy was president and confirmed after Johnson became president.) In sum, then, the Kennedy administration nominated 8 percent of its federal judges from the opposing party. Table 4 provides a useful summary.

Minority Group Representation. As a matter of policy, the team at Justice sought to increase the representation of minority groups on the federal bench. Out of the 130 appointments, 20 were people who identified themselves to the Justice Department as Catholics, 11 as Jews;[25] 5 appointments were Negroes and 5 were foreign born.

The motives for the conscious effort to place minority group members on the courts are subject to two conflicting interpretations. Remember these were the days before the Black Power movement and ideas about compensatory favoritism for minority groups. The pressures for nominating minority group representatives to the bench were not as great as they are today, nor was there as much recognition that strong efforts probably ought to be made to have such representation. One interpretation is that the administration was primarily interested in building its political strength by befriending the minorities in somewhat the same manner and for the same reasons Massachusetts politicians seek to obtain "balanced tickets" to offer the electorate.

Table 4. Kennedy's Republican Appointments

Name	Date Nominated	Date Confirmed*	State	Total No. of Vacancies State	Circuit	Party of Senators
Caffrey† ..	7/31/61	8/9/61	Massachusetts	2	0	1 Dem.; 1 Rep.
Tavares† .	7/31/61	9/21/61	Hawaii	2	2	1 Dem.; 1 Rep.
Eschbach‡	3/12/62	4/2/62	Indiana	3	2	1 Dem.; 1 Rep.
Templar ..	3/22/62	4/11/62	Kansas	2	2	2 Reps.
McLean ..	4/3/62	7/13/62	New York	10	3	2 Reps.
Tyler	5/17/62	8/2/62	New York	10	3	2 Reps.
Hansen ...	6/23/62	7/13/62	Iowa	2	2	2 Reps.
Wiegel§ ..	7/6/62	8/9/62	California	7	2	1 Dem.; 1 Rep.
Cohen ...	7/6/62	8/1/62	New Jersey	4	3	1 Dem.; 1 Rep.
Crary	7/31/62	8/25/62	California	7	2	1 Dem.; 1 Rep.
Decker ..	12/12/62** 1/15/63	3/28/63	Illinois	4	2	1 Dem.; 1 Rep.

* Notice that confirmation in all cases followed quickly after nomination, indicating that the way had been cleared for acceptance before nomination.

† Originally, an Eisenhower recess appointment.

‡ Democratic senator's choice.

§ Had helped Democratic candidates.

** Recess appointment.

As they themselves saw it, Justice officials were motivated by a desire to have a judiciary which better understands the problems of a wider spectrum of the population than might be true of a judiciary whose composition was highly disproportionate in favor of the white Anglo-Saxon Protestant. But even more important, they contended it was necessary to lift the horizons for the youngsters of the minority groups. They felt, for example, that it would be a great inspiration for young Negroes to see Negro federal judges. To the bright young Negro, this would mean that another avenue of opportunity was open to him, that he could aspire to greatness in the field of law just as he could in the sports and entertainment fields. As Dolan saw it, opening opportunities of this kind for the Negro was important for all Americans, since lack of opportunity has been the reason for much of the stereotyping of an adverse nature which has plagued members of minority groups. In this connection, he liked to relate how an old friend used to say, "The Negroes are no good at football because they don't like to get hit." He then would add, "Look what happened to that stereotype when they got a chance!"

It is possible that the reasons offered for seeking increased minority group representation were rationalizations, conscious or subconscious, to put an idealistic gloss on a not-so-handsome political maneuver. Certainly, such an effort could be expected to bear fruit in coming elections, and the men who made the policy were keen politicians and partisans.

On the other hand, it would be the height of cynicism to suspect motives every time political leaders seek to do away with discrimination. If one is truly committed to democratic ideals, he will have an intense interest in helping create conditions where opportunity is not foreclosed on account of race, religion, or ethnic background. Also, the policy-makers involved here, with the exception of Katzenbach, had had a very personal brush with discrimination in the campaign, where it was necessary time after time to counter charges that a Catholic could not be a satisfactory president. The personal anguish which this kind of discrimination caused must have left a mark on those who were deeply involved. Imagine the feelings evoked when candidate Kennedy felt compelled to appear before the Greater Houston Ministerial Association to argue that a Catholic should not be barred from seeking the presidency. Undoubtedly, he laid bare the feelings of those close to him as well as his own when he said: "But if this election is decided on the basis that 40,000,000 Americans lost their chance of being President on the day they were baptized, then it is the whole nation that will be the loser in the eyes of Catholics and non-Catholics around the world, in the eyes of our own people."[26]

In the last analysis, there could have easily been a mixture of motives, for all of them indicated the same course of action. Whether the Kennedy administration sought political advantage in the narrow sense, chose to broaden opportunity, or desired to inspire the young in minority groups, the way to do it was to increase representation from minority groups on the federal bench.

Again, the implicit standard did not require overlooking the explicit standards. A minority group nominee still had to measure up in terms of intellect, professional ability, and character.

A Special Consideration for Appointments in the South: Attitude on Civil Rights. The Justice team took special pains to check on the civil rights attitudes of those under consideration for nomination to posts in the South. They had two reasons for doing so. For one, the attorney general, both by law and by personal inclination, felt impelled to play a leading role in securing the full rights of American citizenship for the Negro. Since much of the struggle was fought out in the federal courts, in cases initiated by the Justice Department, it would have been ludicrous for department officials to knowingly approve avowed segregationists for nomination to those courts. In this connection, it is important to point out that the officials who were involved in the selection process were also involved in civil rights problems. As a matter of fact, Katzenbach and Dolan spent many hours in on-the-spot performance of duty in civil rights controversies in the South. This was not a situation, then, where one arm of an agency did not know what the other was doing. Secondly, as a matter of principle, they felt it would be hard to justify placing on the bench people who would be unwilling to accept the United States Supreme Court's decisions as the law of the land. As they saw it, the failure of lower courts to follow the decisions of the Supreme Court would lead to confusion at best and chaos at worst. But Justice officials were not unaware of the facts of life. As Deputy Attorney General Katzenbach explained, "We do not expect to find and to be able to obtain confirmation for a militant civil rights advocate in the South. What southern senator could afford *not* to oppose confirmation? What we seek is to assure ourselves that nominees will follow the law of the land. We are satisfied with that much."

In an effort to determine the civil rights attitude of a prospective nominee, Dolan frankly asked his regular sources of information to make an evaluation on that specific point. In addition, he consulted with the Civil Rights Division of the department, which acquired both an expertise about the attitudes of southern leaders and connections with so-called "moderates" who, in turn, could advise the division on the attitudes of particular individuals. But, as Dolan pointed out in discussion of the subject, it was frequently impossible to determine a person's attitude if he had not been actively engaged in the struggle on a political level or he had not been on a court where he had had to render decisions in civil rights cases. Not only that; it is possible, of course, for a person seeking to be a judge to assert and manifest acceptable attitudes on civil rights before selection and then to act quite differently once he has acquired the independence of spirit afforded by a lifetime appointment to the federal bench. And, Dolan suggested, there is no foolproof method for predicting which appointments will turn "sour," which judges will become afflicted with "robe-itus"—a term used by Dolan to describe the condition of a judge who is overly impressed with his own wisdom and power.

The charge has been made that the Kennedy appointees rendered decisions which made a mockery of administration efforts to gain civil rights for the Negro.[27] Implicit in the charge is an allegation that the administration did so knowingly. The president supplied his own answer to the charge at his press conference of March 6, 1963, when he was asked:

Mr. President, yesterday Governor Nelson A. Rockefeller of New York charged that you had been appointing "segregationist judges" to the Federal bench in the South. Privately, some NAACP officials have said before that they, too, had been critical of some of the judgeship appointments that you had made in the South, and that that had blunted a certain amount the oppressive stand that the executive branch had taken against segregation and race problems in the South. Will you comment on that?

His reply was:

No, I think that some of the judges may not have ruled as I would have ruled in their cases. In those cases, there is always a possibility for an appeal. On the whole, I believe—and this is not true just of this Administration, but the previous Administration—I think that the men that have been appointed to judgeships in the South, sharing perhaps as they do, the general outlook of the South, have done a remarkable job in fulfilling their oath of office.

So I would not generalize. There are maybe cases where this is not true, and that is unfortunate, but I would say that on the whole it has been an extraordinary and very creditable record and I would say that of Federal judges generally that I have seen in the last—certainly in the last 10 years.[28]

Another view of the performance of Kennedy appointees in the South was given in conversation by John M. Doar, the former chief of the Civil Rights Division whose efforts in behalf of the vindication of Negroes' rights have become legendary. He said that in the beginning of the Kennedy administration, the Department of Justice had to rely on the judgment of local people in the South regarding prospective judges and it was easy to be misled. Once a federal presence was established there, the Department of Justice could turn to people of its own for judgments about members of the bar in the South. Doar himself became an excellent source of information in the period when he was actively engaged in court battles in the South. The Kennedy administration's southern appointments will be compared with those of the Eisenhower administration in the next chapter.

The Use of Negotiation Strategies

As indicated in the first chapter, the president's men have available the strategies of delay, packaging, and making recess appointments in negotiating with other interested parties to judicial selection, particularly with senators. That the Kennedy administration made effective although limited use of delay and packaging can be demonstrated quickly and clearly from the record which is set forth in Table 5.

Of the 111 circuit and district judgeships open following the passage of the law creating new judgeships in May of 1961, 81 (73 percent) were filled within six months. In view of the time required to make the necessary investigations, to consult and negotiate, plus the large number of vacancies to be filled, it seems reasonable to suggest that six months does not represent an inordinate amount of time for department officials to take before committing themselves to a selection by making either a formal nomination or a recess appointment. Consequently, the table focuses on nominations and interim appoint-

Table 5. Number of Months Which Elapsed before Nominations Were Sent to the Senate or Interim Appointments Were Made in the Kennedy Administration

Kind of Judgeship	Total No. of Nominations	0–6 Months	7–9 Months	10–12 Months	13–18 Months	19 + Months
New circuit judgeships (positions created on May 19, 1961)	10	10				
Old circuit judgeships (old positions vacant as of June 30, 1961)	9	5	Edwards, Sixth Circuit	Seth, Tenth Circuit		Mehaffy, Eighth Circuit
New district judgeships*	62	48	Allgood, Ala. Moynahan, Ky.	Beamer, Ind.† TEMPLAR,‡ Kans. TYLER, N.Y.	Carr, Calif.† Curtis, Calif.† HANSEN, Iowa Foley, Nev. Wyatt, N.Y.	DECKER, Ill.
Old district judgeships	30	18	Jones, D.C.† Elliott, Ga. CAFFREY, Mass. Coolahan, N.J.† TAVARES, Hawaii	Roth, Mich.†	CRARY, Calif.	Robinson, D.C.† Higginbotham, Penn.† Davis, Penn.†
Total	111	81				

* Vacancies in Arkansas, Florida, Massachusetts, and Washington were not filled during the Kennedy administration.
† Delay was in some way involved with efforts to obtain a Republican appointment.
‡ Judges whose names are shown in small capital letters are Republicans.

83

ments made after the six-month period. Bear in mind that times indicated in the table do not include the period required for confirmation, for whatever time that process requires cannot be charged against the administration. The extent to which the strategy of delay accounts for the administration's taking more than six months to fill the remaining 30 (27 percent) vacancies can best be determined by exploring the precise reasons for its doing so.

The fact that seven of the tardy appointments were Republican speaks for itself. As indicated earlier, the administration had difficulty obtaining the consent of senators and state party leaders to the appointment of Republicans. Only by holding out was the administration able finally to engineer agreement. It is equally significant that nine other appointments were held up because of the administration's desire to name some Republican judges. The appointments of James A. Coolahan, George N. Beamer, Charles H. Carr, and Jesse W. Curtis were not made until agreement had been reached with other parties in interest that Republican appointments would be accepted at the same time (Mitchell H. Cohen with Coolahan in New Jersey; Jesse E. Eschbach with Beamer in Indiana; E. Avery Crary with Carr and Curtis in California). The appointment of Stephen J. Roth came late because the administration strove unsuccessfully to place John Feikens, a Republican, in the slot Roth eventually filled. The Pennsylvania appointments were delayed because of the desire of Justice officials to make a Republican appointment, which Senator Joseph S. Clark was loathe to agree to. The two District Court vacancies in the District of Columbia were also held up by a desire to fill one of them with a Republican. Although no senator could lay a claim to priority on either of these appointments, a host of them had candidates. Rightly or wrongly, Joseph Dolan attributed much of the difficulty in filling these posts to finding a Republican in the District who would be first-rate.

The appointment of Oliver Seth to the Tenth Circuit Court vacancy was late in coming because, after the department determined that the position should go to the state of New Mexico, Senator Chavez became adamant about having his own candidate named. Since Chavez's candidate was not acceptable to the department, officials there delayed appointment while suggesting other possible nominees to Senators Chavez and Anderson. It eventually required an on-the-spot visit by

Deputy Attorney General Byron White to win agreement that Seth should be nominated.

Senator McClellan's intransigence held up an appointment to the district court in Arkansas and one to the Eighth Circuit Court (the department felt that the post should go to an Arkansan). McClellan proposed candidates unacceptable to the department and would not accept any but his own candidates. Disagreement with the Alabama senators over a district judge for that state resulted in a delay and the subsequent selection of Clarence W. Allgood. J. Robert Elliott's nomination was a little slow in coming because there was a question about his attitudes on civil rights questions, which required additional time for departmental deliberation. The department delayed the appointment of Roger D. Foley in Nevada, although he had the endorsement of the Nevada senators, because department officials knew that he was rated unqualified by the ABA committee and wanted more time to explore alternate possibilities, but they finally did accept him. Inzer B. Wyatt represents a unique case. Department officials wanted to appoint Wyatt much earlier but he was involved in litigation which he felt obliged to see through to a conclusion. It was decided to seek another nominee. But as time passed with no agreement on a nominee, Wyatt concluded the litigation in which he had been involved and became available.

The long-standing vacancies in Florida and the state of Washington were not filled during Kennedy's administration because the Democratic senators had not settled on candidates, nor had the department candidates of its own for those posts. It was assumed by other officials in the department that the attorney general would decide himself who would be the nominee to fill the Massachusetts vacancy and he kept his own counsel during the incumbency of his brother. Apparently he was endeavoring to line up support for the nomination of Judge Morrissey (see Chapter V).

In sum, it would seem a fair estimate that extended delay was consciously employed as a strategy for attaining compliance in at least 19 out of 100 appointments.

The use of "packages" has already been demonstrated in situations involving Republican appointments. The record suggests that there were other situations where the administration negotiated a package. At approximately the same time three nominations were sent up for positions on the bench in Illinois, three in Louisiana, six in New York, three in Ohio, five in Pennsylvania, and four in Texas.

From the outset the Kennedy administration eschewed the use of recess appointments as a strategy for overcoming senatorial resistance to a nomination. Speaking for administration officials, Joseph Dolan asserted that they felt they would have lost more than they would have gained by making recess appointments. They believed that they would only solidify the opposition of a senator by trying to outmaneuver him in such obvious fashion. Yet the administration made a high number of recess appointments, twenty-eight in all (19 percent). (The Eisenhower administration made twenty-two recess appointments in eight years while selecting roughly twice the number of judges that the Kennedy administration selected.) But before drawing the inference from the high incidence of recess appointments that they were used to bring pressure to bear on senators, consider other reasons for making them. One is to save time. Suppose the staff work on an appointment is completed in October or November when Congress is not in session and it is known that the appropriate senator either approves or will not oppose the appointment. Why wait until the following year to make the appointment? The reason for creating new judgeships in 1961 was that the courts were overburdened with cases. In such a situation, there was good reason for putting judges to work as quickly as possible. A second reason for making a recess appointment other than to pressure a senator is to resist pressure from the ABA committee. As indicated in the last chapter, in face of opposition from that committee, it is helpful to be able to offer to the Senate Judiciary Committee statements from judges who have sat on the same court as the recess appointment attesting to his good performance as a judge.

The best way to test the motives of the administration is to study the record. It seems a fair assumption that, if senators felt they were being pressured by recess appointments, they would protest by either word or action. Twenty-two of the twenty-eight recess appointments were confirmed shortly after the nominations were sent to the Senate in the session following the recess appointment and without a hint of protest from a senator indicating that he thought the recess appointment had been used to circumvent him or put him in an embarrassing position. Now, to turn to the six whose confirmations were held up.

Three judges whose confirmations did not come quickly were Louis Rosenberg, Irving B. Cooper, and Ben C. Green. Significantly, all three were rated unqualified by the ABA Committee on Federal Judiciary. Dolan was frank to admit that he felt that it probably helped in obtaining confirmation for at least Cooper and Green that they were sitting judges at the time of Senate consideration, for since neither the Senate Judiciary Committee nor the Senate was importuned to disapprove by a senator seeking to invoke senatorial courtesy they were free to decide on the merits of the candidates alone. In the end, experience on the job counted heavily. The other three recess appointments which encountered stormy weather over confirmation involved opposition from senators. As indicated in the last chapter, Thurgood Marshall's appointment was held up by the southern contingent in the Senate Judiciary Committee. But it is important to note that the senators from his state, both Republicans, supported him. The administration was not, therefore, using the recess appointment as a counter to the possible invocation of senatorial courtesy. As a matter of fact, it was reasonable for them to assume that Marshall would be confirmed without incident or after the southern senators made a short demonstration for the folks back home, since neither the New York senators nor the ABA committee was opposed to his nomination. As to the recess appointment of Lindsay Almond, recall from our earlier discussion that the president indicated that the administration had thought the appointment had been cleared with the appropriate senator. It was not, therefore, a conscious attempt to pressure him. Finally, there was the recess appointment of John Feikens, a Republican, for a judgeship in Michigan. In view of the known opposition of the Democratic senators from Michigan, it is logical to assume that the administration felt that it might be difficult for the senators to persist in their opposition if the recess appointment were made. Conceivably, the appointment could have been the product of another strategy. Assuming that it knew that the Michigan senators would persist in their opposition, the administration could have been anticipating that it would receive credit from the press and public for trying to make a Republican appointment. In this connection, note that the administration did not continue to hold out, as it could have, but rather filled the vacancy with a nomination pleasing to the senators.

In sum, at the most, only five of the twenty-eight recess appointments can be classed as efforts by the administration to force its will in judicial selection. And only one of them was used to pressure senators in the classic sense, i.e., to override the opposition of senators of the state to which the appointment was made. The record then does bear out Dolan's contention that the administration did not use recess appointments in this fashion. At the same time, it is very significant that the recess appointments were employed three times to counter opposition from the ABA committee.

   In summary, the Kennedy administration played a very active role in the selection of judges and was not content to accept candidates suggested by senators. Officials endeavored to make their selections largely from the party faithful, but at the same time they sought to increase the representation of minority groups, to obtain some Republican appointments, and to ensure that appointments in the South would go to people who would uphold the law of the land. The overriding consideration in all appointments, nevertheless, was that whatever else these people might be, they had to meet the high standards set by the president for character, intellect, and professional competence. In this connection, administration officials placed more reliance on their own judgments than on ABA committee judgments. How good were these judgments? Anthony Lewis of the *New York Times* in March of 1962 accurately assessed the intuitive feelings of knowledgeable observers at that time: "Those in a position to appraise the Kennedy judicial appointments expertly and impartially conclude that it has been on the whole a superior performance. In a few cases it has fallen below minimum standards, but the nominees also include a high proportion of the best men."[29] But the difficulties inherent in making judgments about the quality of judicial appointments will be discussed in the concluding chapter.

CHAPTER **III**

The Eisenhower Administration

DESPITE THE LATER views of the Republican judicial appointment-makers that their counterparts in the Kennedy administration had abandoned the guidelines which they, the Republicans, had established and the views of the Kennedy men that the Eisenhower people had a much better press with respect to judicial appointments than they deserved, the truth of the matter is that the procedures developed by the Eisenhower administration and the performance under those procedures were markedly like those of the Kennedy administration, described at length in the last chapter. This is attested to by the detailed description of the process written in 1957 by William P. Rogers, then deputy attorney general:

. . . Mr. Brownell, at the very outset of his tenure as attorney general, established a procedure, which he has followed consistently. It is designed to insure the selection of judges of the highest integrity and professional attainment.

Whenever a vacancy exists many individuals and groups, including United States senators, submit recommendations in support of various lawyers for appointment to the vacancy. These recommendations and endorsements are all gratefully received, acknowledged and given careful consideration. At the same time the department, through bar groups and governmental sources, initiates its own study in order to secure the best available person for the office.

Sometimes, persons wishing to become judges, make known their interest in person. . . .

When the list of qualified persons is complete, the process of recommending one who appears to merit appointment begins. This process is conducted by the Department of Justice under standards which President Eisenhower has affirmed and reaffirmed at his press conferences. . . .

Finally, President Eisenhower has stated that in connection with judicial appointments he places considerable weight on "the recognition of the American Bar Association." . . .[1]

On reflection, it should not be surprising that the two administrations were so much alike with respect to procedure and performance. In a very real sense, the Kennedy administration, like it or not, was to a large extent prisoner of the legacy left it by the Eisenhower administration. Once the Eisenhower administration squarely placed on the shoulders of the president full responsibility for the quality of judicial appointments to the fervent applause of the nation's press as indicated in Chapter I, there was no turning back. It was and is now highly unlikely that any succeeding administration would risk the wrath of the press and public by being visibly less concerned about the quality of appointments. Secondly, once the Eisenhower administration developed its elaborate and close liaison with the Committee on Federal Judiciary of the American Bar Association, no future administration could disengage itself without sustaining critical wounds which might prove lethal in ensuing election-time combat.

Having duly noted the basic similarities of the two administrations with respect to judicial appointments, it is imperative to point out that there were, nonetheless, some significant differences. Unfortunately, this study was not started at a time which would have made it possible to observe at first hand the Eisenhower administration at work as it was possible to observe the Kennedy administration over a period of several months. Consequently, I can only relay what I learned from interviews with the decision-makers in the Eisenhower administration and from the objective record, without the benefit of firsthand observation.

The Role of the President

It is no secret that Dwight D. Eisenhower assumed his duties as president with the fierce conviction that his predecessor had allowed a serious deterioration in the character of the personnel who headed the government. As he wrote some years later in his memoirs, he felt that "by 1952 numerous instances of malfeasance in office, disregard for fiscal responsibility, apparent governmental ignorance or apathy about the penetration of Communists in government, and a willingness to divide industrial America against itself had reduced the prestige of the United States and caused disillusionment and cynicism among our people. These I felt must be erased if we were to remain a people of self-respect, capable of governing ourselves in a world of strife. This fact made it more essential than ever that we find candidates of the highest possible standing in character, integrity, and ability, to assist me in carrying on the proper functions of government."[2]

How deep his convictions were in the matter was made crystal clear to me in the course of a long interview he generously granted me in his office at Gettysburg on a warm and pleasant summer day in 1964. The hackles on his neck rose as he indignantly reasserted in more colorful language what he had written. At times, his indignation was interlarded with parenthetical expressions of sadness about the low estate to which the government of the United States had drifted. In response to questions, he made it clear that he did not think the federal judiciary was at that time all it should be. He was particularly incensed by what he perceived to be the "imbalance" on the federal bench, i.e., the fact that there were so many more Democrats than Republicans. One very knowledgeable and long-time student of the federal judiciary, attorney Ben R. Miller of Louisiana, who served about nine years on the ABA Committee on Federal Judiciary, feels that President Eisenhower and the press were unfair to Truman on his judicial appointments.[3] But to understand what happened in the Eisenhower administration, it is not important to determine whether President Eisenhower was right or wrong in his assessment. For, right or wrong, his perception of the situation was the basis for the guidelines which he laid down for his administration. He was determined that in his administration every effort would be made to appoint to the federal courts men who would measure up to his concept of a first-class appointment. He explained his concept in his memoirs this way:

I told him [the attorney general] also that I would appoint no one who did not have the approval of the American Bar Association and the respect of the community in which he lived. I further directed Brownell to use the FBI in making a thorough investigation of a prospective appointee's reputation and of every important detail of his life, a practice that I followed respecting major appointments from the very beginning. Another qualification I thought important was that of age. I finally fixed sixty-two as the upper age limit for initial appointment to the federal courts, although I said also that I would waive this requirement, allowing a margin of a year or so if other qualifications were unusually impressive. The general health of the person proposed would also be an important factor. Finally, I told Brownell that I placed a great value on solid common sense—a quality hard to define but well understood by most— and that we would exclude from any list of prospects candidates known to hold extreme legal or philosophical views. I wanted federal judges who commanded the respect, confidence, and pride of the population.[4]

In my interview with him, he expanded on these views. He stressed the point that, if one wanted to identify good lawyers, he went to lawyers for advice just as one would go to businessmen to identify men with business talent. Mr. Eisenhower's enormous respect for professional men came through loud and clear. It is not surprising, therefore, that in his administration, the Committee on Federal Judiciary of the American Bar Association came to play such an important role in the selection process. He did not just support or acquiesce in such a development; he strongly urged it. (When the former president read this chapter in manuscript he noted that he had respect for professional men *of character*—it was "not merely because they were professionals but also men of integrity.")

Another point which he emphasized in the interview was the desirability of previous judicial experience for a nominee to the bench, that is, state judicial experience for a nominee to the district court and state or federal district court experience for those nominated to the appellate courts. But this emphasis did not stem primarily from the belief that the experience per se would be valuable. Rather, he pointed out, looking at what a man had done as a judge was the best way to get a good reading on what he would do in his new post. He explained at length how difficult it is for a president to determine how a man who has not been a judge will perform on the bench. He wryly observed that some of his appointments had disappointed him. He shrugged his shoulders and asked, "What can you do? You just can't ask a man point blank how he will decide cases." He thought such a quizzing would be demeaning and probably not very helpful in any event. The same basic points are made but less emphatically in his memoirs: "Early in my administration I added another item to the criteria I had initially established for the appointment of men to our higher courts, particularly to the Supreme Court. . . . I would not thereafter appoint anyone who had not served on a lower federal court or on a state supreme court. . . . [This] would insure that there would be available to us a record of the decisions for which the prospective appointee had been responsible. . . . "5

When queried about his views and actions with respect to providing for representation on the bench from minority groups, Mr. Eisenhower at first seemed puzzled either by the question or by the fact that I should ask it. I explained what I conceived to have been the policy of the Kennedy administration much as I have set it forth in the last chapter and asked whether or not an administration should actively seek representation of minority groups on the federal bench. His answer was a deliberate "no" as he continued thoughtfully to ponder the question. He said that he, too, felt deeply about the need to help and support minority groups in their efforts to share in America's bounties and opportunities but that he did not think that the way to do it was to seek out members of minority groups as representatives of those groups for high office. As he warmed up to his subject, he inveighed against the use of hyphens to describe Americans as Jewish-Americans, Irish-Americans, and so on: "Damn it, it is time we all stopped thinking that way; we're all Americans period." Whereas he did not think a man should be sought out for high office or a judgeship on the basis of his origin, he was emphatically opposed to origin being a bar. He added that in his view all groups save the Negroes had actually succeeded in breaking the ice and were participating in American life as equals. He summed up his views by saying that as president he instructed those about him to seek the appointment of the very best people without regard to religion, the national background of their forebears, or their color, and that he never urged that they seek someone for appointment on that basis either.

Top members of the president's team at Justice attest to the accuracy of his memory with respect to his having served notice on them in no uncertain terms what he wanted by way of judicial appointments. But we know that a president's wish is not automatically treated as a command by his subordinates.6 Unless a president is aware of what is going on and follows up on his instructions to subordinates there is no guarantee that his orders will be followed. With respect to judicial appointments Eisenhower was to me surprisingly knowledge-able. I say "surprisingly" because I came to the interview with the bias nurtured in academe that he had been an inactive president who had not been much interested in the details of government. Despite the possibility that he might become annoyed at what could be re-garded as presumption on my part, I felt it was imperative to this study to plumb the depths of his knowledge about the judicial proc-ess and judicial appointments. Again at the risk of sounding presump-tuous, I should like to testify for the historical record that Mr. Eisen-hower passed this schoolmaster's oral examination with flying colors. It might come as a surprise to many of my colleagues in academe that his knowledge in these matters far surpassed that of Harry Truman to whom I had put many of the same questions several years before. For example, Mr. Eisenhower was familiar in detail with the issues over which the Supreme Court was split in 1963. He had precise and accurate ideas about where each of the justices of that court had in recent years stood. He was still familiar with details concerning many of his appointments of federal judges, remembering which senators he had trouble with over appointments and what the Committee on Federal Judiciary had done with respect to ratings. It was in this con-text that he expanded on his views about "common sense" and "ex-treme legal and philosophical views." In discussing the views of some Supreme Court justices on law enforcement problems, he made the point that it defied common sense to take the position that the gov-ernment law-enforcers were always wrong. The law of averages, he suggested, would seem to indicate that in some cases the government should be right. He objected to the doctrinaire absolutist position of Black with respect to First Amendment freedoms, preferring instead the balancing approach of Justice Harlan which struck him as com-monsensical. (In reviewing this chapter, Mr. Eisenhower pointed out that he objected to Black's position as he perceived it at the time of the interview; later Black had shown "an apparent about-face on the subject.")

As to how a president should perform his onerous duties, Eisen-hower's views were best expressed in the advice he gave to his chief subordinates: "Again and again I emphasized the need for efficient decentralization within each agency of the government. My principal assistants, I insisted, in the interests of sanity and efficiency, should save for themselves time for thinking and study. The only way they could get such time was to delegate as much as possible to their subordinates. 'The marks of a good executive,' I wrote to the heads of agencies on September 29, 1953, 'are courage in delegating work to subordinates and his own skill in coordinating and directing their effort.'"[7] It is beyond the compass of this study to attempt to judge whether or not he acted accordingly with respect to his legion of tasks as president. But with respect to judicial appointments he did. Like other presidents he delegated the task of narrowing the field of possible nominees for federal judgeships to the Justice Department. And senators and others who attempted to approach him on nominations to the bench were directed to get in touch with the team at Justice. He insisted, however, that the attorney general or deputy give him a rundown when the field had been narrowed to a few choices. He expected and received a briefing on the assets and liabilities of those being considered, particularly where the other parties in interest were urging a candidate which did not measure up to presidential standards.

During the course of our interview, Mr. Eisenhower emphasized another issue not touching on appointment which seems important enough to warrant a moment's digression. He expressed the view that something should be done about the tenure of judges. He pointed out that Black and Douglas, for example, would serve in excess of thirty years in their respective lifetimes. He felt that lifetime tenure could give a judge an inordinate amount of time to influence the direction a court takes. Also, he thought there was a problem of their keeping au courant with life about them in view of their isolation while on the bench. He had no fixed notions about what an appropriate length of service should be, but thought that it would be in order to study a possible revision of the constitutional provision granting federal judges virtual lifetime tenure.

As William P. Rogers Saw It

At the age of forty William P. Rogers was appointed to serve as Dwight D. Eisenhower's first deputy attorney general. He remained in that post until late 1957, when he was appointed to succeed Herbert Brownell as attorney general, the position he held for the remainder of Eisenhower's second term. His climb to the heights of political power had been exceedingly swift. Born in 1913 in the small town of Norfolk, New York, he graduated from Colgate University in 1934 and received his law degree from Cornell University in 1937. After being admitted to the bar of New York, he served as assistant district attorney of New York County from 1938 to 1942 under District Attorney Thomas E. Dewey. During the war years he was a lieutenant commander in the navy. In 1946–47 he returned to his post as assistant district attorney, this time under Frank Hogan. From there he moved on to join the staff of the Senate War Investigating Committee in 1947 as counsel and become chief counsel. From 1948 to 1950 he was chief counsel of the Senate Investigations Subcommittee of the Executive Expenditures Committee. From 1950 to 1953 he was a partner in the distinguished law firm of Dwight, Royall, Harris, Koegel and Rogers with offices both in New York City and Washington.

Anthony Lewis of the *New York Times* has described Rogers's rather sudden entry into the arena of partisan politics this way:

He got into politics at the top. When the Eisenhower-Taft fight for the Republican nomination developed in 1952, Rogers walked into Eisenhower headquarters at a Washington hotel and volunteered his services. He was sent to New York to meet Brownell and put to work on what turned out to be the determining factor in the fight—the seating of contested delegations at the convention. Rogers was the tactician who got onto the nation's television sets and front pages the Eisenhower charge of a Taft "steal" of delegates, and it was the promotion of this charge that eventually routed Senator Taft.

During the 1952 convention, Rogers renewed his casual friendship with a member of the credentials committee, Senator Richard M. Nixon. They had met in connection with Nixon's work as a member of the House Committee on Un-American Activities, when the then Congressman asked Rogers' legal advice on the Hiss-Chambers affair. (Rogers told him to push ahead.) Their common interests (golf, for example) and closeness in age (Nixon is a few months older) had thrown them together.

At the end of the 1952 convention Rogers was asked to come along on the Vice Presidential train and help set things up. Before long that train was the focus of the campaign. With disclosure of the expense fund maintained by California supporters for Nixon, several advisers deserted his cause and began talking about substituting another candidate. Rogers counselled standing fast. He handled communications with the Eisenhower advisers—Brownell, Sherman Adams and others. And he helped arrange the television speech that recaptured for Nixon the good opinion of the President and public.[8]

96

To those closely associated with him in the campaign, Rogers had proved himself both in ability and in loyalty to the new team. It was not surprising, therefore, that he should be sought out by Herbert Brownell, the newly designated attorney general, to be his deputy and for the president and his political intimates to find the choice gratifying.

As with all success in human endeavors, luck and happenstance had played a part in the orchestration of events which contributed to the making of William P. Rogers the deputy attorney general, but his rapid rise was no fluke. Rogers is blessed with extraordinary endowments and talents. From his law school days, when he was on the *Law Review*, he has sought to excel in his work and he was born with the intellectual horsepower to drive successfully to that goal. In addition, his looks and personality are assets. He is big and good-looking enough to stand out in a crowd. He conveys an impression of toughness and integrity. Yet he smiles easily, is courteous and warm in manner, and is exceptionally articulate. In a most masculine way, he has charm. He is candid and direct in his dealings with others. The wonder of it is that the Republican party never saw fit to tap the man to seek high *elective* office in the days before he was selected for the post of secretary of state. He would have been a natural. Perhaps the explanation lies in the fact that he had spent so much time in the District of Columbia that there was a problem of residence.

I opened the working part of our interview in 1963 by asking Mr. Rogers how he would describe the process of the selection of federal judges. He made the point emphasized in the opening of the first chapter. Each appointment is different. As he put it, "Each appointment is a little drama of its own." He said that you cannot talk of a process as though it were the same in every case. Rather, you must describe the factors and the general kind of considerations which go into the making of appointments.[9]

I asked him to comment on the observation that is frequently made that senators "own" the judgeships and that the Justice Department merely approves or disapproves the candidates offered them. He snorted in derision and said that it just was not so, that "we made the appointments." He asserted that "of the 106 or so appointments in which I participated, I would state that all but two were presidential (as opposed to senatorial) appointments." "Of course," he added, "some of the appointments were men the senators wanted, too, and we were content to let them have any credit they wanted to claim for them." One of the two "non-presidential appointments" involved Senator Knowland when he was Senate majority leader. Knowland was adamant and the department took a man that they were not happy about but only after delaying for eight months in the hope that Knowland would back down. Later, in another connection, Rogers pointed out that some senators could be very tough to deal with and the men in Justice had no choice but to give way in some few cases. He cited the late Senator McCarran as a case in point. He said that McCarran didn't give a damn about anything save getting his man appointed. When he was chairman of the Judiciary Committee and the Appropriations Committee, he was in a position to sabotage the administration and had no compunctions about doing so if he did not get his way. Rogers wryly observed that he could appreciate the problems the Democrats must have had with McCarran.

Rogers related that at the outset of his incumbency as deputy attorney general, he and Attorney General Brownell decided that they were going to go all out to get the best men they could for judgeships. He said that he felt even at that time that it would be a good idea to have more bipartisanship on the bench. He smiled and asked, "Well, why didn't we?" He pointed out that the ratio of Democrats to Republicans on the bench was 82 to 18 percent when the Republicans took office. When it got near to 50–50, he would have been prepared to try bipartisanship. As if to anticipate my next question, "Why not attempt to get it for the long run by splitting appointments from the start?" he went on to say that they never would have been able to pull it off. The party, long out of power and hungry for jobs, would have called them "idealistically stupid." In short, then, he agreed that getting the best men meant for all practical purposes getting the best Republicans.

How did he go about getting candidates? It varied depending on the state. In some states such as Ohio, the senators were very conscious of the need for first-rate judges. After all, Taft was the son of a former chief justice and was more conscious than most of the importance of the judiciary. Senator Bricker was a lawyer with a profound interest in the law and courts. When Justice officials came up with the names of outstanding men whom they wished to consider for judgeships in Ohio, they would go to Taft and Bricker and suggest them, talk it out, and reach an understanding.

In Indiana, when Indiana had the best claim on a vacancy for the Seventh Circuit Court, Republican Senators Jenner and Capehart both had candidates. (According to Rogers, they never agreed on candidates.) The department would not take them. The department suggested John S. Hastings, a distinguished lawyer, who later did get the post. Senator Jenner threatened to oppose the appointment by declaring that Hastings was "personally obnoxious." The matter was brought to the president's attention and he told the department to go ahead with the Hastings appointment. Rogers said that he then went to Senator Jenner and told him that they were going to make the appointment and that they did not think "that you have the guts to stand up and object to him in the Senate."

In another state with two Republican senators, the senators did not get along. When a vacancy occurred there, both sent in names. Senator A—— sent in the name of the United States attorney and the other senator sent in the name of a man who was thought to be well regarded by the president but who turned out to have a reputation as a heavy drinker. The United States attorney was a mediocrity. Neither was acceptable to the department. Rogers related that he "sat tight," while the senators stewed. Neither would talk to him nor would they even answer his phone calls. The newspapers back in the state began to raise questions about the vacancy. Finally, the senators asked Rogers to suggest a move to break the deadlock. He asked them each to send a list of people they would be willing, if not happy, to see considered. In an aside, Rogers said that if senators do not get along, they always try to avoid putting someone on their list who might turn out to be the favorite of the other, for later the other senator might be able to reap whatever prestige and credit a senator can get from having "his man" appointed. Both senators sent in lists. Z——'s name appeared on both lists and he was the man department officials themselves wanted. At first Z—— was not eager to accept appointment but he was soon persuaded. Neither senator was very happy with the appointment at first. But later, as Z—— was developing a reputation for being an outstanding judge, the senior senator wrote to Rogers to tell him that in retrospect he thought the appointment had been an excellent one. Rogers observed that senators find

99

that a good appointment redounds to their credit locally just as a poor one selected while they are in office becomes an albatross around their necks.

I asked Mr. Rogers how the department went about getting leads on names independently of the senators. He answered that he inquired from everyone, judges, top newspaper people, United States attorneys, and people from the other party. He said he always tried to get the jump by coming to the senator(s) with a name before they came to him. He pointed out that the department frequently had the advantage of knowing well in advance when someone was considering retiring. It is a common practice for a judge considering retirement to alert the department as a matter of courtesy. If Justice officials were dealing with a senator who seemed to resent the fact that he could not name the candidate, they would get someone else, state party leaders or distinguished lawyers who were friends of the senator, to press the department's choice on the senator.

I related the newspaper account of Senator Symington naming a candidate and putting the administration on the spot[10] and asked him if this ever happened and what they did about it. He said several senators had tried it but the administration did not give in.

As to recess appointments, he said that sometimes this was a useful device to get a man by a senator. But it depended upon the senator. If department officials knew that it would only make things more difficult they would not try it. He said that they had used the device successfully on only a few occasions. (It is interesting to note Mr. Eisenhower's reaction to this observation when he read the chapter in manuscript: "The attorney general may have made his recommendations on this timing—but such a thing never occurred to me!")

While on the subject of the role of senators, Rogers made this significant observation: "If you have guts, the administration has far more power than the individual senator." Delay, the interim appointment, and running the risk of being challenged to oppose openly an appointment (a good one, that is) are too much for a senator to cope with. He pointed out that even so powerful a senator as Taft felt compelled to back down on one occasion. After the men of Justice had decided on certain age restrictions, Taft wanted a man who, although outstanding, was beyond the desired age limit. Taft became angry about the decision but he did back down.

I asked Rogers where the idea of an age qualification as enunciated by President Eisenhower came from, indicating that I thought the Committee on Federal Judiciary generally took credit for it. He said it had been the administration's own idea and that the committee did not get into the picture until after the policy had been established.

In answer to a question about the role of the Committee on Federal Judiciary, he said that the department placed great store in the committee's ratings but reserved the right to go against them. He admitted, however, that in the last two years of Eisenhower's incumbency no one had been appointed whom the committee rated "unqualified." But he went on to add that he thought the committee had been a little less important than the committee liked to think it was. In the course of our discussion on this point, Mr. Rogers made the observation that he thought that no man should serve as chairman of the committee for as long as Bernard Segal had.[11] For me the implication was that Mr. Segal had been a thorn in the department's hide. Later, Mr. Rogers emphasized that the ABA committee should never initiate suggestions for nominees. I asked, then, "In view of Segal's close relationship, didn't he ever suggest names?" Rogers replied, "He may have initiated a few—but they were probably for Pennsylvania judgeships; in any case they were not given any special weight."

When I asked him to tell me how decisions were made on nominations, Rogers smiled and said that it was impossible to fix the decision-making process in any precise way. The deputy, whether it was he or Walsh, did the original work. The attorney general would make the department's decision ultimately but he would rely heavily on the deputy's judgment. This was particularly true in cases where the judgeship was for a state, say Utah, where the attorney general would not know much personally about any of the men being considered. If the appointment was for New York, there might be a lively discussion about it, since all the principals in the department were from New York. "Herb Brownell might in a New York situation, after a discussion, say, 'If we can get any one of these three people, it will be fine.'" If the deputy was encountering trouble at any time, he would go to the attorney general and tell him about it and the attorney general might suggest a course of action. Often, where difficulties were arising, the president would be so advised personally. In any case, they would generally check with the president before sending over the papers.

One important point Rogers made about decision-making was this. When Brownell briefed him on his duties, he assured Rogers that he would not be forced by the attorney general to accept a man he felt was not up to standard. In short, Brownell really gave him a veto power. Rogers said that when he moved up to the attorney general's slot, he made the same promise to his successor, Walsh.

According to Rogers, the White House staff never tried to tell him what to do. The attorney general dealt directly with the president on appointments. He did keep General Persons (deputy assistant to the president) informed, particularly about fights they were having, since it was important for Persons, who served as the president's liaison with Congress, to understand who was angry and why.

In response to a query about whether or not they checked the political philosophy of a nominee, Rogers said generally no. I asked about southern appointments. He admitted that they checked to see if prospective nominees had been members of rabid segregationist organizations or if they had made wild statements. When I suggested that there had been evidence in departmental files that on several occasions they had checked for views of prospective appointees on law enforcement procedures, presumably to keep men who might be too "soft" on alleged criminals off the bench, he talked at length about how naive some people are about law enforcement problems. He suggested that it was very easy to become overly concerned about the rights of the accused. He spoke at length of his experience as a prosecutor. He said he was as concerned as anyone about civil rights and civil liberties but he was also concerned about the victims.

In discussing the role played by the candidates themselves, Rogers insisted that it was not true that all of them sought the nominations. He thought a significant proportion, about 20 percent, really were sought out.

In concluding the interview, I asked if he saw ways to improve the system. He replied that he thought it would be helpful if we could find ways to focus attention on the work of the courts. He thought it would be helpful if the chief justice gave an annual report to Congress on the judiciary just as the president gives a State of the Union message. He said that he had pushed such a proposal and that the chief justice liked the idea but that then the Supreme Court decided the *Brown* case,[12] the landmark case dealing with segregation in the schools, and it became in his judgment a bad time to push it further. He thought, also, that it would be a good idea to get a kind of gentleman's agreement between the parties that they would keep the courts bipartisan. He said it would strengthen the appointing officials' position if they could say to people in their own party, "Look, we've got to divide these appointments up; if you don't come up with a strong candidate and the other party does, we'll have to give the appointment to them." Also, the opposing party would be on its mettle to recommend outstanding people.

He did not think much of the idea of making appointments for less than lifetime. He asked, "How could a judge in the South hope to get by the Senate if he decided cases pro civil rights?" He felt that it would be helpful if individual senators did not attempt a veto power. He made it clear that he was cognizant of the practical difficulties involved in getting senators to cut down their prerogatives.

On the way to the door, he remarked how proud he was of the job the Eisenhower administration had done in appointing judges to the federal bench.

Several of Rogers's observations warrant further discussion. Evidently, he did take a much harder line with senators than either his Republican successor, Walsh, or the Kennedy deputies. This was verified in interviews with senators and other close observers of the process. In mulling over the reasons for the hard line and Rogers's apparent ability to engineer the appointments he wanted, I related to Joseph Dolan the account given me about Rogers defying a senator to get up in the Senate and declare that a nominee was "personally obnoxious." Dolan's reaction was "What did he want to do that for?" He said that it is difficult enough for the administration to keep its relations with senators cordial and cooperative without deliberately goading them. He indicated that, although the Kennedy men would also stand up to senators, they tried hard to be conciliatory. Some interesting hypotheses suggest themselves for Rogers's being less conciliatory. Rogers himself suggested one of them. He said that since the Republicans had been so long out of power, some of the Republican senators really did not know exactly what their due was from a Republican in the White House. A second possible explanation was the fact that Eisenhower was an exceptionally popular president, more popular with the electorate than his party. This would make senators a little more timid about crossing swords with him than they would be with a president who was not demonstrably as popular. Also, for a good part of the time Rogers was playing a leading role in the judicial appointment process, the Democrats controlled the Senate. On that basis, one could hypothesize that support from senators of the president's party was not as crucial to the Eisenhower administration as to, say, the Kennedy administration. Further, since Eisenhower was more satisfied with the status quo than Kennedy and was not pushing for vast legislative programs, that, too, could account for less concern for senatorial feelings. Possibly it could be argued that Rogers and company were more highly principled or less sophisticated politically than their Democratic counterparts. But such an assertion does justice neither to the character of the Kennedy men nor to the acumen of the Eisenhower team. Perhaps the answer lies in the personality and experience of Rogers himself. For one thing, he had worked for senatorial committees for several years and was not unduly awed by senators. But more than that, Rogers impresses one as the kind of man who thoroughly enjoys a good scrap, particularly if he can hold the moral high ground. Where his choice appeared to him to be clearly better than a senator's, in his view he was holding the high ground and he could rely on devastating fire support in terms of the unfailing support of a very popular president. It may well be that a combination of these factors best accounts for Rogers's attitude toward senators.

As to the question of checking the philosophical views of prospective nominees, it would seem that there is a large difference in kind between checking a prospect's views on civil rights and checking his views on law enforcement. In the one case, civil rights, it would seem proper for the department to attempt to ascertain if a man who would be a judge would *follow* the Supreme Court's decisions. But, when the department attempted to ascertain what a man might do with respect to law enforcement in the years Rogers was in office, it was apparently seeking to pick men who took a jaundiced view of the Supreme Court's decisions in that field, particularly the decision in the *Mallory* case.[13] In *Mallory* the court construed the federal rule which requires prompt arraignment of a defendant as mandatory.

This meant that even a voluntary confession made between arrest and delayed arraignment was inadmissible at the trial. Most law enforcement officials to this day regard the decision in *Mallory* as a horror. Assuming that department officials in Rogers's time shared that view, and it would appear that they did, it might have been a relevant consideration for a Supreme Court appointment to attempt to determine whether a nominee held another view. But lower court judges cannot reverse Supreme Court decisions per se. Consequently, if the hope was to have lower court judges moderate the Supreme Court's decisions, there was a heavy cost to be reckoned with, the danger of undermining the Supreme Court's authority.

As Lawrence E. Walsh Saw It

Rogers's successor, Lawrence E. Walsh, took office as deputy attorney general at the age of forty-six, making for a relatively young team at the top of Justice (Rogers was just short of forty-five at the time), though certainly not as young as the Democratic teams which followed. In personality, Walsh was a sharp contrast to Rogers. Where Rogers was outgoing and urbane, Walsh was quiet, almost solemn in mien and manner. But like Rogers, he was tall, slender, handsome, and youthful looking. As to character, those who knew him regarded him as a man of unusual integrity.

Like Rogers, Walsh, too, came to the department following a striking career of public service. He was born in 1912, the son of a physician in Nova Scotia. His family moved to the United States when he was two. He worked his way through Columbia College and the Columbia Law School. He received his law degree in 1935 and was admitted to the New York bar in 1936. In 1938 along with a number of other ambitious men, he hitched his star to the crusading district attorney Thomas E. Dewey. He served as deputy assistant district attorney from 1938 to 1941. Later from 1943 to 1949 he was assistant counsel to Governor Dewey and from 1951 to 1953 the counsel. From 1951 to 1953 he was counsel to the New York Public Service Commission and then the general counsel and executive director of the Waterfront Commission of New York Harbor, 1953–54. From that post, he was appointed to a federal district judgeship in the southern district of New York. He served in that position from 1954 until 1957, resigning from what could have been a lifetime post to become the deputy attorney general. As a judge, Walsh quickly acquired an outstanding reputation for both his wisdom and his speed in disposing of cases. Walsh's appointment to and acceptance of the post as deputy came about as a consequence of Rogers's desire to have him and his persuasiveness in selling the idea of coming to Washington to Walsh.

I interviewed Judge Walsh while he was serving his last days in office. I was accompanied by Professor William M. Beaney, then of Princeton University, who had been most helpful in the planning phase of this study. Using one of Walsh's published articles as a jumping-off point, we asked to what extent the department took the initiative in the selection of nominees to the federal bench.[14] He said it depended upon whether or not there was a senator of the president's party from the state where the vacancy existed. If there was, he would check first with the senator. Where there was no senator of the president's party, he would take a great deal of initiative in seeking out candidates directly. But even in those cases there would be a close check with state party leaders. He stressed, however, that the process of appointment varied depending upon the situation, and that there were a number of people who were generally very deeply involved in the process, the president, the attorney general, the deputy, senators, party leaders, American Bar Association officials and members, and sometimes the candidates themselves. He suggested that generally the appointment actually represented a consensus rather than the decision of a single person. He said an ideal appointment was one where "everyone thought his man got the nod." He considered this to be the reason a number of people can and do take credit for a particular appointment.

In response to our questions, Judge Walsh made it clear that he thought the story of how a judge was appointed could not be learned from looking at records and files alone. He felt it would be necessary to go back to the areas from which the appointee came to interview political leaders and members of the local bar associations as well as to interview officials in Washington. He was not sure that even at that it would be possible to get the full story, because so much of the negotiation was on a highly personal basis, i.e., phone calls and private conversations which were not reported.

We asked specifically about the role the Committee on Federal Judiciary played in the appointment process. He answered that he worked closely with Bernard G. Segal, then chairman, for whom he had an exceptionally high regard. Segal would provide him with the assessments of the committee on prospective nominees. In response to our query, Judge Walsh said that it frequently happened that a local bar association would rate a particular prospect far differently from Segal's national committee. But even in face of that fact, he felt it was wise policy to rely on the judgment of the national committee because of an awareness that the local group's assessment might be based on factional differences in the local association.

As to the National Committee of the party, Judge Walsh said that the committee served primarily as a conduit to the state party people. He preferred to work through the committee usually rather than to canvass state party people directly to avoid embarrassment and to avoid undue pressure. He thought that once one started dealing directly with people on the state level, it opened the way for a number of individuals and factions to exert pressure directly. He preferred that that kind of heat be focused on the National Committee. Nonetheless, this did not make the National Committee part of the decision-making apparatus. He emphasized that the committee only served as a means of communication. He indicated that for the same reason he did not want to deal directly with the prospects either. He preferred instead to deal through intermediaries to ascertain a man's willingness to accept appointment, to clear up questions about his health or matters pertaining to his career which came up. These intermediaries might be political leaders, distinguished lawyers, or a senator.

In response to the question "What do you look for in a prospective nominee, or what are the criteria for a 'good' judge?" Judge Walsh answered, "(1) integrity, (2) vigor, (3) temperament, (4) intellectual ability." In expounding on this theme, he conveyed the impression that where you could accept less than the best with respect to ability, a judge must have unquestionable integrity and must have the vigor to do the job.

We asked, "What kind of experience best qualifies a man for a judgeship?" He said that he felt very strongly that previous trial experience was a tremendous asset. He thought an occasional professor or lawyer with no trial experience added a little necessary leavening to an appellate court, but he was convinced that the better judges even on appellate courts were those with trial experience.

As to whether or not a man's general slant politically, whether he was conservative or liberal, should be taken into account in the selection process, he thought not. He said, "It comes out in the wash," a man's slant does not matter much particularly at the district court level.

In discussing his published account of asking seven outstanding trial lawyers in one metropolitan area if they would consider a federal judgeship before he could find one that would,[15] he said that the stumbling block was salary (salaries of judges have been raised since this discussion). He did not think that the retirement program available to judges was attractive enough in itself to a man making $75,-000 a year. Such a man would say, "Hell, my kids are in college now. I need the income now. I'm not thinking about twenty years from now."

When asked about his general appraisal of the appointment process, he responded that it probably was about as good a one as we could have. He indicated that he was very much opposed to election of judges as practiced in some states. This led to a query about his impressions on the quality of federal as against state judges. He felt the federal judges were on the whole superior. He thought salary, tenure, and prestige of the federal judgeships accounted for the difference in the quality of the men who could be attracted. He pointed out, however, that, at that time, the salaries of some of the New York State judges exceeded those of federal judges. Even though he thought that some of the New York judges were exceptionally fine, he felt that the federal posts were still more appealing. He said that it would make an interesting study to get a panel of outstanding lawyers in New York with high incomes ($50,000 a year and up) to indicate what type of judgeships they would be willing to accept. His hunch was that most of them would give up private practice only for a federal judgeship, if at all.

In retrospect, the most striking observation made by Judge Walsh was his assertion that a judge's philosophy, particularly at the district court level, did not really matter. Interestingly enough, about 50 percent of the district judges subsequently interviewed took the same position, asserting that in the type of cases they decide it really does not matter what their philosophy is. There is impressive evidence to the contrary, however.[16] In addition to the studies cited, the other 50 percent of the judges interviewed felt that in certain types of cases like antitrust suits, philosophy made a difference. One judge of liberal persuasion complained that one good measure of the difference between liberal and conservative judges could be found in the sentences given to businessmen for income tax evasion. He asserted that some conservative judges never gave jail sentences in such cases, whereas liberal judges sometimes did. One of my fondest interviewing memories grows out of a discussion with one district judge on the importance of philosophy. The judge had indicated it made no difference. At that point, I said that I had sat in his courtroom that very morning and was not surprised when he, a liberal Democrat before ascending to the bench, was exceptionally solicitous of an indigent defendant eighteen years of age. Before sentencing, the judge had asked not only the lad if he had something to say in mitigation but also his mother and sister if they did. The judge bridled, and said, "Why, do you know that I just two days ago threw the book at a businessman whom a jury had found guilty of fraud." When I suggested that this did not surprise me either in view of his pre-judicial reputation as a liberal Democrat, he first looked puzzled and then grinned broadly acknowledging that I might have a point.

Subsequently, being kind enough to review this chapter in manuscript, Judge Walsh in a letter to me made these significant observations on the foregoing paragraph:

With respect to your discussion of the importance of a judge's underlying philosophy, I think there has been some oversimplification as well as confusion between its effect upon an individual case, its effect upon the court as a whole and its importance as a factor of selection.

There is no doubt that a person's basic slants, political or otherwise, may affect his judgment on an occasional individual case. On the other hand, the cases coming before federal judges are so varied that the biases of the various judges tend to neutralize each other in the long run and in the overall effect upon the nation. As to most cases in the district court level, there is little room for an exercise of bias. District judges are severely curbed in their interpretation of the law by the appellate courts and their view of the facts in any case, even antitrust cases, will be overturned if it is the least bit arbitrary. Further, in at least half of the cases coming before them the ultimate question of fact is resolved by a jury rather than

109

a judge. On the basis of these observations, I should like to clarify my views as follows:

1. As to an occasional individual case, the underlying biases of a judge can have some effect.

2. As to the overall impact of the courts, these biases neutralize each other and are not serious unless a determined effort were made to select judges having only a particular point of view.

3. As a factor in selection, I do not believe that the political slant of a judge should be important unless it is so severe and dogmatic that it would cast doubt upon his temperament and intellectual capacity.

In interviews, Eisenhower, Rogers, and Walsh had been most convincing in asserting their determination to make judicial appointments of high quality; at any rate, I was convinced that they were so determined. Toward that end, they believed that they had set criteria and developed procedures, particularly their liaison with the ABA Committee on Federal Judiciary, which would ensure that they would achieve outstanding results. Does the objective record bear them out?

The Objective Record

PREVIOUS JUDICIAL EXPERIENCE OF JUDGES

It was the explicit policy of the Eisenhower administration to lay stress on previous judicial experience in the appointment of judges particularly to the appellate courts. In the articulation of the policy, an impression was created that this was a new approach. Consequently, the objective record reveals some surprises. First, with respect to choosing district and former district judges for posts on the courts of appeals, surprisingly the Truman administration did better than the Eisenhower administration and the Kennedy administration did almost as well. See Table 6. By way of contrast, the Hoover administration demonstrated what an administration could do when it was dedicated to maximizing judicial experience. Eleven of its sixteen ap-

Table 6. Previous Judicial Experience of Appeals Court Appointments in the Truman, Eisenhower, and Kennedy Administrations

Administration	No. of Appointments	Those Who Had Been Federal District Judges	
		No.	%
Truman	26	12	46
Eisenhower	45	18	40
Kennedy	21	8	38

peals court appointments (69 percent) were men elevated from the ranks of district judges. If judicial experience at the state as well as federal level is taken into account, the Eisenhower administration improves its comparative position only somewhat. See Table 7.

With respect to appointments to the district courts the objective record shows that the Eisenhower administration did not in fact place a higher premium on prior state judicial experience than did its immediate predecessors. And on the record, the Kennedy administration placed somewhat more emphasis on this factor than the Eisenhower administration. See Table 8.

Table 7. Previous Judicial Experience of Circuit Court Appointments in the Truman, Eisenhower, and Kennedy Administrations

Administration	No. of Appointments	Those with Judicial Experience at Federal or State Level	
		No.	%
Truman	26	16	62
Eisenhower	45	28	62
Kennedy	21	11	52

Table 8. Previous Judicial Experience of District Court Appointments in the Truman, Eisenhower, and Kennedy Administrations

Administration	No. of Appointments	Those with Previous Judicial Experience	
		No.	%
Truman	98*	28	29
Eisenhower	128†	33	26
Kennedy	107‡	35	33

* Includes two nominated by Roosevelt and appointed by Truman.

† Includes three recess appointments at end of term.

‡ Includes four nominated by Kennedy and appointed by Johnson.

In reviewing Tables 6–8, Judge Walsh suggested that it was "unfair to compare Presidents who succeed prior Presidents of the same political party with those whose administration represented a change in political party. Of course, a successor Democratic President may be expected to promote more Democratic district judges than a new Republican President." Consequently, in his view to include Truman in the tables and to allude to Hoover is misleading.

With respect to Table 8, Judge Walsh wrote this additional interesting and meaningful comment: "Table 8, I believe, emphasized a relatively insignificant factor, namely prior *judicial* experience for district judges. It was the view of Mr. Rogers and myself that the important factor was prior *trial* experience, whether obtained as a practising lawyer or a judge. In other words, it was important that a large percentage of trial judges be drawn from lawyers and judges having litigation experience rather than those experienced in corporate, real estate and other matters."

PARTY AFFILIATION

Despite the strong statements made by the leaders of the Eisenhower administration on the need for bipartisan selection of judges, their record indicates that like all administrations before and after, they chose overwhelmingly from their own party. Administration officials argued that it was necessary for them to do so to redress the balance, since they came to office after twenty years of Democratic control of the White House and the judiciary was largely composed of Democratic appointees, that in the waning days of the second Eisenhower administration they had proposed splitting appointments if the new judgeship bill was passed. Whatever the merits of that position, of the 182 (includes nine special court appointments) life-term judges appointed by Dwight D. Eisenhower only nine were Democrats. Six of the nine came from southern states and three of them had been "Democrats for Eisenhower" during a presidential campaign. How this record compares with that of other recent administrations can be seen from Table 9.

Table 9. Percentage of Judges Selected
from Opposing Party in the Truman,
Eisenhower, and Kennedy
Administrations

Administration	Percentage
Truman	10
Eisenhower	5
Kennedy	8

AGE OF APPOINTEES

President Eisenhower and his chief subordinates in the selection process placed great emphasis on the need for guarding against the appointment of judges who were well along in age. Although there was a change in the age pattern from the Truman administration it was hardly as dramatic as the rhetoric would have suggested, as indicated in Table 10. In fairness, it should be pointed out that the Eisenhower

Table 10. Percentage of Judicial Appointments in Different Age Groups in the Truman, Eisenhower, and Kennedy Administrations

Administration	District Judges				Circuit Court Judges			
	60 and over	50–59	40–49	30–39	60 and over	50–59	40–49	30–39
Truman	16	40	38	6	35	46	19	0
Eisenhower	10	56	31	3	33	52	13	2
Kennedy	8	54	34	4	19	62	19	0

men evidently made a successful effort to lower the maximum ages at which appointments would be made. None of the Eisenhower district judges was over sixty-three when appointed; Truman placed one sixty-eight-year-old, one sixty-six-year-old, and two sixty-four-year-olds on the district court bench. To the circuit bench, Truman appointed one sixty-nine-year-old; Eisenhower's oldest was sixty-six. Significantly, if there is virtue in appointing judges under sixty years of age, the Kennedy administration did better in this respect than did the Eisenhower administration.

Curiously, the average ages of federal judges on appointment for the administrations of Truman, Eisenhower, and Kennedy were about the same—52.

SOCIOECONOMIC BACKGROUND

In a splendid study of the backgrounds of Eisenhower and Kennedy appointees, Professor Sheldon Goldman examined socioeconomic factors and came up with this interesting conclusion:

. . . both the Eisenhower and Kennedy appointees tended to come from middle-class backgrounds, and . . . whatever mobility did occur was probably predominantly within that class. The route to judicial appointment by mid-twentieth-century America most certainly included a law school education and this rather than social origins was all-important for providing opportunities for occupational as well as social mobility. There was little to support any claim of a class "power elite" either by the schools attended or the occupations of the judges at the time of appointment. What was suggested by the data, however, was that the Eisenhower

Administration appointees tended to be of a higher socio-economic status (determined by education and major occupation at time of appointment) than the Kennedy appointees. While the differences between the two groups were relatively small, the observed differences were thought to reflect the differing social composition and political commitments of the two parties. This was reinforced by the data on the religion of the appointees. However, it is well to keep in mind that the differences were those of degree, and the results, on the whole, underscore the absence on the American scene of a party system built on pronounced class and ethnic cleavages.[17]

Perhaps the best explanation for what difference there was lay in the difference in attitude with respect to ethnic and religious considerations. For example, Judge Walsh commented on these considerations in this way: ". . . Such considerations are to me highly speculative and of dubious relevance in a study having to do with the selection of able judges, unless its point is to suggest that the President who was *least* influenced by so-called ethnic or religious considerations was the best." Compare that attitude with the attitudes attributed to the Kennedy administration in the previous chapter.

APPOINTMENTS FROM THE DEPARTMENT OF JUSTICE

The Eisenhower administration nominated eighteen, or roughly 10 percent, of its judges directly from the ranks of the Justice Department; twelve were United States attorneys and one an assistant United States attorney. The Kennedy administration only elevated three, or fewer than 3 percent, from the department. Appointments from the department can be viewed several ways. They can be looked upon as evidence of recognition of merit or they can be regarded as a mark of departmental favoritism. Perhaps the most valid explanation for the greater number elevated by the Eisenhower administration lies in the emphasis it placed on courtroom experience for men nominated to the district courts. United States attorneys have an opportunity to demonstrate their courtroom abilities.

RECESS APPOINTMENTS

The Eisenhower administration made less use of recess appointments than the Kennedy administration, but in both cases the percentage of recess appointments appears high. See Table 11. Of course, it is difficult to establish in how many cases the recess appointment made

Table 11. Recess Appointments during the Eisenhower
and Kennedy Administrations

Administration	No.	Percentage of All Appointments
Eisenhower	25	14
Kennedy	28*	22

* Includes three nominated by Kennedy but actually appointed by Johnson.

it difficult for a senator to oppose the nominee. Significantly, only one of Eisenhower's recess appointments did not eventually receive a permanent appointment, Feikens of Michigan. And none of the Kennedy recess appointments failed to do so. Presumably, if senators felt that they were being bypassed deliberately, they would have bestirred themselves to protest or to reject some of the nominations beyond the unusual one of Feikens who had been given a recess appointment by a Republican president in the closing days of his administration before being succeeded by a Democrat.

DELAY

The Eisenhower administration made much greater use of the strategy of delaying appointments than the Kennedy administration as Table 12 makes clear. These data suggest that the Eisenhower administration was probably less deferential to senators' wishes than the Kennedy administration, that the president's men, in order to make the appointments they wanted, more frequently applied the strategy of delay. An unexplained memo in the Department of Justice files makes this comparison with the Truman administration regarding delay:

LIFETIME JUDGESHIP APPOINTMENTS

Truman Administration

137 Judges
Average time between vacancy
  and nomination: 133 days
Average time between nomination
  and confirmation: 38 days

*Eisenhower Administration
through May 5, 1959*

144 Judges
Average time between vacancy
  and nomination: 163 days
Average time between nomination
  and confirmation: 39 days

APPOINTMENTS IN THE SOUTH

In his very fine study of southern federal judges and school desegregation, *Fifty-Eight Lonely Men*, published in 1961, Jack Peltason

115

Table 12. Delay in Making Judicial Appointments in the Eisenhower
and Kennedy Administrations

Administration	7–9 Months		9–12 Months		12–18 Months		19+ Months		Total	
	No.	%	No.	%	No.	%	No.	%	No.	%
Eisenhower	13	7	12	7	19	10	4	2	48	26
Kennedy	6	5	5	3	6	5	7	4	24	17

castigated President Eisenhower for his refusal "to provide moral leadership or to use his powers as Chief Executive in support of the Supreme Court decision (*Brown* case)."[18] Peltason documented a bill of particulars which included:

Eisenhower insisted that the refusal to obey the federal courts could not be dealt with by law enforcement, but only by moral conversion, yet he made little attempt to lead the people toward this conversion. . . .

The President made no attempt to answer segregationists who on the floor of Congress, on national television and in public forums, taught that it is honorable and profitable to defy the United States government. . . .

President Eisenhower believed it was desirable to obey the law, but he deliberately refused to endorse the *Brown* decision on its merits. The only time he did state his own views, he gave aid and comfort to the segregationists. . . .

Not only did Eisenhower refuse to lead the forces of civil rights, but when he did speak, whatever his intentions, his words hurt southern moderates. By defining the situation so minimally and by constantly emphasizing the need to go slow, President Eisenhower made it appear that any school board or any district judge calling for integration, no matter how limited, was taking an "extremist" stand. . . .

There is a fundamental public interest in school-entry suits. But President Eisenhower considered them to be only private matters between two parties in which the federal government had no concern.[19]

Peltason concluded: "The President's nonintervention policy has had its impact on the judges as well. If they can find a legitimate reason for postponing an unpopular ruling they are apt to do so. Nor were those judges who did act encouraged by the fact that if they ran into opposition, the President's backing was by no means assured. In this situation the most recalcitrant judge and the most defiant school board were allowed to set the pace. When a judge allowed a school board to get away with its program of 'nothingness,' there was a delaying reverberation throughout the South. Other judges were afraid to get too far out in front of the pack."[20]

In light of Peltason's criticism, it is significant to note that in a thoroughgoing analysis of judicial performance in the Fifth Circuit in civil rights matters, the editors of the *Yale Law Journal* did not single out even one Eisenhower-appointed district judge for criticism.[21] Of the nine district judges faulted in the article, two had been appointed by Franklin D. Roosevelt,[22] three by Harry S. Truman,[23] and four by John F. Kennedy.[24] To the district bench in the four states of the Fifth Circuit covered by the analysis, Georgia, Alabama, Mississippi, and Louisiana (the Fifth Circuit also includes Florida and Texas), Eisenhower had appointed six judges[25] and Kennedy eight.[26] Of two Kennedy appointments to the Circuit Court, the Yale editors criticized one and rated the other inconsistent. Of the five Eisenhower appointments to that bench, three were commended,[27] one criticized,[28] and one rated as inconsistent.[29] Peltason's own work, published before the Kennedy administration had been long in office and which, consequently, does not deal with the Kennedy appointments, contains criticism of five Eisenhower district judges[30] drawn from a wider area than the Yale study and the same circuit judge[31] faulted in the Yale study. Significantly, Peltason singles out for praise four Eisenhower-appointed district judges[32] and seven circuit judges.[33]

(Of interest also is Mr. Eisenhower's own comment on Peltason's bill of particulars against him: "Nuts . . . While in office I never publicly commented on *any* Supreme Court decision. What does this guy think the 'Little Rock' incident was all about? Seems to me he starts off with a preconceived notion, and then *tries* to prove it. Also does he have any idea how hard the attorney general and I worked to get through the first civil rights legislation in 80 years?")

In an interesting doctoral dissertation (Yale), Mary Hannah Curzan classified the judges selected in the Fifth Circuit, 1953–63, as Segregationists, Moderates, and Integrationists. In her words: "Classifications of the judges into Segregationists, Moderates, and Integrationists is done on the basis of the civil rights cases—reported in the *Race Relations Law Reporter*—which each judge has decided; it is broken down into decisions for or against civil rights litigants. A percentage of pro-Negro or pro-civil rights worker decisions can then be related to each judge."[34] Her findings were as indicated below.[35]

On the basis of these findings, Dr. Curzan expressed surprise that there was a general belief that Eisenhower's judges had done better than Kennedy's judges in the matter of civil rights. She attributed

Classification	Eisenhower Appointees	Kennedy Appointees
Segregationists	5	5
Moderates	8	3
Integrationists	2	8

what she regarded as a false perception to three factors. One, two of the most prominent integrationists were Elbert P. Tuttle and John M. Wisdom, appointed by Eisenhower. Two, Kennedy's segregationists attracted the most publicity. Three, the ABA publicly had favored Eisenhower. But then she concluded: "Finally, there is one empirical basis upon which the Eisenhower appointees do appear to be more liberal than the Kennedy appointees to the courts of the Fifth Circuit. If one takes the total number of civil rights cases decided by all the Eisenhower and Kennedy judges in each year and determines the percentage of those cases that favored the Negro plaintiff, the Eisenhower judges have a more liberal record than do the Kennedy judges."[36]

But there is perhaps another more important reason. Using only case decisions and counting them as equal qualitatively is misleading. When I first endeavored to go that route myself, Judge John O. Butzner, an outstanding federal judge whom I consulted, persuaded me that to do so would be deceptive. He pointed out that how the judges rule on motions and objections and a host of other crucial indicators are neglected in such an approach.

In sum, for whatever reasons, the Eisenhower-appointed judges, patently, have at least as good a record as the Kennedy judges with respect to vindicating the Negroes' civil rights.

AMERICAN BAR ASSOCIATION RATINGS OF JUDGES

In view of the deference of officials of the Eisenhower administration toward the American Bar Association and their pride in the quality of their selections, it is interesting to compare the ratings given their appointees with those of the Kennedy administration. See Table 13. It would appear that, at least in the eyes of the ABA raters, qualitatively there was little to choose between the appointments of the Eisenhower and Kennedy administrations.

118

Table 13. Percentage of Judges Appointed during the
Eisenhower and Kennedy Administrations in Each
of the ABA Rating Classifications*

Rating	Eisenhower	Kennedy
Exceptionally well qualified 17.1		16.6
Well qualified 44.6		45.6
Qualified 25.1		30.7
Recommended 6.9		0.8
Neither recommended nor opposed 0.6		0.0
Not qualified or opposed 5.7		6.3

* The interpolations for the Eisenhower appointees have been
borrowed from Joel Grossman, *Lawyers and Judges* (New York:
Wiley, 1965), p. 198. Grossman explained: "Ratings for the
years 1953–1958 have been adapted to fit the rating system in
use at that time. Thus, 'especially' or 'very' well qualified were
equated with 'exceptionally well qualified,' etc."

What emerges from a comparison of the characteristics of the Eisenhower appointments and those of the Kennedy appointments is the
conclusion that they are more alike than different. This suggests the
hypothesis that administrations which basically are concerned to
make appointments of high quality will choose the same kind of people for the same kind of reasons whatever goals and standards they
articulate. In retrospect, the descriptions of the selection process detailed in these first three chapters tend to verify the hypothesis.

CHAPTER IV

The American Bar
Association Committee

AT THE OUTSET, two observations about the Standing Committee on
Federal Judiciary of the American Bar Association come to mind.
First, in view of lawyers' natural interest in and concern about the
quality of the men who serve as judges, and in view of the important,
albeit the changing, role that the committee has come to play, it is
surprising that it was not until 1952, one hundred and sixty-three
years after the Constitution was adopted—seventy-four years after
the ABA was established—that the organized bar was able to insert
itself in the selection of federal judges in a significant way. Second,
it is striking how difficult it is to generalize about the role the committee has played. Like any committee setting out to deal with important substance, this committee had to conceive of a role, organize
and develop it. And, not unlike other committees, this committee has
tended to be dominated by its chairmen and be a reflection of their
ideas and personalities. In view of the purpose of the committee, its
role at any given time is as much a product of what key individuals
in the Department of Justice think it should be as of its own thinking.
Since the work of the committee seems to require a very close relationship between the chairman and at least one official in the Department of Justice, how these people react to each other on a personal

120

basis is critical. Consequently, the role that the committee has played has depended in large measure upon the ideas and personalities of the committee chairmen and the president's men, and the personal and official relationships which have existed between them. No two chairmen have behaved in the same fashion or have interacted in the same way with the president's men, who also have behaved differently from one another. This is not to suggest that events are not important. But more often than not, the events which have an impact are an outgrowth of the ideas and personalities of the individuals involved. Presumably, the committee is here to stay, as are some of the operating procedures of the committee and the methods of interchange between the committee and Justice. But the real impact, at any given time, of the committee's efforts depends, and will continue to depend largely on who the chief actors are.[1]

The Setting

Before 1946, the American Bar Association made only one abortive attempt, in 1932–34, to inject itself into the process of federal judicial selection in any significant way.[2] In 1946, the House of Delegates of the association constituted a Special Committee on the Judiciary with

the duty of considering and reporting as to the nominations made or under consideration for appointments to judicial office in any of the Courts of the United States, and to recommend to the House of Delegates or the Board of Governors such action as it may deem to be advisable to promote the appointment and confirmation of competent and qualified candidates and to oppose the nomination or confirmation of unfit candidates if any such are under consideration. *The committee shall not have the power itself to select and propose particular nominations for any judicial office.* [Italics supplied.][3]

The following year, at the committee's urging three resolutions were passed by the House of Delegates granting the committee an exceptionally broad mandate:

1. . . . to consider and report *to the House of Delegates* concerning all matters relating to appointments of judges of the courts of the United States.
2. . . . to promote the nomination and confirmation of such persons as the committee, after investigation, deems to be competent for appointment *as federal judges.*

3. . . . to oppose the nomination and confirmation of such persons as the committee, after investigation, deems to be unfit or not sufficiently qualified for appointment *as federal judges.*[4]

Particularly noteworthy is the fact that the committee was now empowered to *promote* nominations. Nor was this a happenstance. In the report accompanying the proposed resolutions, the committee told of a conference involving, among others, Senator Forrest C. Donnell, who was a member of the committee as well as a newly appointed member of the Senate Judiciary Committee, and Senator Wiley, the chairman of the Senate committee. Quoting from a statement of Wiley's to the effect that "so long as I am chairman of the Judiciary Committee, full weight will be given to the recommendation of recognized and respected law groups, in contrast to those of public officials," the committee concluded: "It is obvious, not merely from this [Wiley's] statement but from the conference which three members of your committee had with Senator Wiley . . . that if the committee is authorized to promote the confirmation of competent nominees and to oppose the confirmation of unfit candidates, its views will be given great consideration by the Senate Judiciary Committee." The committee went on to add: "If the committee is authorized also *to promote the nomination of competent persons* [italics supplied] and to oppose the nomination of unfit persons, it will endeavor to establish a similarly useful contact with the Attorney General, in order that the American Bar Association's opinions may be accorded weight when nominations are under consideration."[5] The power to promote nominations was not easily won. In the debate on the issue, John G. Buchanan, the committee chairman, argued:

The Committee does not ask for authority itself to select and propose particular nominations for judicial office, but the Committee firmly is of the opinion that the only effective method of opposing a proposed nominee who is believed to be not qualified in the judicial office or not so well qualified as another available person, is to support the qualified nominee; and the Committee asks for itself the power to report to the House of Delegates or the Board of Governors, as the case may be, its recommendation that the House or the Board shall propose or oppose nominations for judicial office.[6]

Two members of the committee protested:

The report of the Committee proposes that the Committee be continued and given the power to propose to the House of Delegates or the Board of Governors the appointment of particular persons to the federal bench. That power was specifically denied the Committee in the Resolution establishing it. We believe that restraint is wise and should not be relaxed if the Committee is continued.

There is no hope, if we are realistic, that either the appointment or confirming power will listen to voluntary advice. Experience would indicate the soundness of this viewpoint. Hence, there must be established some qualification by law. We also believe that the subject is of such pressing importance as to compel immediate action. For these reasons, we cannot concur in the report of the Committee and must register our dissent.[7]

W. Eugene Stanley pointed out that the "language [of the resolution] may be construed by some as giving the authority to the Committee to actually recommend the names of judges for appointment." He said he was concerned that this might be giving the committee "the power to get into what might . . . have considerable political repercussions."[8] But Buchanan and the committee majority came away from the meeting with more than they had evidently been willing to settle for. The resolution spelled out above did *not* require the committee to promote nomination *only* where specific approval had been given or action taken by the House of Delegates or the board.

The committee lost little time in endeavoring to effectuate its new, broad mandate. In a matter of days, the committee briskly moved to establish contact with the attorney general.[9] The stress the committee laid on promoting candidates, the vigor with which it moved, and its basic goals were all well manifested in the candid report the committee gave of its activities in behalf of the nomination of Harold R. Medina to the District Court for the southern district of New York. The committee drew the following conclusion from its endeavors:

The case of Judge Medina is an illustration of what can be done by this committee to aid state and local bar associations which are on the *qui vive,* as soon as a vacancy in a federal judgeship occurs, to obtain the best possible man to fill the place. The relationship of this committee with the committees of the New York State Bar Association and the Association of the Bar of the City of New York is a very close one. If other state and local associations worked so closely with this committee, it is believed that learned, experienced, and able lawyers, rather than men of mediocre capacity who have devoted what talents they have to political rather than professional work, will be appointed in almost every case. A United States Senator may well decide that it is safer to thwart the wishes of a local bar association than to disappoint the ambitions of henchmen for whose help he is indebted; but will a President, constitutionally responsible for the quality of federal judges, appoint a mere politician

123

instead of a learned lawyer when the appointment of the latter is earnestly called for by the duly constituted representatives of the organized American Bar? And if the President should be tempted to yield to the importunities of a particular Senator in favor of a particular politician against such a lawyer, can he expect that the Senate, equally responsible with the President for the quality of the federal judiciary, will confirm the political nominee? No; the time has come when, if the bar speaks for the appointment of truly learned and capable judges, we may expect that Senators and Presidents alike will join in their appointment and confirmation.[10]

In view of what seemed a fast and auspicious start, it is not surprising that the committee was made a standing committee of the association replete with a new name in 1949. Accordingly, the bylaws of the association were amended to include the following paragraphs:

(j) *Committee on Federal Judiciary.* (1) This Committee shall consist of eleven members, one from each federal judicial circuit and one from the District of Columbia, each of whom shall serve until the adjournment of the third annual meeting following his appointment, and until his successor is appointed, and from whom the President shall designate a chairman annually . . .
(2) This Committee shall have power, on behalf of the Association, to promote the nomination and confirmation of competent persons for appointment as judges of courts of the United States and to oppose the nomination and confirmation of persons deemed by it to be not sufficiently qualified. It shall have power also to report to the House of Delegates or the Board of Governors on any questions relating to the behavior of judges of such courts and any matters relating to the sufficiency of the numbers of the federal judiciary.[11]

Significantly, the committee was still in the promotion business. But the going was rough, despite the committee's zeal. As Professor Joel Grossman pointed out in his very fine book on the committee: ". . . although the ABA Committee did contribute to the rejection of four judgeship nominations during this period, it was unable to do much to promote the nomination of high-quality judges."[12] Actually, as Grossman indicates, the committee opposed ten nominations to the federal courts, only four of which were subsequently rejected by the Senate. The partial success that the committee had achieved with the Senate Judiciary Committee can be attributed to events as well as personalities. In the election of 1946, the Republicans won control of the Senate and Senator Wiley became chairman of the Judiciary Committee. Rightly or wrongly, Republicans have tended to be more sympathetic to ABA efforts to involve itself in the selection process and to pay more mind to ABA ratings than Democratic senators who have tended to regard the ABA as a Republican-oriented organization. As Grossman reports: ". . . the Democratic Committee Chairman from 1949–1953 did not hold the ABA in the same affection as had Senator Wiley. Although Senator Pat McCarran of Nevada continued the practice of formally requesting an ABA opinion on each nominee, he declared that he was 'firmly resolved that the bar associations shall not choose the judiciary of the country.' "[13] Grossman attributes the failure of the committee to establish a liaison with the Justice Department at this time to President Harry Truman's hostility to the ABA. But it was not a matter of the president standing alone. His hostility was reinforced and fed by partisan Democrats who headed the Department of Justice and who comprised a good number of the members of the Senate. In any case, the committee did make recommendations to the attorney general when it learned of judicial vacancies, but these recommendations were not given any special weight, nor did the attorney general take up the committee's offer to investigate and report upon candidates other than its own.[14]

Perhaps, as Grossman suggests, the most long-lasting impact of the committee's early activity was its decision to endeavor to work within the system rather than to attempt to change the system.[15] As indicated earlier, two members of the committee had wanted it to urge Congress to set qualifications for judges. Had the committee opted for such a course of action, the subsequent history of judicial selection would probably have been very different.

Enter Ross Malone

In 1951–52, external events had a profound impact on the committee's destiny. As charges and evidence of wrongdoing in the Truman administration began to turn up with disturbing frequency, the Department of Justice came under fire for failure to prosecute, particularly in cases alleging tax evasions. The press of the country howled with indignation. For example, the *Nation,* which was not unfriendly to President Truman generally, complained that "if the President had demanded a higher standard of performance from J. Howard McGrath [the attorney general], and his predecessor Tom Clark, the Justice Department's tax division might never have been headed by Caudle [who was then very heavily under attack and who later was actually indicted and convicted for his part in a conspiracy to aid federal income tax evaders]." It went on to describe Justice "as a department conspicuous for indolence, complacency, low morale, and—it now appears—granting favors to friends in tax trouble."[16] In late January of 1952, the House Judiciary Committee voted unanimously to investigate the Justice Department and the attorney general. Hearings began in late March and then the situation became as zany as it was rotten. Attorney General McGrath had on the first of February named Newbold Morris as a special assistant attorney general with the specific assignment of cleaning up the department. One of the measures taken by Morris was to draw up a comprehensive questionnaire on which he wanted government officials to disclose their financial status. He publicly stated in late March that the attorney general would get the first questionnaire. In short order, on the morning of April 3, McGrath announced that he had fired Morris. The same day, President Truman announced that he had accepted the resignation of McGrath.[17] James P. McGranery, a federal district judge, was appointed as the new attorney general. He now had the unenviable task of seeking first-class men to serve as his chief aides in the wake of ensuing resignations. Understandably, there was a reluctance, if not downright resistance, on the part of top-quality people to join forces with an administration which was at the end of its days and whose reputation and prestige were perilously low.

As fate would have it, the name of Ross Malone, a forty-one-year-old New Mexico attorney, was suggested to the attorney general. Malone, a Democrat, was a member of the House of Delegates and the Board of Governors of the American Bar Association and enjoyed an exceptionally fine reputation in legal circles. In due course, Malone became the deputy attorney general in August of 1952 and as such was in a position to affect very markedly the process of judicial selection. And so he did. As Malone later related to Professor Grossman: "Through my membership in the House of Delegates of the American Bar Association and subsequently on the Board of Governors, I was aware of the fact that the Committee on Federal Judiciary had sought for some time to make its voice heard in the selection of federal judges prior to the time that a decision had been reached in the Department and a name forwarded to the White House. I was also aware that the Committee had been wholly unsuccessful in these

126

efforts."[18] In view of his activity in the association, it is not surprising that Malone felt strongly that the committee should play an important role in judicial selection. Consequently, he suggested to the attorney general that the department obtain the views of the committee on prospective nominees before deciding on nomination. There is some question about how willing McGranery was to go along with such an arrangement;[19] nevertheless, he did. And the committee was also agreeable. In essence, there was now an official agreement between the attorney general and the committee giving the committee a recognized role in the selection process. The agreement was never actually put into play in the Truman administration, since no appointments were made in the waning days of that administration.

After the election of Eisenhower, Malone had the opportunity to meet with Attorney General-designate Herbert Brownell and Deputy Attorney General-designate William Rogers. In his letter to Professor Grossman, he reported that he "was extremely anxious to sell" the arrangement he had devised. Brownell and Rogers bought, but with the stipulation that the committtee would eschew promoting candidates of its own. Grossman records that "the Committee reluctantly accepted this stipulation," and quotes from the committee's Annual Report the observation that "your committee believes that it could be more helpful to the Department of Justice in many instances by affirmatively recommending candidates of outstanding qualifications who have been selected without any regard to political considerations."[20] But Edward J. Fox, who was a member of the committee at the time and the chairman shortly afterward, wrote in 1957 with regard to the arrangement: "A similar arrangement was reached under the Eisenhower Administration with Attorney General Brownell and Deputy Attorney General Rogers. However there was a slight modification in the functioning of the Committee at that point. It was decided to forego the suggestion of names for vacancies and give its undivided effort to the investigation of the names submitted to it by the attorney general. This change in procedure was suggested by the attorney general. *It was not forced on the committee in any way.* The change was agreed to by the full committee and after a trial period it was decided to continue this policy in the belief it was the best way to accomplish its result" (emphasis supplied). He went on to indicate his pleasure with the way the procedure had worked out in those first years: "This decision puts the Committee in a totally objective position. Except on rare occasions, the Committee has always had ample time to complete its investigation and make its report to the Attorney General before the Attorney General made a recommendation to the President."[21]

Enter Bernard Segal

From 1956 through 1963 the story of the committee is the story of Mr. Bernard Segal. He became a member of the committee in 1955 and then for six successive terms served as chairman. Segal is a man of unusual force and physical vigor who at the age of more than sixty displays the kind of energy which would do credit to a man half his age. He has been an inveterate "do-gooder" in the best sense of the word. The list of causes he has battled for or served is as varied as it is impressively long. So effective has Segal been in working *pro bono publico* that even presidents and attorney generals have sought him out for help. From 1953 to 1955, he served at President Eisenhower's request as chairman of the Commission on Judicial and Congressional Salaries. In 1954 and 1955, he was a member of the attorney general's National Committee on Antitrust Laws. More recently, at President Kennedy's request, he agreed to serve as co-chairman of a special committee of lawyers formed to "help open lines of communications between races."[22] For Segal, the law is a religion and judges are the keepers of the faith. It may have sounded a bit much to some when Segal told a congressional subcommittee that a federal district judgeship "constitutes the most important single position in preserving the difference between our way of life and that of the Iron Curtain countries; namely, the protection of the lives and the property of the individual, the emphasis on the individual as the paramount consideration of a whole government and of a whole people, rather than the interest in the collective security which the Iron Curtain countries emphasize. It is to this judge, to the trial judge, to whom we must look to preserve those essential liberties and those essential rights."[23] But anyone who has had an opportunity to spend much time with Mr. Segal would have little doubt that he meant what he said. More than that, there is impressive evidence of his sincerity in the fact that he has devoted a great deal of time in the past twenty years to, in his words, "various phases of judicial organization and administration, with special emphasis on judicial selection at Federal, State, and local levels."[24] Although one might quarrel with his ideas and methods, it would seem a fair assessment that one cannot fault his motives.

As a consequence of his ideas, his zeal, and his vigor, Segal devoted an amazing number of hours to his duties as committee chairman. He told a congressional subcommittee: "I might just remind you that during the period from August 11 to September 27, 1961, 47 days, President Kennedy appointed 69 judges, more than 1 a day, and I might say that during that particular year . . . the time I alone, forgetting the committee, devoted to this single task of investigating and reporting on judges for that year or prospective judges, were 2,080 hours or better than 40 hours for every week of the year."[25] Nor was this a rough estimate. Like all good lawyers, Segal keeps careful track of his time. The fact that Segal devoted so much time to the task has been verified by two deputy attorney generals. Walsh publicly stated in 1959 that "Mr. Segal has become, next to the Attorney General himself . . . my most intimate associate in Washington. I work with him and spend more time with him than anybody else in the Department."[26] In a more jocular fashion, Byron White, when the deputy attorney general, alluded to Segal's penchant for calling him on the phone: "I would like to especially say that Mr. Segal, as the chairman of that committee, has done a magnificent job. I don't know how he finds any time to practice law but perhaps he doesn't because he is always on the phone and I have had less sleep during the past year than I have ever had because of Mr. Segal. He never seems to go to bed at night."[27] This was no exaggeration; it was the way Segal worked. Deeply committed to the idea that his committee had a unique opportunity to encourage a decided improvement in the quality of the federal bench, he was going to leave no stone unturned. The pressure he put on the president's men was unrelenting. Unquestionably, these men could have been less receptive or less hospitable. But it would have been hard to refuse his counsel graciously. Of course, Segal's interest and activity created some difficulties for the president's men. He had to be very much taken into account in the appointment process. At the same time, he was a great help. First, he was a good source of data. As indicated earlier, the president's men with whom he worked were genuinely interested in obtaining high-quality appointments. Segal and his committee were of considerable assistance in assessing talent. Also, Segal and the committee could be and were used as a device for exerting pressure on senators in an indirect way. It was helpful to the president's men when they preferred a candidate other than a senator's if they could tell the senator that his man was not considered qualified by the committee.

As Segal made himself a force to be reckoned with by the Eisenhower administration, he proceeded to strengthen the committee's liaison with the Department of Justice. He complained because the attorney general bypassed the committee in making selections to the bench from the Department of Justice. The president's men argued that they knew these people better than anyone else and, consequently, needed no advice from the committee. Segal countered with the argument that it was precisely because these men were insiders that it was imperative to have them accorded committee approval to sustain public confidence. Administration officials conceded and from that time, 1956, on, they consulted with the committee on all appointments.

The tidying-up operation took on the dimensions of a full-scale breakthrough in procedures as Segal continued to press on. As Segal was to describe it some years later:

Three years ago [1959], in a step of the utmost importance, Judge Walsh agreed to use the Committee at a much earlier point in the selective process—to request of us an *informal* investigation and report on every individual whose name was submitted to the President or the Attorney General by any responsible source, and who therefore was likely to be seriously considered for the nomination. This preliminary screening, conducted by the Chairman and the member of the Committee from the particular circuit in which the vacancy exists, has provided the Attorney General with information concerning the comparative qualifications, early in the appointive process, of all probable candidates. It has in numerous cases enabled the President to hold out for the better or the best of a number of qualified candidates.

The informal requests did not eliminate formal reports. In every case, the Committee is still asked, at the same time as the F.B.I., for a formal report on the qualifications of the person who finally appears most likely to be nominated.[28]

It was in this period that the committee reached the pinnacle of its power in judicial selection. In the last two years of the Eisenhower administration, the committee had a virtual veto power.[29] Only those rated qualified by the committee were nominated and this by design not accident.[30]

In accounting for the development of the committee's power, one cannot stress too much the importance of President Eisenhower's attitude. As related earlier, he felt strongly that the organized bar should play a vigorous role in judicial selection. This created a fertile soil in which the seeds of Segal's efforts could take root and flourish.

After two years of particularly smooth sailing, the committee began to sense the possibility of rough seas. Nineteen sixty might bring a Democratic victory. There was no way of predicting what a Democratic administration might do to the arrangements which had been cultivated during a Republican administration. The committee tried to hedge against a repudiation of its efforts by urging the ABA House of Delegates to pass the following resolution (which it did):

RESOLVED FURTHER, that the incoming President of the United States be urged to continue the program [for seeking committee reports] presently in effect . . .

RESOLVED FURTHER, that after the election, the Secretary of the Association forward copies of this resolution to the incoming President of the United States, and to his appointee as Attorney General of the United States.[31]

As the committee explained: "If we are successful in this attempt [to effectuate the goals of the resolution], and still another administration carries forward the program now established, then we shall be assured that at least our gains to this date have taken root, and may before too long be institutionalized as part of the political system of our country."[32]

Coincident with its effort to win approval by the incoming president of the ongoing arrangement between the committee and the Department of Justice, the committee made what in retrospect was a gross error in strategy. It chose to press once again for the principle of bipartisan selection of federal judges. In conjunction with an ABA special committee, it attempted to convince the major political parties to include a plank on bipartisan selection in their respective 1960 platforms. The Republicans did but the Democrats did not. This attempt as well as subsequent efforts early in the new administration tended to make the Democratic leaders suspicious of the motives of the committee. For the committee had not appeared to them to be

131

as interested in bipartisanship when the Eisenhower administration first came into office. But along with the Republican chiefs, Segal professed to see a great difference in the two situations. As he pointed out later, when Eisenhower came into office, 84 percent of the federal judges had been Democrats when appointed.[33] Now, in 1960–61, "the judges sitting in the Federal courts . . . are just about evenly divided as to their pre-appointment political party affiliation—half of them Democratic, half Republican."[34] Nicholas Katzenbach, then the deputy attorney general, summed up the administration's views retrospectively when he told the ABA House of Delegates in August of 1962:

> I would like to say just a brief word with respect to the remarks made about bipartisanship or non-partisan appointment. . . . I can understand the reasons and arguments for non-partisan or bipartisan appointments to the bench. . . .
>
> If you regard this as a matter of achieving and then keeping a balance, you will put yourselves in the position, which I do not think you should put yourselves in, for being critical of appointments of this Administration that they do not evenly divide Republicans and Democrats, and praising a subsequent Republican Administration, if by any happenstance this should come to pass, for appointing 90 or 100 per cent Republicans for the non-partisan and impartial character of its appointments in striving at a balance, when both administrations will have been doing what every administration has done throughout the years. And I do not think that the motivation of this Administration in appointing largely Democrats should be identical with the motivation of the next Administration that is Republican in appointing mostly Republicans, that we should be subject to the criticism for being partisan for appointing Democrats, and they should be praised for being non-partisan for appointing Republicans.[35]

Recall that it was earlier pointed out that during the campaign, when the president of the ABA had sent a letter asking the candidates to pledge themselves to the principle of bipartisanship, candidate Kennedy carefully promised no more than "I would hope that the *paramount* consideration in the appointment of a judge would not be his political party, but his qualifications for the office" (emphasis supplied), while candidate Nixon asserted that "I believe it is essential . . . that the best qualified lawyers and judges available be appointed to judicial office, and . . . *that the number of judges in Federal courts from each of the major political parties be approximately equal* . . ." (emphasis supplied).[36]

Segal planned to retire as chairman in 1960. He wrote to a friend:

"After holding out quite a while and after much soul-searching, I finally permitted myself to be persuaded to accept the Chairmanship last year, upon the express condition that it be my last and that at the earliest possible opportunity, John Randall advise Whitney Seymour, the President-elect, to be thinking about a new Chairman for this year." He could be well satisfied with the job he had done. Assuming as he did that it was desirable for the organized bar to play a key role in judicial selection, he had accomplished his mission. He had devoted an inordinate amount of time to the task and it was appropriate for someone else to pick up the cudgels. Not only that, he was well aware as an exchange of letters between him and Ross Malone, president of the ABA in 1958, made clear that, in Malone's words, "it is extremely important that no one stay in the position long enough that he comes to be regarded as a 'judge-maker.' Should that occur, I think that the relationship with the Department would suffer and that the prestige of the Committee would suffer." Segal agreed saying: "The problem has caused me some concern as well. . . . I have been extremely careful to avoid any such implication in my activities as Chairman. . . ."[37] But Whitney Seymour was of a different mind. He urged Segal to stay on as chairman on the grounds that with a new administration and with the prospect of a whole host of new judgeships in the offing all of Segal's work could go down the drain if Segal quit. In view of the intensity of Segal's own conviction on the subject, the argument was irresistible. Segal did not have any illusions about the magnitude of the job which confronted him. But like the proverbial firehorse, he was up and running at the sound of the bell.

As Segal later reported: "Two weeks before the Kennedy Administration took office, President Seymour and I visited Attorney General-designate Robert Kennedy and Deputy Attorney General-designate Byron White. We received their unequivocal commitment that the Kennedy Administration would continue the policy of submitting to the ABA Committee, both for preliminary screening and for later formal report all names of persons under consideration for Federal judicial appointment, and of appointing only those who were pronounced clearly qualified."[38] The new administration was less than enchanted with the idea of dealing the committee a hand in judicial selection. But it really had no choice. One of Segal's greatest achieve-

133

ments as chairman had been winning unbelievably enthusiastic and widespread editorial support for the committee's endeavors.[39] To have refused to meet with Segal and agree to continue the working arrangement between the committee and department would surely have evoked a violent reaction among the leading editorial writers in the nation. The new team was not eager to trigger off such a reaction. But something did go amiss. Segal left the meeting certain that the committee still had its veto power, as indicated by his words above. Clearly, from its subsequent actions, the team at Justice was not about to subscribe to such a proposition.

The attitude of the new team at Justice toward Segal and the committee can best be capsulized by saying that, had there been no prior arrangement to which they felt they must give obeisance, they would not have undertaken to make one, nor would they have probably even agreed to one. But as things stood the committee was a factor to reckon with and the ever-present Mr. Segal was looking over their shoulders. Initially this attention from Segal was about as welcome as kibitzing is to one trying to play a difficult bridge hand. It soon became apparent, however, that this particular kibitzer knew the game exceptionally well and could be very helpful in educating neophytes in judicial selection to the problems and subtleties of their task. In a relatively short time, a very close personal relationship based on mutual respect and liking grew up between Segal and the new team at Justice. As a matter of fact, so close was the relationship that Segal for all practical purposes became a part of the team. And, metaphorically speaking, once Segal got into bed with the administration, he could not remain chaste. During the period of *informal* inquiry and rating, Dolan, not unlike his Republican predecessors, was able to challenge by argument and cajolery some of the ratings and to get the committee to change its mind or Segal to change his. Segal acknowledged this fact in testimony before a Senate subcommittee:

To effectuate the practice of submitting several names per vacancy, rather than only one, Judge Walsh and I set up the system of informal reports. What occurs is that the Deputy Attorney General will advise the ABA committee chairman that the following individuals are under consideration. The chairman and the member of the circuit only—not the whole committee—will then conduct an exhaustive investigation, the reasons being that at that point, neither the Senator in most cases, nor the Attorney General wants to have too much talk triggered by an investiga-

134

tion. They want a completely off the record survey. The report is oral and informal. It binds nobody, but it has proved to be a pretty good indication of the ultimate result. *At that point, there is a great deal of give and take in the discussion. I must say that in—and I'm guessing— 95 percent of the cases, the eventual rating in the full committee's formal report is the same as the preliminary informal report.* [Emphasis supplied.][40]

Segal's guess was not very accurate. In a two-year period in the Kennedy administration, by my reckoning, almost 29 percent or 29 of 101 informal ratings differed from the formal ratings. Seventy-two ratings showed no change; 7 which looked not qualified on the informal were qualified on the formal; 1 went from qualified to not qualified; 17 went from qualified to well qualified; 1 from well qualified to qualified; 3 from well qualified to exceptionally well qualified. Perhaps of even more significance is the fact that for 9 qualifieds which I counted in the 72 as unchanged, there was indication (in the informal rating) that the committee had some reservations about the candidate. In short, in the give and take of discussion something happened in nearly 30 percent of the cases, usually resulting in an upgrading. Of course, the informal report was never intended to be a finished product and perhaps the changes were not the consequence of persuasion by the men at Justice. But observation leads to the conclusion that a good part of them were. The purist might assert that a rating is a rating and should not be the subject of negotiation. On the other hand a strong case could be made out for the chairman and representatives of Justice arguing over the merits of a particular nominee before the committee's final choice of a rating. After all, making a rating of this sort is not an exact science and the negotiation involved in this process is of the kind at which lawyers are particularly skilled. In any case, it is understandable that lawyers, for whom negotiation is a way of life, would not be upset by such a procedure. Whether he liked it or not, as deeply involved as he was with the department, Segal had to play the negotiation game. He could not have it all one way. If he wanted to be close to the team at Justice in order to exert his, as he saw it, healthy influence, he could not turn coy when they wanted to influence him. It is important to bear in mind, however, that all parties understood full well that there would be and were times when they would just have to agree to disagree. As Dolan told Professor Grossman with respect to a difference of opinion between Segal and Deputy Katzenbach in their oral statements at the ABA meetings in 1962, "Segal said what he had to say, we said what we had to say, and then we got back to work."[41] So it was with respect to negotiations over ratings. When it got to the point where each side had its say and there was no agreement, each with a shrug of the shoulders and a "so be it" went on to the next item of business.

As pointed out earlier, eight Kennedy appointments became federal judges in the face of a committee rating of "unqualified." One of these appointments had been the occasion of the public donnybrook over Irving Ben Cooper and at the close of Segal's tenure another such donnybrook was in the making over David Rabinovitz. The burden of that battle fell to Segal's successor, however. Despite these differences with the department, Segal's relationship with the men at Justice remained remarkably close. He continued to have enormous influence in the selection process, although he was never again to wield the virtual veto power he had in the last two years of the Eisenhower administration.

Exit Segal

Neither of Segal's immediate successors, Robert Meserve, 1963–66, and Albert E. Jenner, Jr., 1966–68, attempted to ingratiate himself with the team at Justice to the degree that Segal did. It is understandable that they had neither the time nor the inclination to devote the equivalent of a full working week each week to judicial selection. Geographically, they were further afield from Washington than Segal in Philadelphia. Meserve is a Bostonian and Jenner a resident of Chicago. But more important their concept of their role and the committee's effectiveness was very different from Segal's. Of course, Segal was aware of the battles he had lost with the men at Justice, yet by his reckoning his close relationship had paid off in handsome dividends. He reported in July of 1962:

Of the 459 persons whom we were requested by the Attorney General to screen and to report on informally, we reported 158 as Not Qualified. Of these, 150 were not appointed. While the fact that the Attorney General refers a name to the Committee, particularly when this is for preliminary investigation and informal report, does not, of course, mean that he considers this person to be qualified or even that he has as yet conducted any investigation whatever of the person's qualification, nevertheless, many of these persons had strong sponsorship and substantial political support. Under conditions existing not so many years ago, there is no doubt that at least some of them, probably a substantial number, would have been appointed.[42]

In the terms of the hockey goalie, eight goals were scored against him but he had upward to *150* saves! Not a bad record. That was one way to look at the matter. And Segal did. Thus, he could conclude, as he did a year earlier, that "your Committee emphasizes that in the main, we have been securing a very good quality of Federal judges."[43] Meserve and Jenner never criticized Segal's mode of operation but they were never as sanguine about the committee's effectiveness. For example, in his remarks accompanying his 1965 report to the House of Delegates, Meserve, after observing the amenities, was reported to have unburdened himself in the following style: "Mr. Meserve went on to say that there have been many fine appointments, but there are still too many mediocre ones. 'Only when our friends in Congress know that we represent an aroused, organized bar who will fight for the principle of a high grade judiciary can your Committee's efforts be fully successful,' he emphasized."[44] In February of 1966, Jenner used this kind of language in discussing judicial selection:

Your Committee must regretfully if not *dejectedly* report that various additional factors other than judicial qualifications have, unfortunately, continued to play a part in the Federal judgeship selection, nomination, confirmation and appointment process. Without going into detail, these factors embrace personal friendship with one or more of those taking part in the process of preliminary consideration and ultimate appointment by the President, and confirmation by the Senate of the United States; "cronyism"; performance of service to political party organizations or to the United States Senators, or others in high public office, state and federal; ethnic origin; religious faith of the candidate; vigorous personal campaign by the candidate himself; current or prior holding of high public office, state and federal on the part of the candidate or his personal or political friend or sponsor; and other like considerations wholly irrelevant to the matter of judicial qualification. [Emphasis supplied.][45]

Apparently, they felt that nothing major had really been gained by Segal's especially close relationship with the men at Justice and that possibly Segal's hands were somewhat tied by the relationship. In any case, without ever articulating publicly their reasons for doing so, both Meserve and Jenner disengaged from the close liaison with the department and endeavored to be aloof and independent. To some extent this was only a matter of degree, for they continued to have a good and healthy working relationship with the men at Justice, even while seeking to maintain their independence.

As luck would have it, at the start of his incumbency as chairman, Meserve had a big fight on his hands. The administration wanted to appoint David Rabinovitz to a judicial post in Wisconsin; the committee felt that he was unqualified. President Kennedy laid his prestige on the line for this appointment as he never had for any before. In what was to be one of the last questions to which he would address himself in a press conference, President Kennedy answered when he was asked if he would withdraw Rabinovitz's name: "No, I am for David Rabinovitz all the way. I know him very well, in fact for a number of years. And the American Bar Association has been very helpful in making the judgment, but I am sure they would agree that they are not infallible. Mr. Brandeis was very much opposed. There are a good many judges who have been opposed who have been rather distinguished. And I am for David Rabinovitz."[46] President Johnson was not prepared to go "all the way" and eventually nominated someone else for the post, after naming Rabinovitz to a recess appointment. Whatever chance there might have been for a close Segal-like liaison to grow in spite of Meserve's disposition against it was dispelled by the Rabinovitz contest and by the early Johnson administration appointments. By committee count, of the first fifty-six Johnson appointments below the Supreme Court level, six had been rated unqualified by the committee. This was by comparison with the two previous presidents a high percentage and could be taken as a manifestation of disdain for the committee's judgment.[47] On top of this came the bruising battle over the nomination of Judge Francis X. Morrissey. Relationships between committee chairman and Justice continued to be close but the warmth which characterized the Segal incumbency was being dissipated very quickly.

Enter Friesen

In April 1965, Ernest C. Friesen, Jr., burst on the scene like a rush of fresh air. He took over Dolan's duties of bird-dogging judicial appointments. For this assignment he was uniquely equipped. In a short but meteoric career, he had learned much about judges and the business of judging. He had the opportunity to become acquainted with literally hundreds of state judges as well as with a lesser number of federal judges.

Friesen was born in Hutchinson, Kansas, in 1928. He graduated from the University of Kansas in 1950 where he was president of the student government. He entered into active service in the Marine Corps as a regular officer in 1950. After completing Basic School at Quantico, he reported to Camp Lejeune, where he joined an amphibious reconnaissance unit. The work of such an outfit requires an officer who is unusually rugged physically and who has the ability to operate effectively in the field without a great deal of supervision. Among marines, it is a mark of great distinction to be considered good enough for this elite of elite units. Lieutenant Friesen won for himself the accolade of being a "hard-charger," a marine who knows how and can get things done and who will spare no effort in the doing. Friends report that Friesen was impatient to go to Korea and do what he thought a marine officer was supposed to do, be where the action is. He grew impatient at the fact that he like a host of others was being held back in North Carolina as part of the strategic reserve. Exasperated by the Marine Corps' refusal to send him to Korea and with the fighting there grinding to a halt, Friesen decided "to hell with it" and junked a promising career as a professional marine officer to go on to the Columbia Law School where he distinguished himself as a Harlan Fiske Stone Scholar. He practiced law for a short time with a New York law firm and then became a trial attorney in the Tax Division of the Department of Justice. In 1958, he became an assistant professor of law at the University of Cincinnati. Shortly, he advanced to an associateship and conducted a study of the pre-trial conference under a Ford Foundation fellowship. During the years 1961–63, he was a director of the Joint Committee for Effective Justice, a national program for court reform. Then for two years he was dean of the National College of State Trial Judges. This unique college was started in 1962, in Justice Tom Clark's words, "as a school composed of judges, operated by judges for the benefit of judges. Its objective was to acquaint the relatively new state judge of general jurisdiction with the techniques of trial procedure and court administration developed in like courts throughout the country."[48] Toward that end the college offered a twofold program: a four-week summer course for new judges and an extension program consisting of state judicial seminars and distribution of reading material.[49] As dean of such a college, Friesen lived in a world of judges. Beyond thinking about what kind of training program would best befit state trial judges, it would be natural for anyone in that post and in that environment to ponder such questions as Who is a "good" judge? What makes a "good" judge? How should judges be selected? Being more intellectually curious than most, Friesen was irresistibly drawn to do such pondering. Consequently, he was not giving these questions serious thought for the first time when he came to the Department of Justice.

With all due respect to the chairman and members of the ABA committee whom he knew, admired, and respected, Friesen was highly skeptical of the validity of committee ratings. He felt that the committee members stood no better than a 50–50 chance of being right in their evaluations both on those they considered fit and on those they considered unfit to be federal judges. Friesen was quick to point out that this is no better than what can be done by chance selection. Nor was this an off-the-top-of-his-head judgment. To demonstrate his point to me, he went over a list I had compiled of ABA committee "unqualifieds" and "exceptionally well qualifieds," analyzed the ratings, and suggested where he thought the committee had been wrong based on subsequent performance on the bench.

As Friesen saw it, the questionable validity of the committee's ratings stemmed from several factors and difficulties. First, prediction of how a man will perform on the bench is at best hazardous. Friesen felt that there are without doubt better techniques for making such predictions than are currently used. For example, he suggested that an intensive interview by a small group of lawyers and social scientists who know the right questions to ask would be most fruitful. They would first have to construct a list of criteria for a "good" judge and work out a system of giving mathematical weights to each of the criteria. One of the criteria which he thought should be explored was "open-mindedness" both about people and about the individual himself. He felt that for a judge to be too self-centered is lethal and that it is healthy for a judge to have self-doubts concerning his genius. He related that in studies of highly successful business executives the one trait that seems most common to them all is self-doubt about their ability. Among other possible criteria which Friesen felt should be explored were (1) something akin to what the military call "command presence," an ability to run the courtroom; (2) an ability to listen; (3) an ability to stick with a complicated point for a long period of time. Transcending all of these items for Friesen, however, was compassion. Friesen, who had a happy penchant for quantifying by way of illustrating his thoughts and in so doing making them clear to his listener, asserted that sentencing is 70 percent of a trial judge's job much in the manner of the often asserted but unprovable maxim that pitching is 70 percent of the game in major league baseball. To one who would challenge the assertion about the importance of sentencing, Friesen gave a strong answer. He believed that in most trials the judge's use of discretion is limited and that the quality of judicial decision-making on issues arising in a trial will not vary much depending on the judge's wisdom or lack of it. On the other hand, when it comes to sentencing, a judge's wisdom, understanding, and empathy are all important. Most of us never give a thought to the enormous power judges wield in sentencing. I shall never forget my students' reactions, when in an earlier day, the day of smaller classes, I used to take my American government classes to municipal court on a Monday morning. They were shocked and startled by the ease and what seemed to them the arbitrary manner and disinterested way in which the judge could bang the gavel and say "thirty days" and a man would be unceremoniously carted off to the workhouse. Friesen's own compassion and his work with state trial judges had made him exceptionally sensitive to the importance of sentencing and the importance of having men on the bench in trial courts who have understanding. He commented, for example: Suppose a young man is convicted for breach of the peace in a demonstration, would you want a judge who took the absolutist position that law and order must be upheld by giving the maximum sentence without much thought or one who made some effort to understand what kind of person the defendant was and out of what kind of environment he came as well as to attempt to understand the circumstances and purposes of the demonstration itself? The same question can be asked about the host of cases which are tried in federal district courts. Should the tax evader be sent to jail or be fined? And how about the businessman who is convicted of a criminal violation of the antitrust laws?

Couple these ideas on what makes a good judge with Friesen's ideas about the factors which go into a committee's rating and it is easy to see why he viewed the committee's ratings with a high degree of skepticism. For one thing, Friesen felt that members of the committee understandably are likely to believe that lawyers like themselves will make the best judges. Understandable, because it is human nature for people to do so. This means then a house-sized bias in favor of the corporate trial lawyer. There is no reason for believing that these are the men who best understand people. The negligence lawyer, the labor lawyer, the politician, by contrast, might have the very kind of experience which would make them more understanding of the problems of people likely to be in trouble with the law. As he put it in a letter to me:

Though I think you have covered the point well, I would further emphasize that a lawyer's specialty: corporate-business, labor, tax, antitrust, patent, is not as significant as is broad experience in dealing with people. No lawyer practices the full gamut of the federal law. Trial lawyers are usually personal injury lawyers (a very narrow specialty) or antitrust lawyers (an even narrower specialty) and "general practitioners" are usually either corporate-business lawyers or probate lawyers. No lawyers today are unspecialized which makes insignificant a particular specialty which a lawyer may have practiced in regard to his selection for a federal judgeship. (On the Personal Data Questionnaire supplied by each candidate they often list ten personal injury cases which are noted by the ABA Committee as "significant" or "extensive" trial experience. Ten labor or tax trials, however, lead to a conclusion that the attorney is too "narrow" in his specialization.)

Further, he would say, for a prospect to find favor with other lawyers, he must be a "nice guy," one who is courteous to other lawyers. For Friesen, it was most important to have as a judge someone who would run the courtroom and sometimes not be "nice," particularly to lawyers who came in unprepared or half-prepared. My own interviewing of a random sample of lawyers who appeared in federal courts substantiates Friesen's point about the kind of judge lawyers like. I asked lawyers to identify the best judges on the federal bench. After that, I asked why they thought they were exceptionally fine judges. *Almost invariably*, the first answer I received in response to that question was that the judges they cited were courteous to the lawyers. To the non-lawyer this might come as a surprise. But bear in mind what is at stake. The cardinal sin for a judge is to make counsel look inept in front of his client. Friesen, however, arrived at his conclusion by another route. He observed that in committee evaluations of state judges whom he knew and in whose courtrooms he had appeared or observed, the committee through its processes would condemn the "take-charge" judge as lacking in judicial temperament and would be generous with the courteous judge who allowed the lawyers to run the trial.

Friesen objected strongly to the committee's insistence on trial experience as an unalterable qualification for the district bench. He acknowledged that everything else being equal trial experience is a plus factor. But when are other things equal, like capacity for compassion? Friesen cited this emphasis on trial experience as specific evidence of the committeee members subconsciously or consciously seeking men in their own image, pointing out that this is akin to the requirements for membership in the American College of Trial Lawyers which the dominant members of the committee belong to. He raised some intriguing rhetorical questions about trial experience. What if the experience is gathered in a poorly run courtroom, is that really a plus or a minus? Is there an advantage in having a judge whose trial experience has been basically that of the advocate? Isn't it possible that the practiced advocate would have acquired habits and a point of view that would be liabilities rather than assets? As the rhetorical *coup de grace*, he asked, why, if trial experience is so important, does not the committee favor state trial judges over corporate trial lawyers in its ratings? After all, the average state trial judge is in the courtroom about 220 days in the year as opposed to 60 days at most for a trial lawyer and he is doing more of what a federal trial judge must do than the advocate. Yet, he asserted, the committee has not been overly generous in its ratings of state trial judges.

Friesen felt that the committee was biased in another way. He believed that it favored, especially for the rating of exceptionally well qualified, people who had attended prestige law schools and, although a Columbia graduate himself, he objected to this on principle. At his suggestion I made a list of the especially well qualifieds appointed by President Kennedy indicating the law school they attended. The results showed three from Harvard, two from Columbia, and one from Yale out of a total of eighteen. He observed that if we added the University of Virginia that would give us two more, which would make almost half of the eighteen.

At this point in this account, there is no need to attempt to determine whether Friesen was right or wrong in his convictions. It is clear that as long as he served as the primary point of contact between the committee and the department and as long as he enjoyed the confidence of the deputy, the attorney general, and the president (which he did) his convictions were probably more important than reality, if, perchance, there was a disparity. Under the circumstances, the impact of the committee on judicial selection was bound to be far less than in the Segal-Walsh days, when the committee had a virtual veto power.

Lest I have created the impression that Friesen was playing a lone hand in judicial selection, I should like to pass on the words he wrote to me about the then Deputy Attorney General Ramsey Clark and their working relationship:

He [Ramsey Clark] deals occasionally with Mr. Jenner, but more important, I do my best to convey his ideas and represent his special point of view to the committee (though not necessarily attributing the point of view to him).

Ramsey Clark is a special kind of person. He has the courage to recommend what he believes to be right and the instincts to know what is right. He is a rare combination of idealist and pragmatist. Without his constant pressure to seek the most qualified I doubt that our attempts to hold the line for quality would be successful. He does all of the negotiating with the political interests with astonishing results.

Despite disclaimers from all sides that there had been a deterioration in the relations between committee and administration, the old saw that actions speak louder than words has application. When the American Law Institute met in Washington in May of 1966, it was expected that the Board of Governors of the ABA would, according to custom, have an audience with the president. That body felt, however, it was more important that year to have the Committee on Federal Judiciary call on the president instead, and the White House was willing to receive it. The committee described the meeting in this fashion:

Your Committee is pleased to report that in May of this year, during the annual meeting of the American Law Institute in Washington, D.C., the full Committee was privileged to meet with President Johnson at the White House. Accompanying the Committee were President Kuhn, President-Elect Marden, nominee President-Elect Morris and the former distinguished Chairman of your Committee, Bernard G. Segal, Esquire, of Philadelphia. The meeting was a rewarding one for your Committee. We are confident that the meeting was rewarding and helpful to President Johnson, as well. The procedures and work of the Committee were explained to President Johnson and we expounded upon the ideals and objectives of the organized bar, as represented by the American Bar Association, in respect of the need that only qualified members of the bench and bar serve as judges of the courts of the United States. We were at pains to emphasize with the President that the American Bar Association welcomed and sincerely appreciated the opportunity that had been accorded us by him and his predecessors, Presidents Kennedy, Eisenhower and Truman, and by Attorney General Katzenbach and his predecessors, Messrs. Kennedy (Robert), Clark and Brownell, to assist the President in the discharge of what the bar of this nation and, in our opinion, the public as well, regards to be as important a duty, responsibility and privilege as any devolving upon the President. President Johnson not only took a lively interest in the work and procedures of your Committee but evidenced a knowledge and alertness of its work and activities that thoroughly gratified all of us.

There was a healthy exchange of views as to problems which faced the President from time to time as respects the exercise of his important constitutional function, political niceties that relate thereto and, on the other hand, the work problems and objectives of your committee.[50]

The *Washington Post*, presumably with the benefit of a White House source as well as the committee, reported the event this way, under the headline BAR GROUP REPAIRS BREACH WITH JOHNSON:

American Bar Association leaders spent an hour with President Johnson yesterday mending fences over qualifications for the Federal judiciary.

According to the ABA officials the meeting went a long way to heal the wounds left by the battle last fall over the nomination of Francis X. Morrissey to a Boston judgeship. . . .

The ABA officials, who sought the audience with the President, heard Mr. Johnson praise them for supporting the War on Poverty program to extend legal services to the poor. He also thanked them for a House of Delegates resolution in February supporting the Administration's legal position in Vietnam.[51]

Both accounts of the meeting seem to support the notion that something indeed had gone awry in the relationship between committee and administration and nothing in these accounts suggests that the president was prepared to have the administration do anything differently from what it had been doing vis-à-vis the committee.

Mr. Friesen even after his elevation to the post of assistant attorney general for administration continued to have special responsibilities in judicial selection. His stint with the Department of Justice ended in December 1967 when he became director of the United States Courts Administrative Office. For the remainder of the Johnson administration the relationship between the administration and the committee was correct if not cordial.

In generalizing about the committee's role in the past and present or predicting its future, we must conclude on the note on which we began. The committee has played an important role since 1953 and will undoubtedly continue to do so in some fashion or other for the foreseeable future. In that connection, the committee's role was re-affirmed in an exchange of letters between Cloyd Laporte of the committee and President Nixon's attorney general, John N. Mitchell.[52] But in the final analysis, what the committee's role was, is, or will be depends primarily (but not exclusively) upon the individuals who hold the key assignments.

Who Are the Committeemen?

All of the chairmen have dominated the committee, some more than others. Perhaps it need not be that way. But there are factors which move things in that direction. The president of the Bar Association picks the chairman and the committee members. As a practical matter, the president will rely heavily on the chairman in selecting members. So the committee tends to be composed of men of his choice, men with whom he can work. The team at Justice, of course, prefers to deal directly with only one man. The "informal" informal puts a premium on speed and secrecy. Once the chairman gives an indication of what an evaluation of a candidate might be, the men at Justice expect him to be able "to deliver" by getting the full committee to come up with at least the evaluation he has indicated. All these factors favor decision and action by the chairman. Too, there is the further factor that it is in the nature of voluntary organizations big and small to be oligarchic. The ones doing the lion's share of the work expect and are accorded deference in decision-making. So, although Mr. Segal used to describe the committee as "the conduit" between the bench and bar and the attorney general, it is really the chairman who is the conduit. This is not to suggest, however, that the committee is unimportant. For it is the committee upon whom the chairman must rely in large part for the information on which he makes his judgments. Since it is a truism that one's perception is conditioned by who and what he is, as well as by his experience, who the committeemen are and what their experience is becomes important to an understanding of committee ratings.

In his study of the committee, Professor Grossman drew an interesting profile of the fifty-one lawyers who served on the committee from 1946 to 1962.[53] He showed that 90 percent were fifty years or older, with about half that number over sixty years of age. He found that the majority were "associated with firms engaged primarily in general or trial practice. There were no Committee members who had specialized in criminal law, domestic relations, or a host of other special types of law practices." More than half of them were associated with large law firms (six or more members); conversely, only about 6 percent were engaged in individual practice. Grossman found that virtually all of them "were active in bar-association affairs prior to their appointment." The overwhelming majority of them "practiced in cities with populations over 100,000." Contrary to Friesen's contention, only one-third of the committee members were graduates of Ivy League law schools. As Grossman points out, these were generally the representatives from the first three circuits where those schools are located. In fairness to Friesen, however, these are the circuits of the populous northeastern part of the country which accounts for a high proportion of the judicial posts.

The profile provided by Grossman still generally holds for the committee. And as for Friesen's contentions, seven of the twelve members of the committee in 1970 were members of the American College of Trial Lawyers and seven, including those from the first three circuits, were Ivy League law school graduates, three from Harvard, two from Yale, one each from Columbia and the University of Pennsylvania.

Another way of ascertaining who the committeemen are is to see how they perceive themselves. Here is how three of the last five chairmen of the committee introduced themselves to a Senate subcommittee:

MR. JENNER. Since the committee appears to oppose and suggests that Judge Morrissey be not confirmed for this position, I suggest the wisdom of my relating to you distinguished Senators the capacity of the men on this committee to make the judgment, and it is a very awesome and serious judgment that they have made and that they do make.

It is only because of that, that I make a personal reference to myself. I was admitted to practice in the year 1930, in October, so that I have been at my profession for 35 years, admitted by the Supreme Court of Illinois.

During that somewhat in excess of 35 years, I have devoted myself primarily to the trial of cases, civil, criminal, patent, and otherwise in the State courts of Illinois and surrounding States, in the Federal courts all over this Nation, long cases, short cases. The longest criminal case was 3 months before His Honor Judge Devitt in Minneapolis 2 years ago, and my longest civil case was a trade secret patent case tried in St. Louis for 11½ consecutive months. The litigation is of great variety, normally in later years of some importance.

In the early years, I practiced and tried cases in the municipal court of Chicago, the county court that Senator Dirksen referred to, to which Senator Dirksen has made reference, our circuit court which is the equivalent of the superior court that has been mentioned to you gentlemen this morning; the Federal district court.

In addition to that, my advocacy has taken me to courts of review, which we regard as matters of importance with respect to qualifications to serve on the district courts as well.

I have handled a little over 100 cases in courts of review, of last resort in Illinois, in the Federal system, and in the highest courts of other States as well.

I am not unusual on this committee. The other members of the committee have substantially the same background. Some of them are not as extensive litigators as I have been, but they are members, as I am, of the American College of Trial Lawyers, the only general trial lawyers' society in the United States, which welcomes as members and invites as members men whose advocacy takes them into all fields of law, unlike the American Trial Lawyers Association, which is the old NACA mentioned here this morning, that confines its membership to those who try personal injury cases.

Throughout these years I have had an abiding interest and devoted much, very much, of my energy, what little competence I have, and my interests to the improvement of the administration of justice in the courts of my State and the courts of the United States, including the district courts and the courts of appeal.

As a young man, right about the time that Judge Morrissey was seeking admission to the bar of Massachusetts, I was a member of a committee appointed by the Supreme Court of Illinois to draft our modern Civil Practice Act and the rules of that court. I was honored by being appointed chairman by the Supreme Court of Illinois of the committee in 1950 that completely revised the then 1933 Civil Practice Act, the rules of the supreme court and the uniform rules of our appellate courts in Illinois.

I have been a professor of law, a full professor of law, at Northwestern University Law School. Prior to that, I was a member of the faculty of John Marshall Law School.

148

I have taken an interest, and this committee looks to candidates as to whether they take an interest or are active in their bars, in organized bars rendering the essential service that the bar must render to the public in order to justify its existence.

I am past president of the American College of Trial Lawyers, of the American Judicature Society, which is the second largest bar association in the world, and I am past president of the National Conference of Bar Association Presidents of the United States, of which the Massachusetts and the Boston Bar are members.

I am a uniform law commissioner, have the honor to serve with Judge Gene Burdick, who is the brother of your distinguished Member, and also a member of this subcommittee. . . .

I am chairman of the Illinois Commission, and have been for 15 years.

Last year, I served as senior counsel to the Warren Commission here in Washington for 9 months, at the invitation of the Chief Justice of the United States.

I am a member, and have been for 5 years, by appointment also of the Chief Justice, of the U.S. Judicial Conference Advisory on the Federal Civil Rules, which are the rules with which Judge Morrissey will have to wrestle if he is confirmed and appointed.

As you distinguished gentlemen, as lawyers, know, that committee has been extensively revising the Federal rules, and as Members of the U.S. Senate, you have passed upon those rules as they are filed with you by the Chief Justice of the United States on behalf of the Judicial Conference.

I was appointed last spring as chairman of the new Advisory Committee of the U.S. Judicial Conference charged with the duty of drafting Federal rules of evidence to apply in all courts and in all causes in the Federal courts of the United States, bankruptcy, civil, criminal, admirality, whatever it may be; as the Chief Justice said, a monumental project designed to complete the reform of practice and pleading procedure in the United States in district courts and courts of appeal, which commenced under the enabling act which you gentlemen enacted back in the late twenties.

I mention these things in order to indicate what capacity for judgment I have and what other members of my committee have with respect to qualifications to serve in this most important court—and I mean that literally—the most important court in the United States of America.[54]

MR. MESERVE. I might say that, as with the last witness [Mr. Jenner], I am a member of the American College of Trial Lawyers and of its board of regents, and I say these things not to sound important but merely to emphasize the fact that I bring some experience to the task which has been imposed upon me as a member, when I was a member, of the American Bar Association's Standing Committee on the Federal Judiciary.

I am formerly an instructor in the field of trial practice at Harvard Law School, and during the years when I was getting a start at the bar, as an assistant U.S. attorney in Boston, Mass., I had the pleasure of teaching evenings in law school at Boston College Law School for 2 years.

I am presently, by appointment of the Supreme Judicial Court of Massachusetts, a member and secretary of its board of bar examiners, and for 2 years, from 1963 to May of 1965, I was president of the Boston Bar Association.[55]

MR. SEGAL. I should say that I personally spent six terms as Chairman of the Standing Committee on Federal Judiciary. I think the thing that determined me to resist the attempt to get me to continue to serve was a book published by Oxford Press on the judicial process in which a professor who wrote the book referred to our Committee and cited its permanent lifetime Chairman, Bernard Segal. I thought that was the time to end the chairmanship for the good of the cause.

I am currently Chairman of the Standing Committee on Judicial Selection, Tenure, and Compensation, and Senator Dirksen had the privilege of appearing a few weeks ago before the Udall committee on the age-old question not only of what should be congressional and judicial salaries, but whether there is not a better way to fix them than the Constitution now prescribes.

I have been for a great many years, and still am, chairman of the Judiciary Committee of the Pennsylvania Bar Association, and am on the Judiciary Committee of the Philadelphia Bar Association. Most recently I had an unusual experience when Governor Scranton decided by executive order to put into effect in Pennsylvania a system of nonpartisan selection by merit, and created a judicial nominating commission binding himself to make appointments, in this case five judges to our trial courts, solely from the list of our nominating commission.

He did me the honor of appointing me as chairman, and we submitted to him 15 names, from which he selected his 5 appointees.

I have just finished my term as president of the American College of Trial Lawyers, which concerns itself with this matter of judicial selection, and I have the privilege of serving permanently by appointment of the Chief Justice as a member of the Standing Committee on Federal Rules of Practice and Procedure of the Judicial Conference of the United States which, of course, is created by virtue of the act of Congress, and supervises the work of five advisory, now six advisory committees, on the rules and so without laboring the question, I may say that I have continued my interest in this matter of judicial selection.[56]

Curiously, in view of its great interest in bipartisanship in the judiciary, one characteristic of the committee members which the committee seems never to explore and which is rarely, if ever, mentioned in press stories is party identification. Unless one is prepared to argue that party identification does not really mean very much when it comes to judicial selection, this is a factor worth exploring. Doesn't it seem reasonable to hypothesize that the bundle of attitudes that draws a man to identify himself as a Republican or Democrat will have an impact on his perception of what kind of man should be a judge? Would it be surprising if someone who identified himself as a Republican regarded corporation lawyers as sound men and felt

that anyone who represented labor as devotedly as corporation lawyers represent their clients must be lacking in judicial temperament?
Or would it be surprising if someone who identified himself as a liberal Democrat felt that corporation lawyers must put property rights
ahead of human rights and that a man who represented labor organizations must have empathy for the people? Of course, these rhetorical
questions are overdrawn, but if they contain a kernel of truth, then
party identification of the committee members may be relevant.

Of the fifty-four members who served on the committee from 1946
to 1967, sixteen identified themselves for *Who's Who* as Republicans
and fourteen as Democrats. Further inquiry reveals that in all, twenty
are known to be Republicans and seventeen Democrats (six southern
Democrats). If years of service on the committee are taken into account, as they should be to give meaning, the Republican edge widens
considerably. Adding the number of years served by those identifiable
by party, the Republicans total ninety-two as against sixty-five for the
Democrats, including eighteen for southern Democrats (for those not
identifiable by party, the sum is seventy-nine). Another way of looking at the matter is that during a Democratic administration in
1961–62 and 1962–63, the committee was composed of four identifiable Republicans, one Democrat, and six unidentifiables; in 1966–
67, four Republicans, no Democrats, and eight unidentifiables. In
brief, at a time when a majority of the American voters identified
themselves as Democrats and when Democrats controlled both the
White House and Congress, the committee had a distinctly Republican
flavor.

Another interesting characteristic of committee members is the
tendency to remain on the committee for more than one term. Although the term of a committee member is designated as three years,
more than half of the committee as of 1967 had served for more than
three years, some as many as eleven, as shown in the tabulation.
This practice has the advantage, of course, of maximizing experience,
but it also raises the specter of entrenched interest.

Finally, a breakdown of how committeemen identify themselves in
religion is interesting and may have some significance. Of the thirty-
one who had indicated a religious identification for *Who's Who*,
twenty-six listed Protestant (eleven Episcopalian), four Jewish, and
one Catholic.

No. of Years of Service	No. of Members
11	2
10	1
9	3
8	3
6	7
5	2
4	9
3	16
2	3
1	8

How the Committee Does Its Work

Critical to an understanding of the committee's work is the method by which the committee obtains the information on which it bases its judgments. Former Chairman Jenner described to a Senate subcommittee what happens after a request comes from the attorney general in this fashion:

> I then talk to the member of the committee from that particular circuit, and he launches a highly confidential, very confidential inquiry with respect to the gentleman or lady in question. He consults with me, or whoever is the chairman.
>
> If I am—and when and if I am—satisfied that the investigation has been thorough enough to warrant our rendering an opinion in so important an area, a matter that is vital to the individual involved as well as to either of you gentlemen [Senators Dodd and Dirksen were then listening] or any other Member of the Senate performing what I know you regard as a very, very important responsibility, I then report to the Attorney General of the United States that it would appear that when we are, if we are, requested to make a thorough or formal report, with a deep-seated investigation, the odds are that the committee would come to the conclusion he is either not qualified or he is qualified, or he is well qualified, or he is exceptionally well qualified. . . .[57]

That account still leaves open the important questions of whom and how many people the committeeman consults and in what manner before making his evaluation, and how does he weigh conflicting evaluations. Mr. Meserve testified with respect to the inquiry on Judge Morrissey: "I made as thorough an investigation as I thought was warranted, in the course of which I contacted some forty or fifty persons, judges, state and federal, lawyers, old and young, including many who had practiced before the Boston municipal court, and several who had tried cases before Judge Morrissey."[58] Interviews with committee members provide the basis for estimating that they will normally try to get in touch with ten to thirty people to get an assessment of a prospect. They will do this by personal interview or by phone where possible. They do not feel that they will get as frank a response in writing. Most lawyers are more than a little reticent to put derogatory information in writing about someone who one day might be a federal judge. The committee members do, however, receive some gratuitous letters of approval which the letter-writer feels compelled to write.[59]

It has long been the articulated committee policy to ascertain the "views of Federal and State judges, ABA State and local Bar Association officials, and *a cross-section of the lawyers practicing in the particular community*" (emphasis supplied).[60] But it would appear that efforts to survey a cross-section are far from systematic and would hardly meet the test of being a good random or other type of "scientific" sample. Professor Grossman's research, as well as that done by Professors Henderson and Sinclair in Texas, and interviews with committee members all indicate that the sources tend to be cut from the same cloth as the committeemen, lawyers highly active in Bar Association activities.[61]

Whether or not a prospect meets the objective criteria with respect to age and trial experience is relatively easy to evaluate. When it comes to ability, judicial temperament, and character, that is another matter. Committee members are frank to admit that evaluations on these factors are highly subjective. When Mr. Meserve was pressed by Senator Dodd to tell how many of the people he had consulted had been for and against Judge Morrissey he responded this way: "I will say that I have heard at least half a dozen who were favorable, and half a dozen who were opposed. The question of how you evaluate that is a question of the strength of the impression, the basis for the impression, the reasons given for the impression."[62] Mr. Segal concedes that there is no "science" in the committee's method of evaluation but argues for its validity in this way:

"Science," as Alexander Hamilton observed, "has discovered no way of measuring the faculties of the mind." And that, of course, is still so.

But I suggest that all of us have, and as we get more and more into the work we acquire certain experience in appraising evidence.

The FBI says a man who goes into the FBI, Mr. Hoover certainly appraises his 10-year man better than his 1-year man. Why?

153

Because he learns how to appraise the truth from falsity. He learns how to appraise the man who is lying or hiding something from the man who is perfectly openminded.

We learn how to assemble facts and we learn how to explore and appraise objective from subjective opinions and we learn to explore the views of the professional community of judges and lawyers which all of us think, we lawyers, at least, should be taken into consideration both by the appointing and the confirming authority.[63]

Add to the problem of subjectivity the vagaries of the standards set for him by the committee (set forth below) and one can appreciate the difficulties a committeeman has in making his evaluations:

To be rated "Exceptionally Well Qualified," an individual must stand at the top of his profession; he must rank among the very best qualified judges or lawyers available for judicial service. He must have not only outstanding legal ability and background, and wide experience in the Federal court system, but also those indefinable qualities of spirit, wisdom, intellect, insight, and impartiality, which we all treasure in a judge. The Committee employs the classification of Exceptionally Well Qualified very sparingly. To be accorded this high accolade—the Committee's summa cum laude—a prospective nominee should generally also have the breadth of vision and of outlook which derives from participation in the civic, charitable, religious, or political activities of the community and the work of the Organized Bar or other professional organizations. In short, he should be a person whose pre-eminence in the law and as a citizen is widely acknowledged and whose qualifications for the position are virtually unanimously hailed by judges and lawyers.

The rating of "Well Qualified" is also regarded by the Committee as a very high one. Your Committee strictly eschews selecting candidates of its own. The Committee's function is limited exclusively to investigating those persons whose names are submitted to it by the Attorney General. However, a rating of Exceptionally Well Qualified or Well Qualified indicates the Committee's strong, affirmative endorsement of a candidate. These designations are reserved for those individuals whom the Committee would gladly sponsor as its candidates if it were pursuing this practice.

The rating of "Qualified" covers a broad area, so broad that it has sometimes resulted in misunderstanding. For example, an editor of one of the Country's most vigorous and knowledgeable newspapers on the subject of judicial selection has referred to all judges whom the Committee rates as Qualified, as "borderline cases as to competence." This is too general a characterization and is unfair to many of the judges who have been classified as Qualified.

Thus, a number of the persons who have been reported as Qualified have been men quite young in years at the time of their appointment. Most of them appeared to be able men on the threshold of promising careers as practicing lawyers, but they had not yet had very great exposure, nor an opportunity to demonstrate their mature capacities. Your Committee approves the practice of appointing some promising younger

154

lawyers to the Bench when they have had sufficient experience to warrant such appointment, but in most of these cases, the Committee would not be justified in according them, as yet, a rating higher than Qualified. Nevertheless, they do not constitute "borderline cases" as to competence.[64]

The Committee's Explicit Desiderata

Over the years, the committee has developed four specific requirements which it feels must be met for qualification to the federal bench. There has been mention of these previously but in the interest of clarity, some repetition appears useful.

The first requirement, concerning age, was described by Mr. Segal this way:

. . . it has become firmly established that no lawyer 60 years or over, should be appointed to a lifetime judgeship for the first time, unless he is regarded by professional opinion as "Well Qualified" or "Exceptionally Well Qualified," and is in excellent health. This rule has not been applied to a Federal judge under consideration for elevation to an appellate court, but the rule has been that in no event, should anyone, even a judge being elevated to an appellate court, be appointed if he has passed his sixty-fourth birthday.[65]

The second is that the designee "have a reasonable amount of trial experience, preferably at least some of it in the Federal courts."[66] More recently, the committee has added two more requirements which to some degree were really operative from the beginning. One, the committee regards it as essential to qualification that a designee have at least fifteen years of significant legal experience before being chosen for the bench, and, two, that he have the highest rating which Martindale-Hubbell accords to a lawyer.[67] Martindale-Hubbell is a directory of lawyers practicing in the United States which contains ratings on ability, recommendations, and financial worth, where they can be obtained.

Some Disquieting Allegations

In the course of interviews with a number of lawyers and judges, several serious allegations were leveled by responsible persons against two men who have served as members of the committee. In one circuit, more than a few federal judges and lawyers vigorously criticized the way the committeeman for their circuit conducted his inquiry. They described in detail how he came to one of the large cities in the circuit, summoned lawyers to his hotel suite, and proceeded to hold court in a most imperious fashion, which they thought was insulting. They were particularly incensed by what they regarded as the committeeman's anti-Catholic bias. They alleged that with respect to an investigatee who had attended a Catholic university law school, he asked questions like "What could he have learned in that Papist school?" It should be emphasized that this was not an isolated complaint. It was echoed by virtually every one of the sample interviewed in that city.

One United States attorney reported that in the course of a trial, when he "roughed up" the opposing counsel who was a past member of the committee, the counsel took occasion to tell the United States attorney in a corridor during the trial: "I know what you want to be and believe me, I'm going to see to it you never get it." Since the United States attorney had pursued nomination to the federal bench openly and ardently, there was no question in his mind what he was being told. In fairness, it must be reported that several years later the attorney did become a federal judge, the threat notwithstanding.

Whether or not the allegations are true, and no attempt was made to determine their validity, the possibility that such things could happen raises perplexing questions. Human nature being what it is, some few members of the committee are going to be less than wise, some few members will abuse the power which inheres in being a member of the committee. What safeguards are there against arbitrary or foolish actions of committeemen? The "obvious" answer is that arbitrary or foolish actions would be reported to the president of the American Bar Association or the committee chairman and the perpetrator would be removed from the committee. There is good reason to wonder if that would often actually happen. When the first allegation reported here was related by me to the then chairman of the committee, he was genuinely surprised and upset. He was hearing it for the first time, in spite of the fact that it had been the subject of great concern in the large city where the alleged misconduct took place. Further inquiry suggests that among some lawyers, there is the view that the ABA committee represents a clique within the legal profession, and it would not do much good to complain to members or about them. Also, there was a feeling among the lawyers interviewed who made the allegation that to do anything about the matter officially within the ABA framework would require making a "federal case" out of it, i.e., would take an inordinate amount of time and effort. They preferred instead to deal with nominations to the federal bench on an ad hoc basis. If they had ideas about people who should be considered for nomination, they communicated them directly to the United States senators from the state and officials in the Department of Justice. If they felt that someone under active consideration was not getting a "fair shake" from the committee, they conveyed this feeling to the senators and Justice officials.

In short, no procedures have been devised for appealing or disputing committee decisions. This is not to suggest that there should or could be such procedures. What is important is to recognize that it is possible for misuse or abuse of power to occur and that there is currently no ongoing procedural remedy within the committee's mode of operation to prevent it or to cure it if or when it occurs.

Assaying the Committee's Role

The lack of measuring sticks which would be satisfactory from a scientific point of view makes any evaluation of the committee's work a hazardous enterprise. Any assessment made in the present state of the art of social science will involve a high degree of someone's subjectivity or the subjectivity of a collection of someones. The following, therefore, is offered with the warning *caveat emptor*.

On the plus side, and it is a big plus, the committee has in effect performed the function in judicial selection that the Founding Fathers had originally conceived for the Senate. Recall Hamilton's words in *The Federalist*: "To what purpose then require the cooperation of the Senate? I answer, that the necessity of their concurrence would have a powerful, though, in general, a silent operation. It would be an excellent check upon the spirit of favoritism in the President, and would tend greatly to prevent the appointment of unfit characters from State prejudice, from family connection, from personal attachment, or from a view to popularity." For reasons explored in Chapter I, neither the Senate as a whole nor the Judiciary Committee has performed that function. The ABA committee has, and not through any formal grant of power. The committee's power to sanction comes from its ability to gather facts pertaining to a particular selection and to draw the attention of the mass media, leading politicians and other opinion-makers, and ultimately the general public to those facts. Where the facts seem to add up to a conclusion that an appointment grows exclusively out of family connections or narrow personal political connections, there will be a plethora of testy editorials and denunciations from politicians, particularly from the party out of power. Committee action or threat of action to oppose a nomination alone will not stop a nomination which the president's men are determined to make at any cost. The committee has no legal instrument to stop such a selection. Once the committee has lodged its objections with the Senate Judiciary Committee, it has shot its bolt. If the president and the senator(s) involved in the selection persist in the face of committee opposition, the Judiciary Committee and the Senate will approve the nomination, even though a minority of each body might disapprove. In that connection, it is well to remember that the Senate majority leader indicated that Morrissey's appointment would have been approved had President Johnson and Senator Edward Kennedy persisted.[68] Nonetheless, Bernard Segal is undoubtedly right in observing that the very fact that the committee is in business prevents a number of appointments which would be fairly characterized by Mr. Jenner's term of "cronyism." It would, of course, never be possible to quantify accurately just how many such appointments are prevented. But it does seem fair to say that the fact that there is such an organization as the committee will inhibit any administration and senators generally. For, as pointed out earlier, it would be a distinct political liability to appear too often to press and public to be cavalier about judicial selection. To the extent, then, that the committee's operation prevents selection by cronyism or for narrow political considerations, it is decidedly performing a highly desirable function in the public interest. But the committee purports to do much more than to bar rank appointments. The committee purports to be able to determine, above and beyond cronyism and narrow partisan considerations, who is and who is not qualified for the bench, even to the extent of determining the degree to which people are qualified. In this area, the validity of the committee's work is highly questionable and, consequently, of questionable value. Despite the fact that there has been a pronounced tendency on the part of the nation's press and public to regard committee evaluations as sacrosanct, no more can be validly claimed for them than that they reflect the systematic bias of the committee members with respect to what manner of men or women should be appointed to the federal bench. "Bias" here is being employed as a scientific, not a pejorative, term. That is to say that the members of the committee perceive how well a person is qualified through a bundle of attitudes, conscious or subconscious, which, however difficult to specify, are identifiable in a general way. The "bias" is systematic in the sense that the bias tends in most cases to favor an identifiable type of legal experience and disfavor another. In the same spirit that it was urged a moment ago that no more be claimed for the committee than that its evaluations reflect its systematic biases, no less should be claimed than that under prevailing conditions, anyone else's evaluations are also a product of his systematic biases. And so they are. Once this fact of life is taken into account, we can explore the bias of the committee, or the bias of a Friesen for that matter, and decide better on the basis of our own value judgments whose bias we would prefer to prevail.

In order to get a fix on the basic direction of the aggregate of committee members' attitudes, it is essential to recognize that the committee is a piece of and of a piece with the American Bar Association. As Professor Grossman has pointed out, the committee members are people very active in association affairs.[69] Some indication of how close to the leadership of the ABA the committee is, is given by the fact that since 1946–47, three former committee members have gone on to serve as presidents of the association itself; eight have served on the Board of Governors; and one has been chairman of the House of Delegates. Although, as indicated earlier, Bernard Segal liked to think of the committee as serving as a conduit between the bench and bar and the attorney general, a good many lawyers and judges are not members of the ABA. A former president of the association has estimated that the ABA, as of 1965, had a membership of 120,000 out of 296,000 "persons holding a license to practice law." He estimated, however, that only 192,000 of the 296,000 were actually actively engaged in law practice.[70] In no sense then can it be argued that the committee or the ABA represents all lawyers and judges. Nor can it be claimed that the committee is representative of the whole of the ABA. It represents the leadership of the organization. Indeed, as pointed out earlier, committee members and chairmen are selected by the president. The relevance of all this is that the committee is frequently pictured, particularly by the committee itself, as being apolitical. But surely the ABA is not an apolitical organization. It involves itself very deeply in a host of political and partisanly political issues and battles. Professor Schmidhauser in assaying the stands of the ABA on public issues from 1937 through 1960 suggested:

> In contemporary America, the size and complexity of the bar defy simple categorization, but the American Bar Association is comprised of a group whose programs and ideological predilections are a matter of public record. The main thrust of the public policy stands of the American Bar Association has been exemplified in its opposition to the Child Labor Amendment, to the Roosevelt Court Reform Bill, to the Wagner-Murray-Dingell (National Health Insurance) Bill, to the Genocide Convention and the Covenant on Human Rights, to the Ewing Health Bill, the Gore-Holifield Bill (providing for public development of atomic energy for peacetime purposes), and to having an ABA observer with the United States delegation to the United Nations. The programs it supported are equally indicative. . . .[71]

There has been no change in the direction of ABA political thinking since 1960. For example, in 1965, the House of Delegates resolved that "the American Bar Association approves and endorses an amendment to the Constitution of the United States to the effect that one house of a bicameral state legislature may be apportioned in part by reference to geography, county and city lines, economic conditions, history, and other factors in addition to population, provided that such a plan of apportionment is approved by a majority of the voters of the state. . . ."[72] On the great issue of our times, civil rights, the ABA has been markedly more concerned with law and order than the evils of discrimination. When the Special Committee on Civil Rights and Racial Unrest, which was created in response to President Kennedy's call to lawyers "for volunteer citizen action to ease racial tensions," gave its report in 1963, its exhortations to lawyers to do something about helping to end discrimination were preceded and overshadowed by Part I of the report which dealt with the "Necessity for Law and Order."[73]

Relevant, too, is the complaint Senator Hart lodged against the ABA in a journal article for its activity opposing his truth-in-packaging proposal:

Although I underestimated the vehemence of the opposition to the bill, I had anticipated the identity of most of the opponents. However, one member of the group came as a surprise to me: the American Bar Association. The House of Delegates of the ABA, moving as groups of such size frequently do, in 1963 followed the recommendation of its study committee and summarily adopted a resolution against the Truth-in-Packaging Bill. Initially this action confounded me, but subsequently I examined the membership of the seven-man Advisory Committee of the Food, Drug, and Cosmetic Division of the Corporation, Banking, and Business Section that made the recommendation, and discovered a possible explanation—that several of its top members were affiliated with the food industry.[74]

The foregoing has been presented not for the purpose of passing on the merits of the ABA position on these matters but rather for the purpose of substantiating the proposition that the ABA philosophically is on the conservative side of the modern-day American political spectrum. What has this to do with judicial selection? It is possible, of course, that whether or not a person is a conservative or a liberal will make no difference in his perception of who would be a good or poor judge. But it would not be unreasonable to assume otherwise as was suggested in the discussion of committee members' party identification. Let us for the moment hypothesize that party identification and philosophy do make a difference in perception. What kind of candidates would a committee with a Republican and conservative coloration favor for the federal bench? It would be reasonable to assume that they might favor persons who were private practitioners with highly successful corporate practices, sitting judges on prestigious state courts (or federal district courts where nomination is made to a circuit court), and Republicans. It could be expected that they would tend to be less than enchanted with government lawyers, even those with considerable trial experience. Do these assumptions and expectations hold up under analysis? Of the eighteen Kennedy appointments rated as exceptionally well qualified, sixteen were either highly successful private practitioners or judges before appointment. The others had been first assistant solicitor general of the United States (Oscar H. Davis) and city solicitor of Baltimore, Maryland (Harrison Winter). In contrast, of the sixteen United States attorneys elevated to the bench during the Johnson administration, the committee rated three well qualified, twelve qualified, and one not qualified. Too, it is instructive to note what

161

happened with respect to committee ratings for district judges who were elevated to the circuit courts by President Johnson. See Table 14.

Table 14. ABA Committee Ratings of Nominees to District
Courts and Circuit Courts in the Johnson Administration

Judge	Original Rating upon Nomination for District Court	Rating When Considered for Circuit Court
Thornberry	WQ	None asked for
Freedman	EWQ	EWQ
Anderson	WQ	WQ
Tamm	NQ	WQ
Gibson	Q	Q
Feinberg	Favorable (Q)	WQ
Winter	EWQ	EWQ
Craven	WQ	WQ
Peck	WQ	EWQ
Ainsworth	WQ	EWQ
Dyer	EWQ	EWQ
McCree	WQ	WQ
S. Robinson	WQ	WQ
Simpson	No rating	WQ
Van Dusen	Not known	WQ
Butzner	EWQ	EWQ
Clayton	Not known	EWQ
Carter	No rating	WQ
Morgan	WQ	EWQ

Of the fourteen who were rated twice five, or more than one-third, had a better rating after being a judge. This result can be looked at several ways, of course. One, the judges have acquired additional experience since the first rating. Two, the halo effect of being a judge could also be operative. Parenthetically, what does this tell us about the validity of the committee's ratings as predictors, if the second rating can be considered an assessment of performance on the bench? It gives credence to Friesen's suggestion that the committee will only be right half the time.

Of the eleven Republicans appointed by Kennedy, three were rated exceptionally well qualified, five well qualified, and three qualified. Of the ten Republicans nominated by Johnson, two were rated exceptionally well qualified and eight well qualified. In short, Republicans picked by our last two Democratic presidents have fared well in committee ratings. The committee was sensitive to this fact in its 1966 report in which it explained: "All 4 appointees of President Johnson, whose previous political affiliation was of Republican party persuasion, were judged by the Committee to merit its highest ratings. We observe that recognition of the political facts of life dictates that appointees of political persuasion different from the national administration in office necessitates they be highly qualified lawyers or judges in order to withstand political party demurrer."[75]

The labor lawyer David Rabinovitz, despite President Kennedy's strong support, was rated not qualified. Constance B. Motley, the civil rights lawyer, rated only a qualified. Anthony Celebrezze, the secretary of health, education, and welfare and former mayor (1953–62) of Cleveland, and Oren Harris, who had served as a congressman for over twenty years, both rated only qualified. (Another congressman fared better, however. Homer Thornberry rated a well qualified.) George C. Edwards, police commissioner of Detroit who had previously served in the Michigan Supreme Court, 1956–62, rated only a qualified.

Patently, correlations do not prove cause and effect relationships. Nor would it be safe to assume that philosophical orientation was the only factor at work in committee members' evaluations. It is probable that other factors contributed to the committee members' relatively low regard for the United States attorneys elevated to the federal bench by President Johnson. It may even be that by some objective standards they were not up to snuff. Yet taking all the caveats into account, it would seem a fair assessment that committee ratings reflect a systematic philosophical bias. What inferences about the role of the committee can be drawn from such an assessment? First, the committee can serve and probably has served as a healthy check and balance. Our administrations have since 1932 been on the liberal side of the political spectrum, even when the Republicans have had a man in the White House. But in keeping with that role, committee ratings should be recognized by the administration, the press, the public, and the committee itself not as truly objective and absolute ratings, but as the careful and considered opinions of a respected and responsible conservative group of lawyers. As such, the ratings should not be regarded as sacrosanct but should be weighed in the balance.

163

What has been said does not foreclose the possibility that the committee can and may take steps to make its ratings more meaningful. Conceivably, more objective criteria can be developed. Certainly, the committee could do a much better job of sampling the opinions of bench and bar. If the committee were to make use of what is known about drawing up a scientific sample of a population, it could systematically canvass such a sample in order to obtain consensus ratings and lay a better claim that its ratings validly represented the opinion of the appropriate bar than it can under present practice.

CHAPTER V

The Johnson Administration

WITH RESPECT TO judicial selection, Lyndon B. Johnson began his administration under less than auspicious circumstances. Six nominations made by President Kennedy were still awaiting confirmation at the time of the assassination; in addition, one, Thornberry, had been confirmed by the Senate but had not been formally appointed.[1] With understandable and admirable loyalty to the late president, Johnson proceeded with the formalities required to ensure that these appointees would become federal judges. He could have intervened if he had wanted to, to withdraw the names of the six and, presumably, could have refused to make the formal appointment of Thornberry. In any case, he went ahead with efforts to effectuate the Kennedy nominations. Unfortunately for him two of the seven turned out to be highly controversial nominations.

The Kennedy Legacies

As indicated in an earlier chapter, after President Kennedy had nominated David Rabinovitz of Sheboygan to the federal bench in Wisconsin, he let it be known he was for Rabinovitz "all the way."[2] Neither of Wisconsin's Democratic senators favored the appointment.[3]

In addition, the ABA committee was vehemently opposed to the appointment and went on record as judging Rabinovitz to be unqualified for the post. Rabinovitz had been legal counselor for the United Auto Workers in its titanic struggle with the Kohler Company of Wisconsin, and his candidacy had been strongly urged by Walter Reuther.[4] This led to charges from some quarters that the ABA committee opposed the nomination because Rabinovitz was a "labor lawyer." The ABA committee resented these charges and took the highly unusual step of refuting them in its midyear report of 1964.[5]

In view of the opposition of the Wisconsin senators and the ABA committee, the Senate Judiciary Committee had made no move to further confirmation of Rabinovitz in 1963. When Congress recessed, President Johnson dutifully made Rabinovitz a recess appointment on January 7, 1964. With the death of Kennedy, the Wisconsin senators felt freer to staunchly oppose the nomination since they could presume that Johnson did not have the same commitment to it as President Kennedy had felt. Consequently, Congress adjourned on October 4, 1964, without confirming the appointment. The outcome might have been very different had President Kennedy lived. For following the adjournment of Congress, President Johnson allowed the vacancy to go unfilled. The vacancy gave rise to pressures which Kennedy might have exploited to have his way. The *Milwaukee Sentinel* editorialized after a few months: "The vacancy has gone beyond the point of public tolerance. Because of the continued inability or unwillingness of the Johnson Administration to appoint a judge, the very system of justice in that court is breaking down."[6] David Carley, the Wisconsin Democratic national committeeman, complained: "When I go around the state I get blistered for not bringing things to a head. Things are not only deteriorating from the judicial standpoint but the position of the Democratic party is deteriorating and put in jeopardy by the continued delay."[7] Ultimately Johnson succumbed and in May of 1965 appointed James E. Doyle to the judgeship that Kennedy had hoped would go to Rabinovitz.[8]

When George C. Edwards, Jr., was nominated by President Kennedy to be a United States circuit judge, Sixth Circuit, in September of 1963, he had a number of things going for him. He was stamped "qualified" by the ABA committee and had the approval of the two Democratic senators from his state, Michigan, plus a warm endorsement from the Republican governor, George Romney.[9] In addition, he had held a series of posts which on their face would seem to have afforded him with experience eminently fitting him for a federal judicial post. He had been president of the Detroit City Council, 1946–50; judge of probate in Detroit, 1951–54; judge of Wayne County Circuit Court, 1954–56; justice of the Michigan Supreme Court, 1956–62; and police commissioner for the city of Detroit, 1962–63. Despite these impressive credentials, Judge Edwards was subjected to more than a perfunctory questioning when he appeared before a subcommittee of the Senate Judiciary Committee as part of confirmation proceedings. Questions propounded to Judge Edwards from Senators Ervin, Dirksen, and Hruska manifested concern (1) that Edwards's father had been a Socialist, (2) that Edwards had been a member of the American Student Union, (3) that he had been a labor organizer, (4) that he had been "sentenced to thirty days in prison for a contempt arising out of an alleged violation of an injunction issued in connection with a strike," (5) that he had written "a decision of the Michigan Supreme Court which upset a precedent of eighteen years, and favored the union for which [he] had worked as a paid organizer," (6) that he was a deputy judge of the Administrative Tribunal of the International Labor Organization.[10]

In a second day of hearings, representatives of the Tennessee Bar Association (Tennessee is in the Sixth Circuit) appeared to protest the Edwards nomination. Mr. S. Shephard Tate, the president of that association, stated that it was "the position of the Tennessee Bar Association that the admissions by Commissioner Edwards before this subcommittee of certain past activities would show a disqualification for this high judicial office and would create in the public mind and in the bar a lack of confidence in the courts of the United States."[11] The Tennesseans added nothing to the concerns already noted. Judge Edwards handled himself very well—patently well enough to allay fears that he lacked judicial temperament—and was confirmed. But Mr. Tate had laid bare the fact that there had been some reservations on the ABA committee. He testified: ". . . as I understand it . . . from the Chairman of the American Bar Association Standing Committee on the Federal Judiciary, Mr. Robert W. Meserve, from Boston, as I recall—I recall that he wrote to me, and I understood that he wrote to this subcommittee to say that it was one of the relatively rare instances in which the committee was not unanimous, but the majority had stated that the nominee was qualified . . ."[12] So at best, Judge Edwards had been granted begrudgingly a "qualified" and however well he had handled himself in the hearings, the now well-published fact that he had been a militant unionist in an earlier day would leave lingering doubts in many quarters about his judicial temperament.

The 1964 Appointments

In 1964, the Johnson administration made eighteen nominations which were in no way legacies of the late President Kennedy. All but one, an elevation from a district to circuit court, were Democrats; they tended to be a little younger than Eisenhower and Kennedy appointees; a relatively high percentage (33 percent) had attended Ivy League law schools; a relatively high percentage (25 percent) of the district judges had been United States attorneys at the time of nomination; two of the three special court nominees had come up through the ranks, so to speak. But thunderclouds were forming.

By ABA committee standards, the Johnson administration had not covered itself with honors in appointing judges that first year. In comparison with the Eisenhower and Kennedy administrations, the Johnson administration was low in the percentage of exceptionally well qualifieds and well qualifieds, and much higher on unqualifieds, as shown in Table 15. The ABA committee was not pleased. In its 1964 report, it lamented:

Last year's annual report started off with the statement that, during the period covered by it, there had been no nomination for lifetime judicial

Table 15. Percentage of Judges Appointed during the First Year of the Johnson Administration Compared with Judges Appointed during the Eisenhower and Kennedy Administrations in Each of the ABA Rating Classifications

Rating	Eisenhower	Kennedy	Johnson
Exceptionally well qualified	17.1	16.6	5.6
Well qualified	44.6	45.6	22.2
Qualified	32.6*	31.5†	55.5
Not qualified	5.7	6.3	16.7

* Includes qualified, "recommended," and "neither recommended nor opposed."
† Includes "recommended."

office submitted to the United States Senate of any person who had been previously reported by this Committee to the Attorney General as "not qualified." We are told that "pride goeth before a fall." Any feeling of satisfaction which your Committeee may have then had in the practical agreement between its conclusions and those of the appointing authority has surely been lessened by the nominations submitted since last July. . . . Of the nominations in question [those made in late 1963 and the first half of 1964], the substantial majority (18) were made by President Johnson, and, of the number nominated (whether or not confirmed) in the entire year, three, as noted, were found "not qualified" comprising, therefore, almost an eighth of the whole. Of the other 20, on the other hand, 9, or nearly half, were found by the committee to be "well qualified" or "exceptionally well qualified." [13]

The 1965 Appointments

The 1965 Johnson nominations (thirty-two) on the whole fared markedly better in the ABA committee ratings than the earlier ones, but were still not on a par with the Eisenhower and Kennedy appointments: 9.4 percent rated exceptionally well qualified, 40.6 percent well qualified, 43.7 percent qualified, and 6.3 percent not qualified. Ten of the twenty-three nominated to the district and special courts were men who had served in their respective state benches and four of the nine nominees for circuit posts were elevations from district benches. That the ABA committee was generally pleased with these choices can be ascertained by the generally high ratings accorded these appointments, as shown in the tabulation that follows. (The one rated unqualified was Morrissey.) Only two of the nominees were United States attorneys at the time of appointment, although ten had at one time or another served in the Department of Justice.

Rating	No. of State Judges Nominated to District and Special Courts	No. of Judges Elevated from District to Circuit
Exceptionally well qualified	2	0
Well qualified	4	2
Qualified	2	1
Not qualified	1	0
No rating requested	1	1

Normally, a record of ABA ratings the likes of which the Johnson administration received in 1965 would have been enough to merit the praise of the nation's press and give the administration a good public image with respect to judicial appointments. But the biggest news events concerning judicial appointments in 1965 were the nominations of James P. Coleman and Francis X. Morrissey. And deservedly or not, the Johnson administration came out of the fights over those nominations with a fat lip and a black eye.

When President Johnson in June of 1965 nominated Coleman, a former Mississippi governor (1956–60), for a post on the Appeals Court for the Fifth Circuit, it was a foregone conclusion that the nomination would create a furore among liberals and proponents of civil rights. Mrs. Victoria Gray of Hattiesburg, one of the leaders of the Mississippi Freedom Democratic party, raged at a news conference: "Throughout Mr. Coleman's long career, he has held virtually every type of office in the State of Mississippi, all of which have been won only over the rights—and often the bodies—of Negro citizens of that state."[14] Representative Don Edwards (California), chairman of Americans for Democratic Action, issued a strong statement: "It is ironic that at the very point that the American government and people have taken steps to eradicate segregation from this country, the American President should appoint to the court a man committed to frustrating the will of the people and the human rights guaranteed to every man, regardless of race."[15]

It was true, as the *New York Times* reported in a profile on Coleman, that "he was as strong a segregationist as the next fellow, Mr. Coleman told the voters, but his approach was legalistic rather than emotional. The new governor pushed through the Legislature an array of laws intended to preserve rigid separation of the races in schools and in public accommodations."[16] But in all fairness there was much more to the Coleman record, as the *New York Times* was quick to point out in the same profile:

He set out to lead Mississippi further into the mainstream of American life by attempting to write a new state constitution devoid of mention of race—he barely lost in the Legislature—and by supporting John F. Kennedy for President.

He also prevented the Citizens Councils from obtaining tax money, called in the Federal Bureau of Investigation after a lynching in south Mississippi, and publicly supported former Representative Brook Hays of Little Rock when he was unseated by a segregationist.

By the end of his four-year term, Ross R. Barnett was able to brand Mr. Coleman a moderate and, worse than that, "a Kennedy liberal," in his successful campaign for the governor's office. . . .

170

And even though he insisted that he was still a segregationist, Mr. Coleman was defeated in 1963 in his second campaign for the governorship. He was unable to shed the "Kennedy liberal" label pinned on him by Mr. Barnett.[17]

In a strategy conceived to counter or at least to put the swell of criticism in perspective, the attorney general of the United States took the highly unusual step of testifying in behalf of Coleman at the outset of the Senate committee hearings on the nomination. As the *New York Times* reported: "It was believed to be the first time in this century that an Attorney General had given public testimony to a Congressional committee on behalf of an appointment to the Federal judiciary."[18] Attorney General Katzenbach made no effort to deny that Governor Coleman had supported racial segregation. The burden of his testimony was that Coleman's statements in support of segregation

cannot be considered in a vacuum. They must be considered in the context of the society and the times in which they were made. In the second place, there is a full record of other actions taken and other pronouncements made by the same individual.

These other activities give perspective to the picture and alter the surface impression. When the full picture is considered, we see not the caricature of an unyielding white supremacist but a man who was frequently willing to take great political risks to support moderation and respect for law and order when the opposite course would have been the politically expedient one.[19]

The attorney general's appearance and able advocacy did not allay the stronger critics of the nomination. Among others, Congressman John Conyers (Michigan), Congressman William F. Ryan (New York), Professor Thomas R. Emerson (Yale Law School), Professor Louis Lusky (Columbia Law School), and representatives of leading civil rights organizations came before the committee to vigorously protest the nomination.[20] As they read the Coleman record, the best that could be said for him was that he had been subtle in his support of segration rather than extreme. As Professor Emerson put it:

No one would suggest the appointment of a person who advocated the use of force and violence in race relations. That is not the problem. The problem is to appoint persons who will seek to evade, delay, obstruct in various ways enforcement of Federal laws as declared by Congress and the Supreme Court. That is exactly the approach to segregation which Governor Coleman's record indicates he has followed in the past.[21]

Throughout the hearings, Senators Javits and Hart, members of the Judiciary Committee, also demonstrated their reservations about the nomination by the questions they asked.

At length, it was Senator Edward M. Kennedy who put the sixty-four-dollar question to Mr. Coleman. After relating that President Kennedy had asked Coleman to be secretary of the army in 1961 and suggesting that the responsibilities of a federal judge are different because of civil rights questions, Senator Kennedy asked, "Do you hold any personal beliefs or have any doubts that seriously question this national policy [as indicated in the *Brown* decision and the civil rights acts]?"[22]

Mr. Coleman answered:

No, sir, I do not have. I think that the people of Mississippi know that if I go on the Court of Appeals that I am going to do my duty one hundred percent pursuant to the decisions of the Supreme Court which are binding on me and of other judges as well as acts of Congress which have been sustained by the Supreme Court of the United States. I will have no difficulty whatever in doing that. I wouldn't allow my name to be considered for a judgeship, Senator Kennedy, if I did have any difficulty.[23]

Evidently, an overwhelming majority of the Judiciary Committee and the Senate itself felt that the case against the nomination was not so clear or so impressive as to compel a rejection of the nomination. The committee voted its approval 13 to 2 and the Senate 76 to 8.

That liberal elements in the political spectrum were still opposed to the nomination is attested to by the names of the senators who voted against confirmation: Case, Cooper, Douglas, Hart, Javits, Morse, Nelson, and Proxmire (three others were paired against the nomination: Hartke, Mondale, and Neuberger). Significantly, this roster does not include some names that one would expect to find on a list of Senate liberals. Some, like Clark, McNamara, and Tydings, felt compelled to explain their lack of opposition with words not unlike those of Senator Robert Kennedy, who went on record saying, "We have not often agreed, but Governor Coleman is a man of his word and in my judgment a man of high character."[24]

Clearly, administration efforts notwithstanding, there were still significant and articulate elements even in the Senate who regarded the nomination as a poor one to say the least. The attention given in the press to accounts of criticism of the nomination as well as coverage of the hearings tended to create an impression that something was amiss in judicial selection.[25] It does not seem untoward, therefore, to suggest that the administration did not come through the contest unscathed. That battle accounts for the fat lip. Now for the black eye.

In late September of 1965, President Johnson announced the nomination of Francis X. Morrissey to the District Court of Massachusetts. Official Washington, and indeed aficionados of American politics everywhere, were titillated by the riddle: why did President Johnson nominate a Kennedy-sponsored candidate whom the Kennedys manifestly never dared to nominate when one of them was president and another attorney general? Morrissey himself shed some light on the matter by telling friends that shortly before the assassination President Kennedy had promised him the nomination after the 1964 election.[26] Undoubtedly, the Johnson administration would not have selected Morrissey for a judgeship on its own initiative. But when Senator Edward M. Kennedy continually pressed for Morrissey's nomination, President Johnson was induced to go along because of what he perceived were the late president's wishes in the matter (as he had done on his earliest judicial appointments) and because of his predilection for acceding to senators' wishes in regard to appointments where possible.[27] To those most knowledgeable little credence was given to the idea that the president hoped to embarrass the Kennedys by the nomination. As *Washington Post* staffer John P. MacKenzie put it: "Political and bar figures familiar with the Morrissey-Kennedy relationship also discounted another theory that has been prevalent in Washington—that President Johnson sought to 'mousetrap' Edward Kennedy by yielding on an appointment for which the Senator would be criticized."[28] After all, Johnson was politically astute enough to know that he himself would not come through unscathed if the nomination was fiercely contested or if the appointment was made and Morrissey turned out to be a poor federal judge. By the same token, Edward Kennedy was not being enticed unknowingly into sponsoring Morrissey; he, too, was well aware of the pitfalls inherent in the nomination.

The ensuing battle royal over the nomination demonstrated clearly that Edward Kennedy wanted the nomination for Morrissey with all his heart, whatever the reasons. Morrissey had served the Kennedys, father, John, and Edward, long and well.[29] Whether out of personal gratitude, respect for his father, sincere admiration and respect for Morrissey, or, what is more likely, a combination of all, Senator Edward Kennedy fought prodigiously for Judge Morrissey's appointment.

Battle lines were quickly drawn. The ABA committee and important elements of the nation's press expressed their opposition immediately and in no uncertain terms.[30] The *New York Herald Tribune* called the nomination "nauseous."[31] In a highly unusual step, Judge Wyzanski of the District Court of Massachusetts—one of the most highly regarded albeit controversial federal judges—wrote to the Senate Judiciary Committee urging disapproval of the nomination on the grounds that Morrissey "has neither the familiarity with the law nor the industry to learn it."[32] Morrissey was not without supporters, however. For the edification of the Senate Judiciary subcommittee which held the hearings on the nomination, Senator Edward Kennedy was able to trot out an impressive array of supporters including the president of the Massachusetts Bar Association who testified that that organization endorsed the nomination[33] and Speaker of the House John W. McCormack.

There apparently were many in and around Boston who saw the ABA committee–Wyzanski opposition as a kind of snobbery because of Morrissey's humble beginnings and his lack of posh educational credentials. MacKenzie of the *Washington Post* captured the flavor of these feelings when he visited Boston several weeks before the hearings. He wrote:

> The home of "The Last Hurrah" could not care less what the American Bar Association thinks of Francis Joseph Xavier Morrissey.
> To a degree, the same opinion holds for the view of Chief Judge Charles E. Wyzanski, Jr. that Morrissey is unqualified to sit in his Federal District Court.
> In fact, if there is any strong feeling around the courthouses and Democratic parlors, it is one of wry satisfaction that the organized bar will probably go down swinging this week in its fight to block Morrissey's Senate confirmation.
> The elevation of Morrissey from the Boston Municipal (pronounced "muni-CIP-al" here) Court represents to many an "inspiration," a wonderful success story.[34]

For counterfire, the ABA committee rolled out before the subcommittee hearings its three biggest guns, the last three chairman, Jenner, Meserve, and Segal. Their testimony bit hard at the chinks in Morrissey's armor.[35] They pointed out that he had poor legal credentials by contemporary standards. He acquired a law degree from a school which was unaccredited at the time he attended. In the course of his work there he had failed four important courses. He had failed his bar examination twice. He had had very little significant legal experience before being appointed a municipal judge. The ABA committeemen made it abundantly clear that they did not regard the municipal judgeship as being particularly valuable experience for one going on the federal bench.

Despite the lacing Morrissey received at the hands of the ABA committee's big three, it was not his lack of credentials and lack of significant legal experience which did him in. In 1933, for purposes not altogether clear, Judge Morrissey obtained a law "degree" from a diploma mill in Georgia and on the basis of that degree was admitted to the bar of Georgia.[36] To gain admission to the bar, Morrissey had claimed that he was a resident of Georgia.[37] Mr. Jenner asserted that Morrissey had remained in Georgia only long enough to gain admission to the bar and returned to Boston. Although he never explicitly said so, Jenner implied that this action reflected on Morrissey's integrity. Jenner stated to the subcommittee: ". . . it is this course of events that led us to reach the considered judgment that Judge Morrissey is not qualified to serve in this high important office."[38] Later in the hearings, Judge Morrissey asserted that "I honestly and sincerely thought that I could practice law and be successful practicing law in the State of Georgia." When Senator Tydings asked Morrissey how long he had stayed in Georgia, Morrissey replied, "Totally about nine months." When Tydings asked, "How long after you were admitted to the bar?" Morrissey replied, "I would say about six months or a little less than six months."[39]

The fat was now in the fire. Evidence was brought to light that Morrissey was a candidate for a seat in the Massachusetts legislature during the period he claimed to be resident in Georgia.[40] The Justice Department undertook an FBI investigation, in Edward Kennedy's words, "to find out what really happened in Georgia."[41] Strangely, the confirmation now seemed to hinge on what should have been a peripheral issue. As the *Washington Post* observed in its news story: "The issue was principally whether he utilized a short-cut 'diploma mill' route to win his legal spurs—he never used the Georgia credentials as a passport to Massachusetts practice. Rather, it was whether Morrissey, who pleaded loss of memory in crucial points, had been completely open with the Senators who had to pass judgment on his qualifications."[42]

Within a matter of several days, Attorney General Katzenbach sent a letter to Senator Eastland, chairman of the Senate Judiciary Committee, stating that the FBI investigation substantiated Morrissey's version of his Georgia caper.[43] Then with a large number of its members abstaining, the Senate Judiciary Committee voted 6–3 recommending confirmation.[44] See the accompanying tabulation of votes.

For Confirmation	Against Confirmation	Not Voting
Eastland	Dirksen	McClellan
Burdick	Ervin	Long
Dodd	Scott	Bayh
Hart		Tydings
E. Kennedy		Hruska
Smathers		Fong
		Javits (absent; said he would have voted against)

The committee action did little to dispel growing Senate uneasiness over the nomination. A story alleging Morrissey's association with a deported Mafia figure became the object of wide speculation.[45] In a dramatic surprise move, Senator Edward Kennedy rose in the Senate on October 21, 1965, to ask that the nomination be sent back to the Judiciary Committee.[46] With a voice described as "choked with emotion" and "near tears," Senator Kennedy lashed out at the critics of the nomination.[47] He asserted that the FBI had backed Morrissey "on every controverted point. No one who knew Frank Morrissey could doubt that he was telling the truth." He upbraided the ABA committee for its posture on Morrissey's qualifications:

> The ABA was not satisfied with Judge Morrissey's legal education and training, perhaps because he attended a local law school at night, rather than a national law school by day.
> I think it is well to point out, however, good judges are not found only in great law schools. And to restrict judicial appointments to the graduates of such schools is to adopt a selection system which is profoundly undemocratic.[48]

Pulling out all the stops, Senator Kennedy went on:

> His father a dockworker, the family living in a home without gas,

electricity or heat in a bedroom; their shoes held together with wooden pegs their father made.

As a child of this family Frank Morrissey could not afford to study law full time, but had to study at night, snatching what time he could for his family.[49]

Senator Mansfield, Senate majority leader, rose to commend Senator Kennedy and to assert that there were votes enough to confirm the nomination.[50] (Senator Dirksen later claimed that this was not so.[51]) In any case, it is not clear that Senator Kennedy was actually giving up the fight. He asked only that the nomination be recommitted to the Judiciary Committee so that "if any Senators have any questions at all, they should have the chance to air them fully and seek the answer through the proven process of our committee system . . . I would wish any man placed on the court on my recommendation to be able to take his seat free of unresolved controversy."[52] Presumably, the action to recommit would give time to air the FBI report and to refute or explain the allegation of association with an underworld character and still leave the way open for confirmation. The president had reassured Senator Kennedy before the dramatic Senate action that "he himself was very much behind Morrissey's nomination or he wouldn't have submitted it, but it was a Senate matter and he would abide by the Senator's judgment."[53] But Judge Morrissey had had enough. Within a fortnight, he wrote to the president that he wanted his name removed from further consideration. The president lauded him for his courage and agreed to comply with his wishes in the matter.[54]

Whatever the merits (or lack of them) of attempting to put Judge Morrissey on the federal bench, the carnage of the battle was monumental.[55]

The Appointments of 1966–68

Despite its position that it was not much impressed with ABA ratings, and its posture with respect to the climatic meeting of the president and the ABA committee in May of 1966, described in the last chapter, the administration apparently was concerned about the need to make appointments which would deserve high ratings from the committee. Understandably stung by the criticism which had been heaped upon it as a result of the Coleman and Morrissey nominations, the administration had good reason to seek to regain the confidence of the press and public, if not the committee. In any case, for whatever reasons, the nominations in 1966 through May were excellent by ABA committee standards. Of twelve nominations, two (16.7 percent) were rated exceptionally well qualified, six (50 percent) well qualified, four (33.3 percent) qualified, and none unqualified. For all of 1966, the score for sixty-three nominations was as shown in the accompanying tabulation.

Rating	No.	Percentage
Exceptionally well qualified	9	14.3
Well qualified	30	47.6
Qualified	23	36.5
Not qualified	0	0
No rating given	1	1.6

Comparisons with the Eisenhower and Kennedy Administrations

The ratings of the Johnson nominations in 1966 and after made the over-all Johnson record with the ABA compare more favorably with the records of his immediate predecessors on both the high and low points of the scale, as shown in Table 16.

Table 16. Percentage of Judges Appointed during the Eisenhower, Kennedy, and Johnson Administrations in Each of the ABA Rating Classifications

Rating	Eisenhower	Kennedy	Johnson
Exceptionally well qualified	17.1	16.6	12.2
Well qualified	44.6	45.6	43.3
Qualified	32.6*	31.5†	41.7
Not qualified	5.7	6.3	2.8

* Includes qualified, "recommended," and "neither recommended nor opposed."
† Includes "recommended."

On other significant characteristics, the Johnson appointments were not markedly different from those of his immediate predecessors. Previous judicial experience of appeals court appointees is shown in Table 17. It is significant that five of the Johnson appeals court appointees who did not have previous judicial experience were men of considerable stature. The controversial James P. Coleman, after all, had been the governor of Mississippi (rated well qualified by the ABA committee). Anthony J. Celebrezze had been secretary of health,

Table 17. Previous Judicial Experience of Appointees to Appeals Courts
in the Eisenhower, Kennedy, and Johnson Administrations

Administration	No. of Appointments	Those Who Had Been Federal District Judges		Those with Judicial Experience at Federal or State Level	
		No.	%	No.	%
Eisenhower	45	18	40	28	62
Kennedy	21	8	38	11	52
Johnson	40	19	48	24	60

education, and welfare (rated qualified), Frank M. Coffin at forty-six had been a well-regarded congressman and a high-ranking United States foreign aid official (rated exceptionally well qualified), and Otto Kerner had been governor of Illinois and Bert T. Combs had been governor of Kentucky (both rated well qualified). Thirty-four percent of Johnson's district court appointees had previous judicial experience as against 26 percent of Eisenhower's and 33 percent of Kennedy's.

The Johnson judges included 6 percent from the opposing party, which compares with 5 percent for Eisenhower and 8 percent for Kennedy. The Johnson administration showed a small margin of greater partiality for younger appointees than its predecessors, as shown in Table 18.

Table 18. Percentage of District and Circuit Court Appointees in Various
Age Groups in the Eisenhower, Kennedy, and Johnson Administrations

Administration	District Judges				Circuit Court Judges			
	60 and Over	50–59	40–49	30–39	60 and Over	50–59	40–49	30–39
Eisenhower	10	56	31	3	33	52	13	2
Kennedy	8	54	34	4	19	62	19	0
Johnson	9	49	39	3	8	57	33	2

A slightly larger percentage of the Johnson appointees identified themselves as Catholics or Jews than did the Eisenhower and Kennedy appointees:

Administration	Catholics	Jews
Eisenhower	13%	7%
Kennedy	15	8
Johnson	18	9

179

The Johnson administration also showed some partiality toward graduates of Ivy League law schools:

Administration	District Judges	Appeals Court Judges
Eisenhower	21%	29%
Kennedy	18	19
Johnson	23	30

Eight percent of the Johnson appointments were made from the ranks of United States attorneys as compared with 7 percent in the Eisenhower administration and less than 3 percent in the Kennedy administration.

For whatever it is worth, which admittedly may not be very much, another piece of interesting data is offered, the percentage of those appointed who appeared in *Who's Who* the year before appointment: in the Eisenhower administration, 35 percent, in the Kennedy administration, 27 percent, and in the Johnson administration, 42 percent.

Despite the over-all comparability of Johnson's judicial appointments with those of his predecessors, it was to be his lot to end as he began in controversy. The agonizing struggle to make Fortas chief justice of the Supreme Court, itself beyond the scope of this study, gave impetus to the idea that all federal judicial appointments in the late hours of the Johnson administration were tainted. Nan Robertson of the *New York Times* charged in August of 1968 that "Mr. Johnson has also paid off debts of varying kinds by nominating 35 Federal judges for lifetime jobs. Fifteen vacancies are still to be filled, and it is considered certain the President will leave none of them empty."[56] Then, in his last days in office, well after the election, President Johnson made five nominations for judgeships, apparently thinking that an arrangement had been reached with President Nixon not to withdraw them before the Senate had a chance to confirm.[57] President Nixon subsequently did withdraw them and brought on the wrath of Johnson's attorney general, Ramsey Clark.

Clark, by this time a private citizen, issued a public statement on January 27, 1969, insisting that he had telephoned John Mitchell (to be Nixon's attorney general) on January 9 to tell him that five judicial nominations still pending would be sent to Congress. According to Clark, "During this conversation Mr. Mitchell said that he had been asked by Mr. Nixon to request that I inform President Johnson that

the President elect understood the submission of the judicial nominations, that he did not object, and that he would not withdraw them."[58]

Attorney General Mitchell said that Clark had "failed to understand
that definitive approval of the nominations was not expressed during
the telephone conversation . . ."[59] In a press conference later in the
day, President Nixon sought to close the controversy by answering
a query in the following way:

> What happened was that Ramsey Clark discussed this matter during the
> period between the election and the inauguration with Attorney General
> Mitchell. He asked Attorney General Mitchell to ask me whether I would
> object to action on the part of President Johnson in the event that he did
> submit these appointments to the Senate.
>
> My reply was that I would not object to President Johnson's submitting
> such—submitting names to the Senate. . . .
>
> However, I did not have any understanding with the President directly
> and no one including Attorney General Mitchell as far as I was concerned
> had any discretion to agree to a deal that those nominations having been
> made would be approved by me.[60]

The LBJ Brand on Judicial Selection

Understandably, at the beginning of his administration, President
Johnson was too preoccupied with other matters to give much attention to judicial selection. The team at the Department of Justice remained the same, and they continued to carry on their activities con-
nected with judicial selection as they had done while President Kennedy was alive. There were, however, some signs of restiveness on the
part of the White House staff. Joseph Dolan was asked to meet with
White House staffers Walter Jenkins, Ralph Dungan, and Jack Valenti. Dolan outlined the procedures in use for the selection of nominees to the bench, and it was agreed that they should be followed as
usual. At that time Walter Jenkins, the president's key aid, assured
me as he had Dolan that no changes in procedure were contemplated.
There seemed to me, nonetheless, a greater effort on the part of Dolan
to keep White House staffers informed in an informal way of significant developments leading up to the departmental recommendations
of nominees. It is significant, too, that of the three White House staffers with whom Dolan dealt, only Dungan was a carryover from the
Kennedy administration. Jenkins and Valenti were brought to the
White House by Johnson.

It was not long before President Johnson began to put his individual mark on the appointment process. Robert Kennedy resigned from his post as attorney general in early September of 1964 to embark on his quest for a seat in the Senate. Joseph Dolan followed soon after to become the victorious Robert Kennedy's administrative assistant. In the meantime, as noted earlier, John Macy, chairman of the Civil Service Commission, was brought over to the White House to serve also as a personnel adviser to the president. His role was "to pull all appointment matters together."[61] At first, Dungan continued to be concerned with nonjudicial appointments, but he was destined to leave soon to become ambassador to Chile.

Giving a White House staffer, John Macy, a role in judicial selection was a marked departure from the method of operation which prevailed during the Kennedy administration, when the White House staff members were reluctant to insert themselves between the brothers Kennedy. Needless to say, circumstances had changed markedly. From the time of Robert Kennedy's resignation in September 1964 to the middle of February 1965, Nicholas Katzenbach was acting attorney general. Katzenbach was closely identified as a Robert Kennedy man. Political alignments and enmities being what they were, there was good reason for the president to desire to protect his own political interests by having a member of his staff active in judicial selection. A case can, of course, also be made for the logic and wisdom of having one man in the White House office review all high-level appointments, since some being considered for federal judgeships might also be fit for other important posts and vice versa. At any rate this was the president's reason, in Macy's view, for giving him this role. President Johnson's special feelings for John Macy began when Johnson, as vice-president, was serving as chairman of the Committee on Equal Opportunity in Federal Hiring. Macy gave him a great deal of help at a time when Johnson felt slighted by other members of the Kennedy administration.[62] In any event, for whatever reasons, John Macy was given a role to play in judicial selection, and he continued to play that role to the end of 1968.

After lengthy deliberation, the president appointed Katzenbach as the attorney general. Three things were noteworthy about the appointment. First was the time Johnson took to make it. Second was the president's announcement of it. As the *New York Times* reported it:

Mr. Johnson said he . . . called Mr. Katzenbach in and asked him what he would like to do with his future. The President revealed that he had asked Mr. Katzenbach if he would like a "high judicial appointment" or another important job in the Government, outside the Cabinet. He said that Mr. Katzenbach had indicated a desire to stay in the executive branch.

The President, without saying so flatly, left the impression that he had only been testing Mr. Katzenbach. He said that a few days later he told him he would like him to be the President's lawyer.[63]

Third was his appointment, at the same time he appointed Katzenbach attorney general, of Ramsey Clark, about whose political loyalties he could be surer, as the deputy attorney general.

According to Macy, the bulk of the work and negotiation with senators was still done at the Justice Department. Macy worked with officials there informally, largely over the telephone. In considering a judicial nomination, Macy's office, as a matter of routine, checked out the candidates with its own sources. These were people whom Macy, in a long and distinguished government career, had come to know personally and whose judgments about personnel he had come to trust. The president himself took an unusual personal as well as official interest in every high-level appointment. A former staffer attributed his personal interest to three factors. First, the president by nature was people-oriented, i.e., he thought in terms of people rather than in terms of things. He had an inordinate range of acquaintanceships, and he knew personally or knew about a larger percentage of the people considered for high office than any previous president in recent history. Second, because of his humble origins, Johnson, more than most presidents, had a feeling that high posts in government, aside from their importance, were exceptionally good jobs and should go to only the most deserving and meritorious contenders. Therefore he was personally curious about those being considered for these choice prizes. Third, his penchant for consulting with everyone who might be able to add something to a presidential decision or who might consider himself a party in interest meant that the president frequently requested that Macy consult with named individuals.

Since checking and consulting with people tends to create reciprocal expectations, it was not surprising that Macy's office received a great deal of gratuitous advice from those he consulted about people who should be considered when a vacancy occurred. Such suggestions were passed on to Justice for investigation.

In contrast to his recent predecessors, President Johnson had indicated to his team that he wanted greater deference to senatorial prerogative in judicial selection. Whereas Joseph Dolan in the Kennedy administration and William Rogers in the Eisenhower administration sought "to take as much ground" as they could for the president in jockeying with senators over judicial selection, Ernest C. Friesen, who replaced Dolan, explained that his orders were to go along with the senators of the president's party unless the senators urged unacceptable appointments. It is not difficult to reconstruct reasons for President Johnson's deference to senators. Johnson, both as a senator and as Senate majority leader, insisted on his senatorial prerogatives because he believed in them. Further, perhaps more than any other president in our history, he was closely attuned to the political process in which senatorial prerogative plays a crucial part. This deference manifested itself in one very significant way. President Johnson was most reluctant to use the recess appointment as a means of forcing administration choices for judgeships on reluctant senators. Whereas 14 percent of Eisenhower's appointments were first recess appointments and 22 percent of Kennedy's appointments were first recess appointments, not one of the purely Johnson appointments in his first two years of office was a recess appointment. When the Senate did not act on three appointments in 1965, Johnson waited until the next year to offer their names to the Senate again rather than make recess appointments. Surprisingly, of the first eighty-one appointments in the Johnson administration twenty-six, or 32 percent, were appointments to vacancies which had been open for seven months or more; this may be compared with 26 percent and 18 percent of the nominations by Presidents Eisenhower and Kennedy which were delayed seven months or longer. This can be partly explained by the fact that it took the "new" team awhile to get its bearings. While the incidence of delayed appointments diminished the longer the Johnson administration was in power, it did not do so significantly when compared with the Eisenhower and Kennedy administrations.

What emerges from this account of the Johnson administration's selection of federal judges and the comparisons of the characteristics of its selections with those of the Eisenhower and Kennedy administrations further supports the hypothesis suggested at the conclusion of Chapter III that the dynamics of judicial selection are such that administrations which are basically concerned with making appointments of high quality will choose the same kinds of people for the same kinds of reasons whatever goals and standards they articulate. Furthermore, though the procedures employed will vary, the parameters within which administrations must work make the procedural differences differences of degree rather than of kind: they must contend with the same forces, like senators and the ABA committee. Consequently, they face the same problems and tend to face up to them in parallel ways.

CHAPTER VI

Conclusions

EVALUATING THE appointing process is no easy matter. *On its face,* the process appears plausible enough, but one which inevitably allows the courts to be infested with mediocrities and more than occasionally plagued by the appointment of scoundrels. Many an august voice has been raised to give credence to such an assessment. Erwin Griswold, while dean of the Harvard Law School, did not exempt the federal judiciary from his condemnation of the selection of judges in his annual report of 1964:

> The basic complaint goes back to the fact that the generally controlling basis for the selection of judges in this country is political, whether they are chosen by appointment or by election. The result is that many persons become judges who, no matter what their other qualifications may be, are not well qualified for judicial office.
> It is clear that this has a serious adverse effect on the administration of justice, and that this is well known and generally resented by large numbers of practicing lawyers.[1]

Likewise, former Attorney General Herbert Brownell presumably did not exempt the federal judges from his jaundiced evaluation of the American judiciary:

> Justice in this country is suffering because we are not getting the best qualified lawyers as judges. . . .

Let's look at the present state of our judicial establishment. The real trouble is not venality or corruption. True, there probably are a few corrupt judges. . . . But the incidence of wrongdoers is probably lower among the judiciary than elsewhere. . . .

The problem, then, is not corrupt judges. The problem is mediocre judges—the men whom one distinguished judge has described as the "gray mice" of the judicial establishment. What are the characteristics of these many "gray mice"? Like other mice they are unobtrusive, they have not distinguished themselves in law school or college. Their practice has generally been a limited one and their general legal experience not well rounded. Although they rarely win distinction in professional or learned organizations, they do belong to an astonishing array of fraternal, military and other groups.

But above all else they belong to their local political club and are cheerful in performing the interesting assignments their "leader" has for them. They are exemplary in their loyalty to their political party. They look on judicial appointment as the reward for their loyalty and devotion to the party, and they look forward to judicial service as socially and financially rewarding. To them the courthouse is a cozy rest home. In other words, they are ordinary, likable people of small talent. They are not venal, not corrupt, but they can do a great deal to debase and cheapen the entire administration of American justice.[2]

As these critics see it, the vice of the present system is the political nature of the process of judicial selection in America. To quote Brownell again:

Why are there so many of these mediocre judges? Because of the way judges are selected. In theory, some judges are appointed by a President (in the federal system), a governor (in a state system) or by a mayor. Others are elected. As a matter of hard fact, judges are in most instances *picked* by political leaders. This is quite obvious in the case of selected judges . . .

But isn't the situation different where the judges are appointed by a President, governor or mayor? Surely these leaders take seriously their high responsibility for the administration of justice and make their own appointments. In general, it may be assumed this is so. But these appointing officials are under many pressures, political and otherwise. Even the President still must have his candidate approved by the two senators from the candidate's state. By virtue of "senatorial courtesy," these senators may successfully prevent confirmation of the candidate by the Senate. Senators are rightly highly political animals and do not lightly disregard the desires of the political leaders back home.[3]

Do the facts support such alarming assessments as they pertain to the federal bench? Unfortunately, no satisfactory objective or "scientific" method has been devised to answer that question. At an early stage in this study, valiant efforts were made to establish objective criteria for rating sitting judges. It was thought that in view of the hierarchical arrangement of the federal courts which permit higher courts to review cases brought to them from lower courts, the percentage of cases in which a lower court was reversed by a higher court might be a valid objective indicator of performance by the lower court. Experimentation and consultation with sitting judges made it clear that such was probably not the case. First, such analysis assumes that the higher courts are usually "right" when they reverse—and there is no objective basis for such an assumption. Second, as many judges pointed out, such an analysis does not take into account that it is the creative judge and the innovator in the law who is often reversed, that the timid judge who relies heavily on precedent will be least likely to be reversed. In lieu of better methods beyond the ken of this researcher, it was decided to take a random sample of thirty lawyers who appeared in the federal courts in each of seven states (California, New York, Georgia, Virginia, Missouri, Texas, and Minnesota) and ask them to rate the sitting federal judges. The sample was procured by making a visit to clerks of the appropriate courts and taking a random selection from their card files or lists. The sample was then interviewed. Candor was not lacking. Once assured of confidentiality, the seriousness of the enterprise, and the fact that this was not a muckraking enterprise, respondents were very frank in their appraisals. To be concise, these responses were reassuring. No one suggested that their federal courts were beyond criticism, but *all respondents were satisfied that the federal courts in which they practiced were on the whole good or better than others.* One very curious and common observation made to me upon conclusion of an interview was that "we've been very lucky in our federal courts here in California, but they are very bad in New York," and in New York they would say they were lucky in New York but the courts were poor in some other state. To repeat, my interviews led me to conclude that probably those who actually practiced in particular federal courts were generally satisfied with them.

As I write, I am reminded of my ungallant friend who always replies to the question "How is your wife?" with "Compared to what?" The fact that lawyers practicing before federal courts find them "good" does not necessarily mean very much. What is their measure? An obvious comparison to make is between federal and state judiciaries. Without fail, the sample I interviewed rated the federal bench superior to the state bench. In several jurisdictions, the state's highest court was pointed to as a conspicuous exception to the lower rating of the state bench generally.[4]

The limited nature of the data makes any strong conclusion hazardous. I would not go beyond stating that the federal courts are probably in pretty good shape in respect to the general quality of judges. This is not to suggest that there is no room for improvement and no room for suggestions about changes in processes to bring that about. The rest of this chapter will be devoted to those matters. Suffice it to say here that in my studied opinion, there is no grave emergency situation with respect to *selection* of federal judges. I feel that if there were, it would have become apparent in my interviewing just as it became apparent that in some *state* jurisdictions, judicial selection has become a disaster. Interestingly enough, interviews and observation have led me to the conclusion that, where a judge is regarded as unfit for the federal bench, it is not the fault of the selection process, but rather of the constitutional provision granting that federal judges "shall hold their offices during good behavior." I would estimate that roughly 10 percent of the federal judges are incapable of doing a first-rate job due to disabilities of illness (including failing eyesight and defective hearing) and old age. Everywhere I visited, I was regaled with stories about at least one present or recent sitting judge who had to be "wired for sound and still couldn't hear," or "who had to feel his way around the courtroom because he couldn't see." But the important point to bear in mind is that in virtually every case when I asked what these judges were like in their early days on the bench, considered judgments were that they had been good judges. In some cases they had been among the most distinguished judges on the federal bench. Patently, old age is the real culprit. To get some measure of the problem, Table 19 indicates the ages of the federal circuit and district judges sitting as of the first of the year 1966. The ages of judges sitting in the special courts were as follows:

Court	68 and Over	60–67	50–59	40–49
Claims	1	3	3	0
Customs and Patent Appeals..	0	3	1	0
Customs	1	1	3	1

189

Table 19. Number of Circuit and District Judges in Given
Age Groups on January 1, 1966

Circuit	Circuit Judges				District Judges				
	68 and Over	60–67	50–59	40–49	68 and Over	60–67	50–59	40–49	30–39
D.C.	1	2	6	0	3	6	3	1	0
First	0	1	1	1	2	3	2	2	0
Second ...	1	6	1	1	5	14	15	3	1
Third	2	4	1	0	3	15	10	3	1
Fourth ...	2	2	1	2	2	7	10	3	0
Fifth	1	3	6	2	5	12	25	10	0
Sixth	1	1	4	1	2	10	11	6	0
Seventh ...	3	3	0	2	3	10	7	4	0
Eighth	1	3	2	2	3	5	11	4	0
Ninth	1	2	5	1	2	18	19	8	0
Tenth	0	2	4	0	1	8	7	2	0
Total	13	29	31	12	31	108	120	46	2
Percentage of total judges	15	34	37	14	10	35	39	15	1

It is significant that at a time when universities have found it imperative to save themselves from the disabilities of aging professors by making retirement mandatory at age sixty-eight, 15 percent of all sitting circuit judges in January 1966 were over that age. Note too, that almost half of the sitting circuit judges and 45 percent of all sitting district judges were over sixty. Perhaps the problem of disability due to illness and age would not be so great if there were practical and easy ways to remove federal judges who had become unfit. But there are none.

Senator Joseph D. Tydings has explained fully and well why impeachment is not a suitable remedy for the problem:

Historically the only method of actually removing a Federal judge from office, so that he is deprived of his title and his right to salary, has been impeachment by the House of Representatives and conviction on the impeachment charge by the Senate of the United States. This has created many difficulties . . . First, constitutionally impeachment lies only for "treason, bribery, or other high crimes and misdemeanors." It is uncertain whether senility, insanity, physical disability, alcoholism, or laziness—all of which are forms of unfitness that require remedial action —are covered by the impeachment process.

The second difficulty lies in the nature of the impeachment machinery. Even in the early years of the Republic the inadequacy of this process was recognized. As early as 1819, Thomas Jefferson said: "Experience has already shown that the impeachment the Constitution has provided is not even a scarecrow." It is a cumbersome, archaic process which requires one House of Congress, the House of Representatives, to act as a grand jury, and the other House, the Senate, to sit in judgement as a court. The House of Representatives can perhaps do its share of the work effectively through the Judiciary Committee, but what of the Senate? We all know that the Members of the Senate are hard pressed to fulfill the many demands of the office and of the constituents. If the Senate were required to do nothing but listen to testimony in an impeachment case for several weeks—the average time has been 17 days—the Legislative Calendar would be completely and absolutely disrupted. Obviously, few Senators would be able to spend so much of their time thus occupied, yet I submit that an impeachment trial before an empty Senate Chamber would be little more than a farce. History has shown that in some impeachment trials, as few as three Senators were present listening to the testimony, and one of the three was writing a letter. This would hardly comport with modern standards of justice. No conviction of a criminal defendant would be tolerated if it came after a trial at which most of the jurors were not present to hear the testimony and two or three trial judges were absent during the testimony.

Impeachment is perhaps the sole method of removal of Federal judges that may be constitutionally employed by the Congress, for the principle of an independent judiciary, free from interference by the legislative or executive branches, is central to the concept of a government of separated powers. But this is not to say that impeachment is the only constitutionally permissible method of removing a Federal judge from office. It should be borne in mind that a judge is to serve "during good behavior," while impeachment lies only for bribery, treason, "high crimes and misdemeanors." It may be that the framers of the Constitution intended to permit other methods of removal not inconsistent with the principle of separation of powers. The scholarship on this question is disappointingly sparse, and I hope that one of the effects of our study will be to stimulate some scholarly reexamination of the arguments for and against the exclusivity of impeachment as a removal process from the Federal bench.[5]

Congress has attempted to deal with the disability problem in statutory provisions which enable a majority of a circuit's judicial council (composed of all the circuit judges of the circuit with the chief judge of the circuit serving as the presiding officer)[6] to certify to the president that a judge is disabled and if "the President finds that such judge is unable to discharge efficiently all the duties of his office by reason of permanent or physical disability and that appointment of an additional judge is necessary for the efficient dispatch of business, the President may make such appointment by and with the advice and consent of the Senate."[7] Note that this does not *remove* the judge. Note, too, the exchange between Senator Tydings and Judge Biggs in hearings before Tyding's committee:

SENATOR TYDINGS. Has not 372(b), although drafted to be used as an involuntary method of removal, as a matter of practice, only been used when requested by a disabled judge to the Judicial Council?

JUDGE BIGGS. It has only been used once [as of 1966], to my knowledge, and that was at the request of the particular district judge involved.[8]

Presumably, if a judge were designated as disabled, the council could forbid him to work by proceeding to issue "all necessary orders for the effective and expeditious administration of the business of the courts within its circuits," and the district judges "shall promptly carry into effect all orders of the judicial council."[9] But this, too, is questionable as a consequence of the ruckus over Judge Stephen S. Chandler.

In December of 1965, Judge Chandler, United States district judge for the western district of Oklahoma, was ordered by the judicial council of the Tenth Circuit to "take no action whatsoever in any case or proceeding now or hereafter pending 'in his court.' "[10] After four years of intense contention leading to several actions in the Supreme Court, the Supreme Court decided that "whether the Council's action was administrative action not reviewable in this Court, or whether it is reviewable here, plainly petitioner has not made a case for the extraordinary relief of mandamus or prohibition." Consequently, the Court denied the particular petition which Chandler had brought to it. The Court, however, recognized that it was not facing up to the basic questions involved regarding the powers of the judicial council: "These questions have long been discussed and debated; they are not easy questions and the risks suggested by the dissents are not to be lightly cast aside. But for the reasons that follow we do not find it necessary to answer them because the threshold question in this case is whether we have jurisdiction to entertain the petition for extraordinary relief." Justices Douglas and Black dissented, asserting that "there is no power under our Constitution for one group of federal judges to censor or discipline any federal judge and no power to declare him inefficient and strip him of his power to act as a judge."[11] Until the Supreme Court clears up this matter, the present law does not provide a satisfactory remedy for removing disabled judges. Nor is the informal remedy of trying to persuade elderly judges to retire voluntarily very satisfactory, as indicated by the candid testimony of Judge Biggs:

SENATOR TYDINGS. Judge Buffington at that time was actually senile and could not read, is that right?

JUDGE BIGGS. Well, he was blind and could not read and had great difficulty hearing. And he would not—he did not—employ a law clerk. This made for very considerable difficulties.

When Judge Maris came on the bench followed by Judge William Clark of New Jersey, we persuaded these elderly gentlemen [Judge Buffington and others] to retire, which they did, all at the same time. And I, over the last 28 years, have had a rather considerable experience in getting old and sick judges to retire.

SENATOR TYDINGS. How would you go about doing that?

JUDGE BIGGS. Well, what one does, one goes up and talks to them in a perfectly frank way about it. I do not want to mention names, if the committee will excuse me from doing that, but it is a rather tortuous proceeding and one which is rather unpleasant, both for the person who goes to see the the aged judge, and, I imagine, I am quite sure for the aged judge himself. One requires—one may make several trips to see him and one tries to persuade him that if he will go on senior-judge status, he will be allowed to do such work, be authorized to do such work as he wants to do, to which the chief judge of the circuit or the judicial council will designate

193

him. Eventually, generally, eventually we can persuade the elderly judge
to retire.

But to put it frankly, it takes a good deal of effort and quite a long
time.[12]

It is beyond the scope of this study of the appointment process to
discuss and analyze the various proposals and state plans for removing unfit judges which attracted the attention of the Tydings committee and later the House Judiciary Committee.[13] I cannot resist,
however, mention of one proposal which came to my attention and
which I had the opportunity to discuss at length with judges and
lawyers. That is the suggestion of Judge J. Earl Major that there be
compulsory retirement of federal judges at age seventy.[14] Former
President Eisenhower suggested a variation: "that tenure for all
federal judges . . . be limited to 20 years in the same court or to
the time when the judge reaches the age of 72, whichever comes
first."[15] It would seem desirable to have a constitutional amendment
concerning compulsory retirement rather than to argue that giving
retired judges limited duties and maintaining their pay and allowances
does not technically offend the current constitutional provisions regarding tenure.

Mandatory retirement ends all the problems inherent in processes
which attempt to single out those who should retire and then to prove
it some objective way. Not only that, under present law retired judges
can be employed as long as the chief judges who do the assigning
feel that they are capable of handling the duties assigned to them. In
terms of human dynamics, it is much easier not to give someone
assignments than it is to take official action to remove him. This
suggests that there is much to be gained and little to be lost by mandatory retirement. The retired judge who continues to be in good health
and mentally alert can be given assignments until such time as he is
truly incapable of performing them.

Interestingly enough, when Chief Justice Warren was asked about
compulsory retirement for federal judges, he said he would only
be for it if the same requirement were in effect for officials in other
branches of government.[16] With all due respect, such a position does
not take into account the limited tenure of elected officials which
affords the electorate the opportunity to pass judgment on fitness
periodically. This, of course, is not so with respect to federal judges.

To return again to the process of selection, even if the present process nets a pretty good result, we should not be satisfied. In view of the importance of federal judges to our system of governance, we should settle for nothing less than the procurement of the very best judges that it is humanly possible to select. (As noted earlier this is not to suggest that we should try to get *the* best judges.) At the same time we should bear in mind the conclusion Professor Joel Grossman reached in his excellent study of the ABA committee and selection of federal judges: "The existing selection system is far from perfect. But it has the virutes of being flexible, predictable, politically responsive, and battle-tested."[17]

We have never been bereft of suggestions for improving the selection process.[18] By and large, these suggestions stem from a genuine concern over the political nature of the present process and the fear that such a process results inevitably in the selection of inferior people. There is no gainsaying the fact that the process is political. As Ben R. Miller so well demonstrated, partisan political considerations are important:

It was my privilege to have served almost nine years on the Federal Judiciary Committee of the American Bar Association—during the last three and one-half years of President Eisenhower's Administration. As incomplete as our data were on the political background of the various appointees, the active partisan background of most appointees under both administrations is rather clearly shown by these facts:

Appointments by Mr. Truman during that period include these:

One was a brother of a Democratic United States Senator.

One was a son of a Democratic United States Senator.

One had himself served an interim appointment as a Democratic United States Senator.

Two were former Democratic attorneys general of their state.

One was a former Democratic governor.

One had managed a Democratic governor's successful campaign.

Two had been delegates to the Democratic National Convention.

Six had been Democratic members of their state legislature.

Two others had occupied responsible Democratic party positions in their state.

Similar appointments by Mr. Eisenhower included these:

One was a former Republican Senator.

One was the law partner of a Republican Senator.

One was the campaign partner of a Republican Senator.

One was a former Republican governor.

Four were former Republican Congressmen.

One was the law partner of a former chairman of the Republican National Committee.
One was at the time of his nomination, Republican National Committeeman.
One was a former member of the Republican National Committee.
Six were delegates to Republican National conventions.
Five were former Republican members of their state legislatures.
Three were campaign directors for, appointees to special positions by, an unsuccessful Republican nominee for president.
One was an unsuccessful Republican candidate for Congress and later for state attorney general.
One is the husband of a Republican National Committeewoman.[19]

But the fact that the process by which judges are selected is political does not mean *ipso facto* that those selected are not men of good character and high ability, as explained in Chapter I. There is much to be said for the political process at its best. In addition to the comments in Chapter I, the words of Professor Grossman speaking to the same point are worth pondering:

> But the argument against eliminating partisanship from the recruitment equation need not rest entirely on a negative basis. It could be argued that considerations of partisanship (excluding only the more blatant uses of it) make a positive contribution to the rationality of the selection process. First, they insure the selection process will be indirectly responsive to popular sentiment. More important, they insure that the important question of the social and political philosophies of the judicial candidate will be considered.
>
> Although most judges appointed for life tend to shed previous party identifications, there is substantial evidence that prior political affiliation is associated with decision-making tendencies. Since a proper and inevitable factor in the selection is not only the manner in which a judge will conduct his duties, but the types of decisions he will make, and since there are some fairly clear though not mutually exclusive distinctions between members of the two major political parties, political party label is often as good a key (though by no means an infallible one) to the mind of the prospect judge as is available. Although partisanship may be a pernicious influence in the actual rendering of judicial decisions, it *may* also be a desirable feature of the recruitment process . . .[20]

Whether or not it is presently the case, it is certainly possible for judges of outstanding ability and character to be selected under the political process now employed. And discussions deriding the political nature of the process do not specify why the process must inevitably lead to less than excellent appointments. Yet this study has convinced me that there are inherent in the process factors which will inevitably produce less than optimum results for the judicial system as a whole.

If my young lawyer son were to say to me, "Dad, some day I'd like to be a federal judge. You've been studying for a long time how federal judges are appointed. How about advising me how I can get to be one?" I would have to give him this answer: "Son, get active in the party of your choice and I mean really active. Start young— right away. Devote a lot of time to it. Ingratiate yourself by your activity with your party's senatorial candidates and work very hard for likely presidential nominees and for presidential candidates once nominated. In addition, work as hard as you can to acquire a reputation as a good sound lawyer, preferably as a corporation lawyer." If my advice is good—and I think it is—what it means is this. First, judicial selection is made from a relatively small pool of all legal talent. A veritable host of lawyers deal themselves out of likely consideration for the federal bench right from the start of their legal careers because they have neither the time nor the inclination to invest much of themselves in political activity. Nor is there any reason to believe that the most able of the young lawyers or those with the best potential for being judges would opt for entry into the political arena. Indeed, there is good reason to believe that the most prudent of the young lawyers would feel that it was imperative for them to establish themselves in practice first. Second, unless extensive experience in the political arena is the best preparation for the duties of a judge, the process requires our future federal judges to devote an inordinate amount of time to less than the best preparation for the post. Among the judges I interviewed there were some who argued that politics was in fact the best preparation for the bench, since it enabled a judge to meet people from all walks of life and to understand them and that this was most important in being a good judge. But such respondents constituted a minority of the judges interviewed. It is hardly likely that such is the case. Also, it is hard to test this proposition empirically. Because all but a few of the present judges have been politically active, it would be difficult to have a control group against which to match them. In sum, I would suggest that, although there is nothing evil about the political nature of the present process, there are real disabilities to which we would be wise to address ourselves.

One of the most widely proposed reforms has been the suggestion that nominees for the federal bench have extensive judicial or courtroom experience. We saw in an earlier chapter how strongly the ABA

197

committee feels about the value of courtroom experience.[21] Senator
Stennis has long urged that "the United States Senate could set up
standards for approval of nominations of the Courts of Appeals, in
which case, I think the requirements for trial practice should be at
least ten years experience or at least five years of judicial experience.
And by the same method, standards could be established for the approval of nominations to the District Courts, which would include ten
years of actual courtroom practice and trial experience."[22] Ben R.
Miller has written: ". . . we may feel that filling federal judicial positions almost exclusively with men without prior judicial experience
and often in their later years is not too unsound. But the lay public
wonders why more promotions—from the state judiciary as well as
the federal judiciary itself—would not be a wise principle of judicial
selection, inasmuch as sound promotion systems are observed in all
phases of our life and industry; and why men should be first named
to our courts and expected to learn a most difficult and strenuous job
at ages near those at which their 'counterparts' in business and industry are being retired."[23] We saw earlier that President Eisenhower
also thought that there was virtue in selecting judges with previous
judicial experience.[24]

In assessing this proposal, it is well to bear in mind the following.
First, a fair number of the judges have had previous judicial experience and a considerable number have had extensive courtroom experience as indicated earlier and as evidenced by ABA committee
ratings. Second, merely superimposing this requirement on the present
selection process would not eliminate the disabilities of the political
nature of the process. Becoming a judge in the first instance, whether
state or federal, would have been the result of a political process.
Third, there is no magic in judicial experience per se. A man without
talent or strength of character would still be such even with judicial
experience. Fourth, a mandatory requirement of judicial experience
would rigorously narrow the pool of talent from which judges could
be drawn. Fifth, there is no empirical evidence that our best judges
have been those who have had previous judicial experience. On the
contrary, there is good reason to believe that this is not so.[25] The
ratings of judges which I procured from my sample of interviews
revealed no significant differences in the ratings of judges with and
without previous judicial experience. In view of the above, I conclude

that any attempt to make mandatory a requirement of judicial experience would be unwise.

In my interviewing, I found that in the two southern states there was much concern over the role of the attorney general and the Department of Justice in the selection process. In retrospect, I suspect that this kind of regional concern stems from the fact that those who have been the most articulate critics of the role have been prestigious southerners, men such as Senator Stennis, Ben R. Miller, and Charles Bloch.[26] Their basic argument was stated by Senator Stennis in the following manner:

The Department's other duties frequently call for it to be the agency of government which hales American citizens into our federal courts. In the majority of federal cases the citizen is the defendant. When he is involved in a suit against the United States he is forced to appear in a United States court; against United States attorneys—selected and employed by the Department of Justice; before a United States judge who owes his appointment to selection by the Department of Justice. This judge is sometimes a candidate for promotion, dependent upon recommendations of the Department of Justice. Many defendants are bound to feel that the cards are pretty well stacked against them.[27]

Direct observation in the Department of Justice leads me to conclude that normally whether or not a judge decided for or against the government in particular cases was not an important factor in considerations of selection. Nonetheless, impressions about the competence and demeanor of judges sitting on important cases are freely circulated within the department. For example, all the top officers including the attorney general will know which judges are troublesome (to the department) in civil rights cases. Should a southern district judge be considered for elevation, most certainly lawyers in the Civil Rights Division of the department would be consulted about his competence. As pointed out earlier, in the Eisenhower administration some thought was given to how judges had performed in cases involving law enforcement procedures. Surely, judges are not unmindful that assessments of their work are being made. Nor can we rely on the proposition that the department will be scrupulously objective in its assessments. We know only too well that no one can be truly objective, as much as one tries. It is most human for an attorney general and his aides sometimes to view with less than honor and respect a judge who consistently rules against them, say, in civil rights cases where it might be that if a truly objective assessment could be made it would be found that the judge and not the department was right. Added to what I have just said, I must report that at least one attorney general, Robert Kennedy, felt compelled by the critical nature of the times and the civil rights issue to visit and have lunch with certain district judges in the South. Presumably, he urged on them that they "do their jobs." What impact such a visit had could only be known by probing the inner recesses of the judges' minds. In any case, the fact that the Department of Justice is the chief litigant before judges whose "promotions" will in large part depend upon the department should give cause for concern. But in and of itself, this kind of dual involvement, "conflict of interest" if you will, may not be enough to warrant changing the process. As a former secretary of defense, Robert McNamara, so frequently used to say about decisions on complex issues, "You have to add up the pluses and minuses." No process which we could devise would be perfect. So even though there are distinct disadvantages in having the Department of Justice so heavily involved in judicial selection the real question is Will a proposed alternative (which will also be imperfect) have more pluses and fewer minuses? We will come back to the question later.

In recent years those who have sought a remedy for the disabilities in the political nature of the selection process—and their number is legion—have been attracted to the idea of setting up a special commission to play a central role in the selection of federal judges. The idea is an outgrowth of experience on the state level with so-called "merit plans," particularly the apparent success of the vaunted Missouri Plan. Former Judge Royce H. Savage described the merit plan this way: "The Merit Plan in simple form is a three-stage process consisting of: First—the nomination of all judges by an impartial commission; Second—mandatory appointment of judges by the governor from the commission's slate; and Third—periodic non-competitive election of the appointed judges after serving on the bench."[28] The plan has a distinguished lineage, an interesting history, and considerable support as indicated in these words of Judge Elmo B. Hunter:

In recent months, I have participated in citizens' conferences on the courts in ten different states. In the course of these conferences, I have met and discussed this problem of securing and retaining qualified judicial personnel with over a thousand non-lawyers representing all segments of state life. Their response to the merit selection and tenure plan, advocated by the American Judicature Society since 1937, and first adopted in Missouri in 1940, has been consistently enthusiastic after they had an understanding of the basic elements of the plan and how it has worked for almost 25 years in Missouri.[29]

Indeed, by the end of 1964, eleven states had adopted aspects of a merit plan and none had repealed their plans.[30] It is not surprising then that there would be those who would come to feel that a merit plan would be appropriate for the federal government. As the *Journal of the American Judicature Society* editorialized in August of 1965: ". . . the practical success of the nonpartisan judicial nominating commission has so proved itself in a dozen states that it is now under active consideration for adoption in some two dozen more. The great prestige of the federal judicial system, which has an enviable record of national leadership in court organization, court administration and procedural reform, should now be placed at the head of the national movement for nonpolitical merit judicial selection."[31]

Into the breech stepped Senator Scott of Pennsylvania in June of 1966 to introduce a bill to establish a Judicial Service Commission. In doing so, he pointed out that "a Gallup poll released on April 6 of this year revealed the dissatisfaction of most Americans with the present system of selecting Federal judges. Sixty-one percent, nearly two-thirds, of those asked approved a suggestion that the American Bar Association be permitted to draw up a list of approved candidates from which the President would select his nominees."[32] Senator Scott's bill follows:

Be it enacted by the Senate and House of Representatives of the United States of America in Congress assembled, That chapter 21 of title 28, United States Code, is amended by adding at the end thereof a new section as follows:

"§461. Judicial Service Commission.

"(a) There is hereby established in the executive branch of the Government an agency to be known as the 'Judicial Service Commission,' hereinafter referred to as the 'Commission.'

"(b) The Commission shall be composed of seven members appointed by the President, by and with the advice and consent of the Senate. At least three of the members of the Commission shall be selected from among persons who are serving or shall have served as members of a committee of the American Bar Association dealing with the Federal judiciary, and at least two shall be members of the Federal judiciary who have retired from regular active service. Not more than four members shall be from the same political party. The Commission shall elect a chairman from among its members. Each member of the Commission shall be appointed for a term of three years, except that (1) the terms of the members first appointed shall expire, as designated by the President at the time of their appointments, two at the end of one year, two at the end of two years, and three at the end of three years, following the date of such appointments, and (2) a member appointed to fill a vacancy occurring before the expiration of the term of his predecessor shall serve under such appointment only for the remainder of such term.

"(c) It shall be the duty of the Commission to ascertain the qualifications of prospective appointees to positions as justices or judges of the United States and, upon the occurrence of a vacancy in any such position, to make recommendations to the President for the filling of such vacancy.

"(d) It is the sense of the Congress that in any case in which the President nominates for appointment as a justice or judge of the United States a person not recommended by the Commission for such appointment, he should transmit to the Senate at the time of such nomination a statement of his reasons for failing to nominate a person recommended by the Commission for such appointment.

"(e) The Commission is authorized to appoint and fix the compensation of such employees, and to make such expenditures, as may be necessary to enable it to perform its functions. With the consent of the head of the department or agency concerned, the Commission may utilize, on a reimbursable basis or otherwise, the services or facilities of any department or agency in the Executive branch of the Government.

"(f) Members of the Commission who are not otherwise receiving compensation as officers or employees of the United States shall be entitled to receive compensation at the rate of $—— per diem while engaged in carrying out their duties as members, including travel time. All members of the Commission shall be allowed travel expenses, including per diem in lieu of subsistence, as authorized by law for persons in the Government service employed intermittently, while away from their homes or regular places of business."

SEC. 2. The analysis at the beginning of chapter 21 of title 28, United States Code, is amended by adding the following new item:
"461. Judicial Service Commission."[33]

Note that under the Scott bill three of the seven members of the commission shall be or shall have been members of the ABA Committee on Federal Judiciary. Also note that in contrast to state plans the chief executive is not required to accept commission recommendations. Presumably this is to avoid the need for a change in the Constitution.

Before making a judgment about the wisdom of seeking a variation of the merit plan for federal selection, it would be wise to ask just how good the merit plan is on the state level. Despite all the laudatory rhetoric quoted above, there is good reason to believe that the merit plan is not all it is cracked up to be. Perhaps Glenn R. Winters, executive director of the American Judicature Society, is right when he calls the plan the "greatest single event of this century in the field of judicial administration."[34] But again we see the relevance of the question "compared to what?" As against the state systems (like popular elections) which prevailed in particular states before they opted for the merit plan, the merit plan could be and indeed has been a quantum-jump improvement. Does that necessarily mean that it would be better for the federal judiciary than the system which is now operative? The one in-depth study of the Missouri Plan in operation—a superb job done by Professors Watson, Downing, and Spiegel of the University of Missouri—casts real doubt that a merit plan would be an improvement over what we have at present. They conclude that the Missouri Plan does not eliminate politics; it just changes the nature of them:

The Bar politics examined in this article demonstrates that significant cleavages have developed in the Missouri legal community on the matter of choosing judges. In both Kansas City and St. Louis, a practice has evolved whereby rival bar groups nominate candidates and mount campaigns to get their man elected as lawyer members to the circuit and appellate commissions which nominate candidates for the bench. These lawyers' elections have taken on many of the features of a general party system. The bar organizations not only assume the role of parties in the election process, but they also possess characteristics that differentiate them from mere "factions": they are durable and visible; they have not been dependent for their existence upon individual personalities or cliques; and they represent important economic and social divisions in the Bar supported by conflicting ideologies. Moreover, a competitive "two-party" system has developed, since no other group enters candidates, and both the Bar Association and Lawyers' Association have been able to elect their candidates at reasonably frequent intervals over the years.[35]

This is not to suggest that Watson, Downing, and Spiegel find that the political action manifested in the plan in operation is deleterious. As they put it: "the question is whether lawyers as 'client caretakers' adequately represent the various 'publics' that utilize the courts, that is, the social and economic interests involved in litigation." They conclude: "It is our judgement that in Missouri the rival Bar Associations and Lawyers Associations have acted as effective surrogates of the respective interests they represent."[36]

Would it be better to give a greater role to bar association politics in the process of federal judicial selection? I think not. As indicated in the chapter on the ABA committee, on the national level, unlike Missouri, the conservative elements predominate. There is not the kind of interplay of countervailing forces within the legal community that there has been in Missouri. If we are to rely on a political system at the federal level we would be unwise to think in terms of "client caretakers." The issues in many an important federal case involve questions of the greatest magnitude for all of us, not just the clients. Who in our society does not have a stake in a case involving the constitutional meaning of free speech, for instance?

Although it is probably true that a federal merit plan would not require aspirants for judgeships to make the early and heavy commitment to politics as is now the case, one who would aspire to be a judge under a merit plan would still have to devote an inordinate amount of time to politicking, albeit in a different way.[37]

Finally, I am impressed by the fact that when I asked my small sample of lawyers in Missouri, all of whom practiced in both federal and state courts, what they thought of the Missouri Plan, virtually all of them felt it was overrated and virtually none of them were eager to see such a proposal advanced for selection of federal judges.

A Modest Proposal

At this point, readers may well be wondering whether or not there really is a better way than the present process for selecting federal judges. And in my opinion this is all to the good. As I like to point out to my students, in matters of public policy, we rarely have a choice between a perfect solution and a demonstrably poor one. Frequently, we only have a real choice between two or more poor alternatives and we have to settle for the lesser of evils in this imperfect world. Not only that, we can profit from the profound observation of Reinhold Niebuhr that "democracy is a method of finding proximate solutions for insoluble problems."[38] We must make policy decisions, but we should do so in the full knowledge that we are only finding solutions which seem best at the time for problems which generally are not susceptible to solution now for all time. It is in this spirit that I offer two proposals, a modest one and a less modest one.

204

It is my studied conclusion that a great improvement would be made in the current selection process by the simple expedient of senators eschewing a role in *picking* and *pushing* candidates for the federal bench. Much would be gained by having the president and his men clearly and unequivocally responsible for the quality of the federal bench as indicated in Chapter I. For one thing, the Department of Justice has more resources at its disposal than a senator for making determinations about qualifications. The Senate should play the role originally conceived for it with respect to presidential appointments—to keep the president and his men honest.[39] It is significant that in the state of Virginia when Harry Byrd, Sr., was the senior senator and did leave it to the administration to select the candidates (though insisting on a veto power), the quality of appointments there was exceptionally high.

It would probably be helpful if individual senators would forego even a veto power for *personal* political considerations. But the stakes being what they are, it is highly unlikely that senators would be willing to give up the custom of senatorial courtesy.

On the other hand, I do not regard it as hopeless to attempt to convince senators that it is in their interest to let the president and his men make the initial selection. As indicated in Chapter I, a senator more frequently than not "makes a hundred enemies and one ingrate" every time he pushes a particular candidacy.

No laws or constitutional changes are needed to effect this modest proposal. What would be necessary is an effective promotion particularly on the part of the American Bar Association to convince senators that it is in the public interest as well as their own political interest to place full responsibility for *nominations* on the presidency.

A Less Modest Proposal

A more radical proposal for meeting head-on the disabilities of the political process dealt with a few pages ago would be to lodge judicial selection for federal courts *below the Supreme Court level* in the Supreme Court of the United States. Despite what was written in Chapter I, it appears to me clear that it is within the province of the Constitution for Congress to pass a law so doing. Article III states that "the Congress may by Law vest the Appointment of such inferior

Officers, as they think proper, in the President alone, in the Courts of Law, or in the Heads of Departments." Patently, the Supreme Court could not itself perform all the staff work involved in screening possibilities nor would members of the Court have personal knowledge of more than a very few of those who should logically be considered for such a post. The Court would have to replicate the bureaucratic apparatus now doing the leg work in judicial selection in the Department of Justice. What then are the supposed advantages of lodging the final selection of federal judges in the Court? It is my guess that the *criteria* for selection would be radically changed and in a healthy direction. The Court would have to spell out for its agents what qualities it was seeking and then make its final selections from among those whom the staff offered as possibilities. I suspect that the usual political considerations would be of no moment to the Court, that there would be instead great concern for the purely professional capabilities and character of prospective judges. Who could better make judgments about the professional credentials of prospects than the Court? Just as in our large and great universities it is assumed that the best evaluators of the credentials of a prospective faculty member are those already established in the field, so I think sitting judges are probably best able to evaluate credentials of prospects. This is not to say that faculties never make mistakes. But woe unto anyone who proposed that departmental members should be selected (and would be better selected) by the president and central administration of the university. In any case, it would seem reasonable to suppose that there would be an improvement in the quality of the federal bench. If the criteria and selection favored professional accomplishment, it would mean that those who aspire to judgeships would prepare themselves for candidacy by demonstrating professional competence. This would meet the problem mentioned earlier about aspirants devoting great time and energy to political tasks which are probably not the best preparation for a career on the bench. Also, the pool of lawyers from which selections would be made would predictably be much larger than it now is.

Perhaps surprisingly, in a sample of forty federal judges to whom I put the idea, I received no enthusiastic response. About half were strongly opposed on two grounds. One, they felt that the Court was already overburdened and, two, they had considerable misgivings about what they feared would be the growth of a self-perpetuating oligarchy. On reflection, I am impressed that no one offered specific reasons which rendered the proposal infeasible. In view of the novelty of the proposal I am not surprised that first reactions were only lukewarm, if not downright hostile. It is of course true that the Supreme Court is overburdened[40] but I do not see this proposal as being a cruel additional burden. After all, the president and the attorney general who also have their considerable burdens now must give some attention to judicial selection. Further, it is the kind of work which would afford a change of pace from the other duties which the justices must now perform and might not be as onerous as hearing and deciding additional cases. I understand the uneasiness about having judges pick judges. But having professionals select their own is a common practice in American life. As a practical matter, academics pick academics and flag officers in our services pick other flag officers and no one has seriously suggested that there are better processes for making these selections.

This proposal assumes that Supreme Court justices will continue to be appointed by the president with the advice and consent of the Senate. In this way, the president and the Senate would be able to exercise some leverage on the directions the Court takes with respect to judicial selection, as they now do with respect to decision-making on issues affecting important public policy. Presumably, if a president does not approve of the direction the Court is taking, he can select Supreme Court justices who he predicts will change the direction. Furthermore, if there is validity to the notion that a president receives a mandate from the people to move in a particular general direction, and I would suggest there is, then this is as it should be in a democratic society.

Of course, there are those who would question the wisdom of tasking the Supreme Court to choose lower court judges on the grounds that Supreme Court justices are no paragons and that there is something awry about the process by which they are selected. In that connection, the ill-advised nominations of Fortas, Haynesworth, and Carswell come to mind. But it can be argued that the fact that these nominations were rejected actually is a plus for the system. This observation relates back to the modest proposal made earlier. Supreme Court nominations are made by the president and the Senate *does* play the role in Supreme Court selections that Hamilton urged on it. In any case, since we do not have paragons anywhere in the system, the real question is Who, given the resources, will be better able to identify what and who makes for the best selection of federal judges?

In conclusion, I would want to reiterate that my research leads me to believe that our present appointment system nets a good but not outstanding array of federal judges. If we aspire to excellence, the only hope is a radical departure from the present *system* to one in which selection is made the responsibility of the Supreme Court. I am aware of the predictable reluctance of the Senate and the president to give up political power but that should not preclude discussion and debate over the merits of the proposal.

NOTES

Notes

Chapter I. An Overview

1. Joseph Story, *Commentaries on the Constitution of the United States* (Boston: Little, Brown, 1833), sec. 1599.

2. *Ibid.*, footnote 2.

3. 26 Stat. 826 (1891).

4. 62 Stat. 895 (1948).

5. 28 U.S.C. 44 and 133.

6. Burke Shartel, "Federal Judges—Appointment, Supervision, and Removal—Some Possibilities under the Constitution," 28 *Michigan Law Review*, 485, 500–501, 723, 870 (1930).

7. See Collins v. United States, 14 Ct. Cls. 568 (1878). Shartel found support for his position in United States v. Germaine, 99 U.S. 508 (1878); see Shartel, "Federal Judges," pp. 500–501. But for a pithy comment suggesting the difficulty of relying on that decision for such purpose see Edward S. Corwin, *The President: Office and Powers* (New York: New York University Press, 1957, 4th ed.), pp. 365–366.

8. Article I, sec. 8, para. 9, and Article III, sec. 1.

9. For one such speculation, see Joseph P. Harris, *The Advice and Consent of the Senate* (Berkeley: University of California Press, 1953), p. 15. Harris suggests that the courts would leave it to Congress to decide: "The decision concerning which officers should be appointed by the President and confirmed by the Senate is essentially political in character and has appropriately been left to legislative rather than judicial determination." But the fact remains that the courts have never dealt squarely with the issue and, consequently, have never clearly indicated that they would leave it to Congress to decide whether federal judges are "inferior" or "other" officers if the question were presented to them in an appropriate case.

10. *Ibid.*, pp. 17–35, and Charles E. Morganston, *The Appointing and Re-*

moval Power of the President, S. Rept. 172, 70 Cong. 2 sess. (1929), pp. 1–13.

11. Harris, *The Advice and Consent of the Senate*, pp. 215–237, and George H. Haynes, *The Senate of the United States* (New York: Russell, 1960 reissue), Vol. II, pp. 736–748.

12. 93 *Congressional Record* 7991 (1947).

13. Dooley was confirmed. See *ibid.*, p. 8421. Also, F. Roy Yoke's appointment as collector of internal revenue for West Virginia was confirmed in 1938 although Senator Holt of West Virginia protested that he was personally obnoxious. See 83 *Congressional Record* 319–326 (1938).

14. Lawrence E. Walsh, "The Federal Judiciary," 43 *Journal of the American Judicature Society* 155 (1960).

15. Harris, *The Advice and Consent of the Senate*, p. 224.

16. *Ibid.*

17. *Ibid.*, pp. 40–41.

18. *Ibid.*, pp. 90–92 and 93–98.

19. *Ibid.*, pp. 91–92 and 228–237.

20. 97 *Congressional Record* 12838 (1951).

21. Harris, *The Advice and Consent of the Senate*, pp. 321–324.

22. Evan Haynes, *Selection and Tenure of Judges* (Newark: National Conference of Judicial Councils, 1944), p. 23.

23. Harris, *The Advice and Consent of the Senate*, p. 380.

24. *Ibid.*, pp. 91, 96, 317–318.

25. Dean Acheson, *Morning and Noon* (Boston: Houghton Mifflin, 1965), p. 212.

26. 87 *A.B.A. Reports* 601, 610 (1962).

27. Harris, *The Advice and Consent of the Senate*, pp. 255–257.

28. U.S. v. Allocco, 305 F. 2d 704, 712 (1962), *cert. denied*, 371 U.S. 964 (1963).

29. 12 Stat. 646 (1863).

30. 5 U.S.C. 5503. The text of the provision reads: "(a) Payment for services may not be made from the Treasury of the United States to an individual appointed during a recess of the Senate to fill a vacancy in an existing office, if the vacancy existed while the Senate was in session and was by law required to be filled by and with the advice and consent of the Senate, until the appointee has been confirmed by the Senate. This subsection does not apply—(1) if the vacancy arose within 30 days before the end of the session of the Senate; (2) if, at the end of the session, a nomination for the office, other than the nomination of an individual appointed during the preceding recess of the Senate, was pending before the Senate for its advice and consent; or (3) if a nomination for the office was rejected by the Senate within 30 days before the end of the session and an individual other than the one whose nomination was rejected thereafter receives a recess appointment. (b) A nomination to fill a vacancy referred to by . . . (1), (2), or (3) of subsection (a) of this section shall be submitted to the Senate not later than 40 days after the beginning of the next session of the Senate."

31. *Nomination of Irving Ben Cooper*, Hearings before a Subcommittee of the Committee on the Judiciary, United States Senate, 87 Cong. 2 sess. (1962).

32. Interestingly enough, one of the New York senators, Keating, was a member of the Judiciary Committee. As he saw it, his function as a member of the subcommittee was "not to determine whether Judge Cooper should have been nominated by the President or whether you [the chairman of the subcommittee] or I would have made his selection, but only whether, having been nominated, his selection should be vetoed by the Senate." *Nomination of Irving Ben Cooper*, p. 335.   Although Keating endeavored to be impartial, his line of questioning in the hearings made it appear that he was favorably disposed

to Cooper. Javits submitted a statement to the Judiciary Committee in Cooper's behalf. *Ibid.,* p. 19.

33. *Ibid.,* pp. 41 and 43–51.

34. *Ibid.,* pp. 18–19.

35. *Christian Science Monitor,* July 14, 1961. See also *New York Times,* July 3, 1961.

36. *Christian Science Monitor,* July 14, 1961; *New York Times,* July 3, 1961; *Chicago Daily Tribune,* July 6, 1961.

37. William P. Rogers, "Judicial Appointments in the Eisenhower Administration," 41 *Journal of the American Judicature Society* 40 (1957).

38. Recall how long President Johnson deliberated about elevating Deputy Attorney General Nicholas Katzenbach, a Kennedy appointee, to the post of attorney general. This is discussed more fully in Chapter V on the Johnson administration.

39. 71 A.B.A. Reports (1946).

40. *Nomination of Irving Ben Cooper,* p. 40.

41. *Ibid.,* p. 206.

42. *Ibid.,* pp. 361–367.

43. FBI, *Testimony of the Director on February 3 and February 7, 1950 before the Senate Subcommittee on Appropriations Regarding the 1951 Appropriations Estimate for the Federal Bureau of Investigation* (mimeographed).

44. J. Edgar Hoover, "The Confidential Nature of F.B.I. Reports," 8 *Syracuse Law Review* 2 (1956), p. 3.

45. *Ibid.*

46. James A. Farley, *Behind the Ballots* (New York: Harcourt, Brace, 1938), p. 237.

47. *New York Times,* February 20, 1962, and *Minneapolis Star,* February 20, 1962.

48. Quoted in Walter Murphy and C. Herman Pritchett, *Courts, Judges and Politics* (New York: Random House, 1961), p. 95.

49. For a good account of Chief Justice Taft's activities in pushing judicial candidacies, see Walter F. Murphy, "Chief Justice Taft and the Lower Court Bureaucracy: A Study in Judicial Administration," 24 *Journal of Politics* 453 (1962).

50. *St. Louis Post-Dispatch,* November 26, 1961.

51. *St. Louis Post-Dispatch,* November 30, 1961.

52. James A. Farley, "Why I Broke with Roosevelt," *Collier's,* June 21, 1947, p. 13.

53. *Washington Post,* August 7, 1961. Buttressing Alsop's contention that judgeships are a tradable commodity is the following report from a story written by Willard Edwards for the *Chicago Tribune,* April 24, 1962:

"There was almost unanimous agreement that Dirksen played an indispensable part in rolling up the big Senate vote of 70 to 22 for the bill authorizing a $100,000,000 loan to the United Nations.

"At a subsequent White House meeting, Dirksen asked the President: 'When is Illinois going to get a Republican judge?' 'You're going to get a Republican judge,' replied the President. 'If you want, I'll put that in writing to [Vice-President] Lyndon Johnson.'

"*The exchange was in jest,* but [Senator] Douglas, in lodging his later objection to the timing of the Decker nomination, discovered that the President meant to keep his promise" (emphasis added).

54. See Sheldon Goldman, "Judicial Appointments to the United States Courts of Appeals," *Wisconsin Law Review,* 1967, p. 186.

55. *New York Times,* October 25, 1962.

56. *New York Times,* August 23, 1962.

Chapter II. The Kennedy Administration

1. *Oral Statement of Bernard G. Segal, Chairman, Standing Committee on Federal Judiciary of the American Bar Association, to the House of Delegates of the Association, August 7, 1962* (mimeographed), pp. 1–2.

2. P. O. O'Neil, "No. 2 Man in Washington," *Life*, January 26, 1962, p. 92; R. Manning, "Someone the President Can Talk To," *New York Times Magazine*, May 28, 1961, p. 22; "More Than a Brother," *Time*, February 16, 1962, p. 16; Marquis Childs, "Bobby and the President," *Good Housekeeping*, May 1962, p. 80; "Robert Kennedy Speaks His Mind," *U.S. News*, January 28, 1963, p. 56.

3. *New York Times*, May 20, 1961.

4. Morton A. Kaplan and Nicholas deB. Katzenbach, *The Political Foundations of International Law* (New York: Wiley, 1961).

5. Martin B. Travis, "Book Reviews," 341 *Annals* 113 (1962).

6. Richard A. Falk, "The Reality of International Law," 14 *World Politics* 353, 361 (1962). For a strongly critical review, see 55 *American Political Science Review* 968 (1961).

7. For an accounting of Katzenbach's activities see the *New York Times* reports on the following dates: October 1, 2, 3, 4, 5, 6, and 9, 1962.

8. See Chapter IV on the ABA committee.

9. 85 *A.B.A. Reports* 454 (1960).

10. William P. Rogers, "Judicial Appointments in the Eisenhower Administration," 41 *Journal of the American Judicature Society* 39–40 (1957). Quotations from this article are reprinted by permission.

11. Bernard G. Segal, "Federal Judicial Selection—Progress and the Promise of the Future," 46 *Massachusetts Law Quarterly* 142–143 (1961).

12. *New York Times*, August 8, 1962.

13. 48 *American Bar Association Journal* 980 (1962).

14. *New York Times*, August 31, 1960.

15. Rogers, "Judicial Appointments in the Eisenhower Administration," pp. 40–41.

16. 86 *A.B.A. Reports* 509 (1961).

17. 85 *A.B.A. Reports* 597 (1960).

18. *Ibid.*

19. *Ibid.*, p. 455.

20. *New York Times*, August 31, 1960.

21. 15 *Congressional Quarterly Weekly Report* 1206 (1959).

22. *Federal Courts and Judges*, Hearings before Subcommittee No. 5 of the House Judiciary Committee, 86 Cong. 2 sess. (February 2, 3, and 29, 1960), p. 51. The following is the verbatim exchange between the chairman, Representative Celler, and Deputy Attorney General Walsh on the subject:

"THE CHAIRMAN. Yes, and when you use the term 'Democrat,' I hope you are using the term not in the symbolic sense, namely, Eisenhower Democrats.

"MR. WALSH. Mr. Chairman, I can assure you that when we approach a person seeking him to serve on the bench, we are not going to ask whether he voted for President Eisenhower or for Mr. Stevenson, regardless of which party—

"THE CHAIRMAN. On the other hand, however, we have the right to inquire whether the gentleman is a true Democrat, and I think that consideration is going to be very important, probably it is going to be of paramount importance, because it is the other body [the Senate] which will or will not confirm.

"MR. WALSH. I have no doubt, Mr. Chairman, they will be satisfied, and that everyone who closely watches the administration action which follows this bill, if it is enacted, will be satisfied with the good faith and spirit in which this pledge [to split the appointments] is carried out. There are no weasel words in it."

23. See Annual Report of the ABA Committee on Federal Judiciary, 1961, in 86 *A.B.A. Reports* 503 (1961).

24. *Federal Courts and Judges*, Hearings before Subcommittee No. 5 of the House Judiciary Committee, 87 Cong. 1 sess. (March 1 and 2, 1961).

25. It can be established by consulting *Who's Who* and other references that at least six more were Catholics and one more Jewish. I feel, however, there is significance in a person's willingness or unwillingness to answer a question about his religious affiliation. Should someone who does not identify himself as a Jew or Catholic (or who may not be identified by others as such) be counted as a Jew or Catholic in assaying the effort to achieve *visible* minority representation?

26. Theodore H. White, *The Making of the President 1960* (New York: Pocket Books, 1961), p. 471.

27. *Washington Star*, editorial, March 10, 1963.

28. *New York Times*, March 7, 1963.

29. *New York Times*, March 25, 1962.

Chapter III. The Eisenhower Administration

1. William P. Rogers, "Judicial Appointments in the Eisenhower Administration," 41 *Journal of the American Judicature Society* 38 (1957), pp. 39–40.

2. Dwight D. Eisenhower, *Mandate for Change* (Garden City, N.Y.: Doubleday, copyright 1963), p. 83.

3. For his evidence, note these excerpts from a letter Mr. Miller wrote to me when I asked him to review parts of the book in manuscript:

". . . you state that Presidents Eisenhower and Kennedy were 'very concerned' that 'the quality of appointments made during their incumbency be high.' This, and other statements here and there, gives the impression that their judicial appointments were of much higher quality than, for example, those of Mr. Truman. I believe this gives far greater credit than is deserved. In fact, strange as it may appear, from my files as a member of the ABA Federal Judiciary Committee for the last four years of Mr. Truman's administration and the first four years of Mr. Eisenhower's, as well as from information I gathered after leaving that committee, it is my candid opinion that nationwide Mr. Truman in his last four years had a fair size edge over Mr. Eisenhower's first four years. (I said 'strange as it seems' because Mr. Eisenhower had a far better 'press' than did Mr. Truman, both in the lay press and in that of the organized bar. More of those of the bar interested in the methods by which federal judges were selected were supporters of Mr. Eisenhower as was I than of Mr. Truman.) What with Republican Senators hungry for all patronage possible after so many lean years, with respect to their states, and with Mr. Brownell being about as 'political' in the admittedly highly political office of Attorney General as any modern time Attorney General . . . this was perhaps but to be expected!

"Without the wealth of material which had been available to me as a member of that ABA Committee, I can not be as accurate in making comparisons with the last four years of the Eisenhower administration or with Mr. Kennedy's administration. But Robert Kennedy, for example, had few if any equals in using the Office of the Attorney General for political purposes. . . .

"But back to the last four years of Mr. Truman and the first four years of Mr. Eisenhower: My article in the May, 1959 issue of the ABA Journal, Vol. 45, pp. 445–447, gives certain facets of the comparison for these particular

years. Another analysis, based on my files and using a 'standard' comparable to that used in recent years by the ABA Federal Judiciary Committee, shows:
I. Of Mr. Truman's some 47 appointments who were confirmed during his last 4 years:

Exceptionally Well Qualified	Well Qualified	Qualified	Not Qualified
11	15	19	2

II. Of Mr. Eisenhower's some 82 appointments who were confirmed through November 4, 1955 (the date to which I made a résumé from my files):

Exceptionally Well Qualified	Well Qualified	Qualified	Not Qualified
10	10	49	13

(Although I did not carry forward from November 4, 1955, a résumé in all these categories except those considered 'not qualified,' my files indicate that between November 4, 1955, and the end of my term on the ABA Federal Judiciary Committee, two more of Mr. Eisenhower's appointments were considered 'not qualified' and four others were considered very marginal.)"

4. Eisenhower, *Mandate for Change*, pp. 226-227.

5. *Ibid.*, p. 230.

6. Richard E. Neustadt, *Presidential Power* (New York: Wiley, 1960).

7. Eisenhower, *Mandate for Change*, p. 135.

8. Anthony Lewis, "Close-Up of Our Lawyer in Chief," *New York Times Magazine*, April 6, 1958, p. 22.

9. For Rogers's own brief but uninterpolated description of the process, see Rogers, "Judicial Appointments in the Eisenhower Administration."

10. See above, p. 39.

11. For a full discussion of the role of the Committee on Federal Judiciary, see Chapter IV.

12. 347 U.S. 483 (1954).

13. 354 U.S. 449 (1957).

14. Lawrence E. Walsh, "The Federal Judiciary," 43 *Journal of the American Judicature Society* 155 (1960).

15. *Ibid.* He subsequently wrote another article which is also relevant. See "Two Basic Steps toward the Better Selection of Federal Judges," 12 *American University Law Review* 14 (1963).

16. See the following written by Stuart S. Nagel: "Judicial Backgrounds and Criminal Cases," 53 *Journal of Criminal Law* 333 (1962); "Ethnic Affiliations and Judicial Propensities," 24 *Journal of Politics* 92 (1962); "Judicial Characteristics and Judicial Decision-Making," Northwestern University Ph.D. dissertation in political science (1961); "Off-the-Bench Judicial Attitudes," in Glendon Schubert, ed., *Judicial Decision-Making* (Glencoe: Free Press, 1963), pp. 29–47; "Political Party Affiliation and Judges' Decisions," 55 *American Political Science Review* 843 (1961); "Political Parties and Judicial Review," 11 *Journal of Public Law* 328 (1962). See also Glendon Schubert, *The Judicial Mind* (Evanston: Northwestern University Press, 1965); Joel Grossman, "Social Backgrounds and Judicial Decision-Making," 79 *Harvard Law Review* 1551 (1966); Sidney S. Ulmer, "The Political Party Variable in the Michigan Supreme Court," 11 *Journal of Public Law* 352 (1962); Joel Grossman, "Social Backgrounds and Judicial Decisions: Notes for a Theory," 29 *Journal of Politics* 334 (1967). But compare with Sheldon Goldman, "Voting Behavior on the U.S. Courts of Appeals, 1961–1964," 60 *American Political Science Review* 374 (1966), and "Conflict and Consensus in the United States Courts of Appeals," *Wisconsin Law Review*, 1968, p. 460.

17. Sheldon Goldman, "Characteristics of Eisenhower and Kennedy Appointees to the Lower Federal Courts," 18 *Western Political Quarterly* 755 (1965), and his Ph.D. dissertation, "Politics, Judges and the Administration of Justice: The Backgrounds, Recruitment and Decisional Tendencies of the Judges on the United States Courts of Appeals, 1961–4," Harvard University (1965).

18. Jack Peltason, *Fifty-Eight Lonely Men* (New York: Harcourt, 1961), p. 46.

19. *Ibid.*, pp. 46–51.

20. *Ibid.*, p. 55.

21. "Judicial Performance in the Fifth Circuit," 73 *Yale Law Journal* 90 (1963).

22. Sidney C. Mize, Mississippi; and Harry J. Lemley, Arkansas (not in Fifth Circuit). See *ibid.*, pp. 90–92 and 98n.

23. Daniel H. Thomas, Alabama; Frank M. Scarlett, Georgia; and Seybourn H. Lynne, Alabama. See *ibid.*, pp. 97–98 and 114n.

24. William H. Cox, Mississippi; J. Robert Elliott, Georgia; E. Gordon West, Louisiana; and Clarence W. Allgood, Alabama. See *ibid.*, pp. 93, 96–97, 101, 102, and 106n.

25. Harlan H. Grooms, Alabama; Frank M. Johnson, Alabama; William A. Boone, Georgia; Benjamin C. Dawkins, Louisiana; Edwin F. Hunter, Louisiana; and Claude F. Clayton, Mississippi.

26. Clarence W. Allgood, Alabama; J. Robert Elliott, Georgia; Lewis R. Morgan, Georgia; Robert A. Ainsworth, Louisiana; E. Gordon West, Louisiana; Frank B. Ellis, Louisiana; Richard J. Putnam, Louisiana; William H. Cox, Mississippi.

27. Elbert P. Tuttle, John R. Brown, and John M. Wisdom. See "Judicial Performance in the Fifth Circuit," pp. 120 and 121n.

28. Ben F. Cameron. See *ibid.*

29. Warren L. Jones. See *ibid.*

30. Harlan H. Grooms, Alabama; J. Smith Henley, Arkansas; Emmett C. Choats, Florida; Benjamin C. Dawkins, Louisiana; and Joe E. Estes, Texas. See Peltason, *Fifty-Eight Lonely Men*, pp. 84, 87, 115, 133, 140–144.

31. Ben F. Cameron. See *ibid.*, p. 26.

32. Frank M. Johnson, Alabama; William A. Bootle, Georgia; William E. Miller, Tennessee; Walter E. Hoffman, Virginia. See *ibid.*, pp. 11, 12, 23–27, 77, 113–114, and 127–128.

33. Simon E. Sobeloff, Fourth Circuit; Clement Haynesworth, Fourth Circuit; Herbert S. Boreman, Fourth Circuit; Elbert P. Tuttle, Fifth Circuit; John R. Brown, Fifth Circuit; Warren L. Jones, Fifth Circuit; John Wisdom, Fifth Circuit. See *ibid.*, pp. 23–27.

34. Mary Hannah Curzan, *A Case Study in the Selection of Federal Judges in the Fifth Circuit, 1953–1963* (Ann Arbor: University Microfilms, 1968), p. 27.

35. *Ibid.*, p. 36.

36. *Ibid.*, p. 60; see further discussion on pp. 60–62.

Chapter IV. The American Bar Association Committee

1. As Ernest C. Friesen, Jr., who played a leading role in the appointment process and about whom much will be said later in this chapter, observed in a letter to me:

"I feel constrained to observe that no one influence can ever be set forth as decisive in the selection process. The appointment of federal judges is a complex process and no two ever follow the same pattern. We sometimes push harder to get a candidate found 'qualified' than others. The ABA sometimes presses harder to investigate in detail for one candidate than another. The pressures on the parts of the Quadrangle vary in each case with differing amounts of effort expended toward different results. The result may well turn on the degree of resistance encountered in a particular quarter rather than on the absolute merits. The lack of an objective standard makes it possible to exert and resist many pressures that would be less effective in a more objective system."

2. Joel Grossman, *Lawyers and Judges* (New York: Wiley, 1965), pp. 49–58.

3. 71 *A.B.A. Reports* 330–331 (1946). For background, see Grossman, *Lawyers and Judges*, pp. 59–64.

4. 72 *A.B.A. Reports* 411 (1947).

5. *Ibid.*, pp. 411–412.

6. 33 *A.B.A. Journal* 191 (1947).

7. *Ibid.*

8. *Ibid.*

9. 72 *A.B.A. Reports* 256–257 (1947).

10. *Ibid.*, pp. 258–259.

11. 74 *A.B.A. Reports* 528–529 (1949).

12. Grossman, *Lawyers and Judges*, p. 66.

13. *Ibid.*

14. *Ibid.*, pp. 68–69.

15. 77 *A.B.A. Reports* 215 (1952); Grossman, *Lawyers and Judges,* pp. 69–70. Also see Bernard G. Segal, "Federal Judicial Selection—Progress and Promise of the Future," 46 *Massachusetts Law Quarterly* 139 (1961); Edward J. Fox, Jr., "The Selection of Federal Judges: The Work of the Federal Judiciary Committee," 43 *A.B.A. Journal* 685 (1957).

16. *Nation*, December 8, 1951, p. 492.

17. For a good short account of these events, see 8 *Congressional Quarterly Almanac* 263–268 (1952).

18. Grossman, *Lawyers and Judges*, p. 70.

19. *Ibid.,* p. 71.

20. *Ibid.*

21. Fox, "The Selection of Federal Judges," p. 686.

22. *New York Times,* June 22, 1963.

23. *On the Nomination of Francis X. Morrissey of Massachusetts to Be U.S. District Judge for the District of Massachusetts,* Hearings before the Senate Subcommittee of the Committee on the Judiciary, 89 Cong. 1 sess. (October 12, 1965), p. 90.

24. *Ibid.*, p. 89.

25. *Ibid.*, p. 92.

26. *Oral Reply of Lawrence Walsh to the House of Delegates,* Mid-Year Meetings of the American Bar Association (Chicago, 1959; mimeographed), p. 17.

27. *Transcript of Remarks of Hon. Byron R. White before the National Conference of Bar Presidents* (Chicago, February 17, 1962; mimeographed), p. 3.

28. Segal, "Federal Judicial Selection," pp. 143–144.

29. See above, p. 101; see also Grossman, *Lawyers and Judges,* p. 77.

30. "Report of the Standing Committee on Federal Judiciary," 85 *A.B.A. Reports* 453 (1960).

31. *Ibid.*, p. 452.

32. *Ibid.*, p. 454.

33. Segal, "Federal Judicial Selection," p. 146.

34. *Ibid.*, p. 147.

35. *Response of Hon. Nicholas deB. Katzenbach, the Deputy Attorney General of the United States, to Oral Statement of Bernard G. Segal, Chairman,*

218

Standing Committee on Federal Judiciary, House of Delegates of the American Bar Association (San Francisco, August 7, 1962; mimeographed), pp. 3–5.

36. *New York Times,* August 31, 1960.

37. Grossman, *Lawyers and Judges,* pp. 100–101.

38. Segal, "Federal Judicial Selection," pp. 147–148.

39. For a sampling of such editorial approval, see the committee's report of 1961, 86 *A.B.A. Reports* 509–510 (1961).

40. *Procedures for the Removal, Retirement, and Disciplining of Unfit Federal Judges,* Hearings before the Senate Committee on the Judiciary, Subcommittee on Improvement in Judicial Machinery, 89 Cong. 2 sess. (February 15, 1966), p. 48.

41. Grossman, *Lawyers and Judges,* p. 137n.

42. 87 *A.B.A. Reports* 606 (1962).

43. 86 *A.B.A. Reports* 513 (1961).

44. 90 *A.B.A. Reports* 317 (1965).

45. 91 *A.B.A. Reports* 159 (1966).

46. Harold W. Chase and Allen H. Lerman, eds., *Kennedy and the Press* (New York: Crowell, 1965), p. 521.

47. 91 *A.B.A. Reports* 157–158 (1966).

48. *National College of State Trial Judges* (announcement; National Conference of State Trial Judges, 1966), p. 2.

49. *Ibid.,* p. 4.

50. 91 *A.B.A. Reports* 487 (1966).

51. *Washington Post,* May 19, 1966.

52. 94 *A.B.A. Reports* 566–467 (1969).

53. Grossman, *Lawyers and Judges,* pp. 82–92.

54. *On the Nomination of Francis X. Morrissey,* pp. 46–48.

55. *Ibid.,* p. 70.

56. *Ibid.,* pp. 90–91.

57. *Ibid.,* p. 49.

58. *Ibid.,* p. 76.

59. *Ibid.,* p. 49.

60. 87 *A.B.A. Reports* 602 (1962).

61. Grossman, *Lawyers and Judges,* pp. 108–111. Bancroft C. Henderson and T. C. Sinclair, *The Selection of Judges in Texas* (Houston: Public Affairs Research Center, University of Houston, 1965), p. 42.

62. *On the Nomination of Francis X. Morrissey,* p. 82.

63. *Ibid.,* p. 91.

64. 87 *A.B.A. Reports* 604 (1962).

65. Segal, "Federal Judicial Selection," p. 142.

66. *Ibid.,* p. 143.

67. 94 *A.B.A. Reports* 466–467 (1969).

68. 111 *Congressional Record* 27935–27936 (1965).

69. Grossman, *Lawyers and Judges,* pp. 88–90.

70. Edward W. Kuhn, "American Bar Association," 33 *Tennessee Law Review* 6 (1965).

71. John R. Schmidhauser, *The Supreme Court* (New York: Holt, Rinehart and Winston, 1960), pp. 77–78.

72. 90 *A.B.A. Reports* 104 (1965).

73. 88 *A.B.A. Reports* 614–615 (1963).

74. Philip A. Hart, "Can Federal Legislation Affecting Consumers' Economic Interests Be Enacted?" 64 *Michigan Law Review* 1266 (1966).

75. 91 *A.B.A. Reports* 488 (1966).

Chapter V. The Johnson Administration

1. The six were David Rabinovitz (district of Wisconsin); George C. Edwards, Jr. (Sixth Circuit); Charles H. Tenney (southern district of New York); A. Leon Higginbotham (eastern district of Pennsylvania); Spottswood Robinson (district of District of Columbia); and John M. Davis (eastern district of Pennsylvania). Homer Thornberry was nominated for the western district of Texas.

2. Harold W. Chase and A. H. Lerman, eds., *Kennedy and the Press* (New York: Crowell, 1965), p. 521.

3. See Jerry Landauer, "Judgeships and Politics," *Wall Street Journal*, July 11, 1966; editorial, *St. Paul Dispatch*, May 5, 1965; news items in *Minneapolis Tribune*, May 1, 1965, and *New York Times*, March 21, 1965.

4. Editorial, *St. Paul Dispatch*, May 5, 1965.

5. 89 *A.B.A. Reports* 188 (1964).

6. Quoted in *New York Times*, March 21, 1965.

7. *Ibid.*

8. For an excellent detailed account of the politics of recent appointments to federal judgeships in Wisconsin, see Landauer, "Judgeships and Politics."

9. *On the Nomination of George Clifton Edwards, Jr. to Be United States Circuit Judge, Sixth Circuit*, Hearings before the Senate Committee on the Judiciary, 88 Cong. 1 sess. (1963), pp. 1, 47–48.

10. *Ibid.*, pp. 13–19.

11. *Ibid.*, p. 44.

12. *Ibid.*, p. 45.

13. 89 *A.B.A. Reports* 483 (1964).

14. *New York Times,* June 19, 1965.

15. *Ibid.*

16. *Ibid.* Senator Wayne Morse (D.-Ore.) inserted a full dossier on Coleman's segregationist positions into the *Congressional Record*. 111 *Congressional Record* 18235–18241 (1965).

17. *Ibid.*

18. *New York Times*, July 13, 1965. In 1929, however, Attorney General William D. Mitchell had spoken during an executive session in support of the appointment by President Hoover of Albert L. Watson to a district judgeship in Pennsylvania. In addition Attorney General Herbert Brownell, Jr., sent a statement which was read to the committee by an assistant in support of President Eisenhower's appointment of Simon E. Sobeloff to the Court of Appeals in the Fourth Circuit. *Ibid.*

19. *On the Nomination of James P. Coleman of Mississippi, to Be U.S. Circuit Judge for the Fifth Circuit*, Hearings before the Senate Committee on the Judiciary, 89 Cong. 1 sess. (1965), p. 4.

20. *Ibid.*, pp. 17–119.

21. *Ibid.*, p. 48.

22. *Ibid.*, p. 128.

23. *Ibid.*, pp. 128–129.

24. 111 *Congressional Record* 18243 (1965).

25. See, for example, *New York Times*, June 30, 1965, and July 3, 1965.

26. *Washington Post*, October 1, 1965.

27. A *Los Angeles Times* (September 30, 1965) story stated:

"President Johnson informed Democratic congressional leaders Wednesday that he will stand behind the controversial nomination of Francis X. Morrissey.
. . .

"Mr. Johnson reportedly believes . . . that the late President made a private commitment to his father [Joseph P. Kennedy] to nominate Morrissey [for the judgeship] after the 1964 election.

"The President is said to feel that he should move forward with the nomination out of respect for his predecessor and as a special favor to [former] Ambassador Kennedy."

28. *Washington Post,* October 1, 1965.

29. *Washington Post,* October 3, 1965, and *On the Nomination of Francis X. Morrissey of Massachusetts to Be U.S. District Judge for the District of Massachusetts,* Hearings before the Senate Subcommittee of the Committee on the Judiciary, 89 Cong. 1 sess. (October 12, 1965), pp. 11 and 16.

30. *Washington Post,* September 27 and 29, 1965.

31. Quoted in *Washington Post,* September 29, 1965.

32. *Ibid.*

33. *On the Nomination of Francis X. Morrissey,* pp. 31–38.

34. *Washington Post,* October 3, 1965.

35. *On the Nomination of Francis X. Morrissey,* pp. 45–48.

36. *Ibid.,* pp. 56–66 (testimony of Albert E. Jenner). For Morrissey's version of these events, see *ibid.,* pp. 98–103.

37. *Ibid.,* pp. 55–66.

38. *Ibid.,* p. 59.

39. *Ibid.,* pp. 101 and 103.

40. *Washington Post,* October 16, 1965. See also *Washington Post,* October 15, 1965.

41. *Washington Post,* October 16, 1965.

42. *Ibid.*

43. Fred Graham, "F.B.I. Report Backs Morrissey's Story of Stay in Georgia," *New York Times,* October 19, 1965.

44. 21 *Congressional Quarterly Almanac* 1432 (1965).

45. Tom Wicker, "The Morrissey Affair," *New York Times,* October 22, 1965.

46. 111 *Congressional Record* 27935–27936 (1965).

47. *Boston Herald,* October 22, 1965, and *Washington Post,* October 22, 1965.

48. 111 *Congressional Record* 27935–27936 (1965).

49. *Ibid.*

50. *Ibid.*

51. *New York Times,* November 6, 1965.

52. 111 *Congressional Record* 27935–27936 (1965).

53. *Boston Herald,* October 22, 1965.

54. *New York Times,* November 6, 1965.

55. John P. MacKenzie assessed the damage accurately in a perceptive post-battle account in the *Washington Post* (October 25, 1965):

"Senator Edward M. Kennedy (D.-Mass.), Morrissey's sponsor, suffered a variety of injuries. Only by dropping the fight in the showdown Senate session Thursday did he cut his losses in strained relationships and political I.O.U.'s. His allies were grateful and they warmed to his emotional withdrawal speech, but their gratitude was of the it-feels-so-good-when-the-beating-stops variety.

"Only the Senator's reputation for political loyalty was enhanced. The affair did nothing to boost his influence at the White House, for he risked injuring President Johnson. His ability to concede defeat showed a new phase of his political maturity, but he did lose. . . . His standing in Boston may actually have improved, but in the last analysis he did dump Morrissey.

"Senator Robert F. Kennedy (D.-N.Y.), who dispensed more Federal judicial appointments than any Attorney General in history, did no good for his own legal reputation by trying to rescue a nomination he never consummated while at the Justice Department.

"President Johnson who nominated Morrissey after John F. Kennedy could not or would not bring himself to do it, was injured in a vital area—pride in the quality of executive appointments. . . .

"The American Bar Association is not unscathed in victory. Handicapped by its own mechanical standards for qualifications, the ABA failed to persuade politicians at the nominating and early confirmation stages. It blocked confirmation only by taking off the gloves with the Kennedys, by dredging records and by testimony off-limits in paneled law office waiting rooms.

"The ABA entered the thicket without hope of victory but with determination to frame an issue for future appointments to the Federal bench. It ended up playing a fierce political game and the victory may have been costly in terms of the prestige and disinterestedness of its judgment on nominees.

"In the Senate itself, only the unanimously opposed Republicans and their leader Everett M. Dirksen of Illinois, seem to have emerged free of scratches.

"But Senate Democrats will be licking their wounds for a long time. The nomination was exposed to public view just long enough so that Senators could not avoid looking at it. Some of them were revolted, and others who have made lofty statements on the need for a strong judiciary were in an embarrassing predicament.

"Perhaps the biggest loser in the whole affair is Attorney General Nicholas deB. Katzenbach, whose summary of the last-minute FBI check into the Georgia incident carried so little weight on Capitol Hill. Instead of rehabilitating the nominee and the defunct Athens, Ga. 'law school' Morrissey attended, Katzenbach's action brought the charges that the FBI had been politically invoked.

"Katzenbach, who only a year ago was Bobby Kennedy's indispensable deputy at Justice, found his name used in ardent support of the nomination. In vouching stoutly for the credibility of the nominee, Katzenbach left a cloud over the investigative process that screens nominees for high office."

56. *New York Times,* August 4, 1968.

57. Harold B. Sanders, James P. Alger, David G. Bress, William M. Byrne, and Cecil F. Poole.

58. *New York Times*, January 28, 1969.

59. *Ibid.*

60. *Ibid.*

61. *New York Times,* June 28, 1965.

62. *Ibid.*

63. *New York Times,* February 14, 1965.

Chapter VI. Conclusions

1. *Washington Post*, September 18, 1964.

2. Herbert Brownell, "Too Many Judges Are Political Hacks," *Saturday Evening Post,* April 18, 1964, p. 10.

3. *Ibid.*

4. Cf. the more detailed comparison of the rating of federal and state judges by Texas lawyers done in the exceptionally fine work of Bancroft C. Henderson and T. C. Sinclair, *The Selection of Judges in Texas* (Houston: Public Affairs Research Center, University of Houston, 1965). But note that they write that "62 per cent of the lawyers in the sample said their practices were non-trial . . ." (p. 75). Their results were not so clearly in favor of the federal courts as I indicate, but they conclude: "Thus in general the federal courts occupy positions of greater prestige than do the state courts" (p. 76).

222

5. *Judicial Fitness,* Hearings before the Senate Committee on the Judiciary, 89 Cong. 2 sess. (February 15, 1966), pp. 3–4. For difficulties in impeaching even corrupt judges, see Joseph Borkin, *The Corrupt Judge* (New York: Potter, 1962), pp. 189–204.

6. 28 U.S. Code 332.

7. 28 U.S. Code 372(b).

8. *Judicial Fitness.*

9. 28 U.S. Code 332.

10. 398 U.S. 74 (1970). Rehearing denied, 399 U.S. 937 (1970).

11. 398 U.S. 137 (1970). For a good account of the Chandler controversy, see James E. Clayton, "A U.S. Judge Deprived of His Gavel," *Washington Post,* January 2, 1966.

12. *Judicial Fitness,* pp. 15–16.

13. *Ibid.* See especially the testimony of Bernard G. Segal, pp. 24–51. See also *Retirement of Justices and Judges,* Hearings before the House Committee on the Judiciary, 91 Cong., 2 sess. (1970); and an excellent article by Judge Roger J. Traynor, "Who Can Best Judge the Judges," 53 *Virginia Law Review* 1266 (1967).

14. J. Earl Major, "Why Not Mandatory Retirement for Federal Judges?" 52 *A.B.A. Journal* 29 (1966).

15. Dwight D. Eisenhower, "Let's Make Government Work Better!" *Reader's Digest,* January 1967, p. 64.

16. *New York Times,* March 19, 1966.

17. Joel Grossman, *Lawyers and Judges* (New York: Wiley, 1965), p. 221.

18. *Ibid.,* pp. 196–221.

19. Ben R. Miller, "The Selection of the Federal Judiciary," 45 *A.B.A. Journal* 446 (1959).

20. Grossman, *Lawyers and Judges,* p. 219.

21. See above, p. 155.

22. John Stennis, "Federal Judiciary Selection," 44 *A.B.A. Journal* 1179 (1958).

23. Miller, "The Selection of the Federal Judiciary," pp. 445–446.

24. See above, Chapter IV.

25. Grossman, *Lawyers and Judges,* pp. 219–221 and 139. Felix Frankfurter, "The Supreme Court in the Mirror of the Justices," 105 *University of Pennsylvania Law Review* 791–793 (1956–57); John Schmidhauser, "Stare Decisis, Dissent, and the Background of the Justices of the Supreme Court of the United States," 14 *University of Toronto Law Review* 194 (1962).

26. Stennis, "Federal Judiciary Selection"; Miller, "The Selection of the Federal Judiciary"; and Charles J. Bloch, "The Selection of Federal Judges," 41 *A.B.A. Journal* 510 (1955).

27. Stennis, "Federal Judiciary Selection," p. 1180.

28. Royce H. Savage, "Justice for a New Era," 49 *Journal of the American Judicature Society* 126 (1964).

29. Elmo B. Hunter, "A Missouri Judge Views Judicial Selection and Tenure," 48 *Journal of the American Judicature Society* 126 (1964).

30. Savage, "Justice for a New Era," p. 48.

31. "Coming—Merit Selection of Federal Judges," 44 *Journal of the American Judicature Society* 32 (1965).

32. 112 *Congressional Record* 14774 (1966)

33. *Ibid.,* p. 14775. See also Hugh Scott, "The Selection of Federal Judges," 24 *Washington and Lee Law Review* 205 (1967). For a variation on the Scott proposal, see Sheldon Goldman, "The Views of a Political Scientist: Political Selection of Federal Judges and the Proposal in a Judicial Service Commission," 52 *Judicature* 94 (1968).

34. As quoted in Richard A. Watson, Randal G. Downing, and Frederick G. Spiegel, "Bar Politics, Judicial Selection and the Representation of Social Interests," 61 *American Political Science Review* 54 (1967). See also the fine study done by Watson and Downing, *The Politics of the Bench and the Bar* (New York: Wiley, 1969).

35. Watson, Downing, and Spiegel, "Bar Politics, Judicial Selection and the Representation of Social Interests," p. 69.

36. *Ibid.*, p. 70.

37. *Ibid.*, pp. 63–67.

38. Reinhold Niebuhr, *The Children of Light and the Children of Darkness* (New York: Scribner's, 1960), p. 118.

39. See the quotation from Alexander Hamilton in Chapter I, p. 6 above.

40. Henry Hart, "The Time Chart of the Justices," 73 *Harvard Law Review* 84 (1960). But see also Thurman Arnold, "Professor Hart's Theology," 73 *Harvard Law Review* 1298 (1960).

INDEX

Index

Acheson, Dean, 12
Age: factor in judicial selection in Eisenhower administration, 68, 92, 101, 112–113; factor in judicial selection in Kennedy administration, 68, 69; criterion of ABA Committee on Federal Judiciary, 68, 155; comparison of Truman, Eisenhower, and Kennedy appointments, 113; comparison of Eisenhower, Kennedy, and Johnson appointments, 168, 179; of sitting judges, 189, 190, 191
Ainsworth, Robert A., 162, 217n26
Alger, James P., 222n57
Allgood, Clarence W., 83, 85, 217n24, 217n26
Almond, J. Lindsay, 46–47, 87
Alsop, Joseph, 41–42, 213n53
American Bar Association (ABA), 3, 66, 106, 122, 138, 205: relation with Committee on Federal Judiciary, 20, 121–131 *passim*, 146, 159—*see also* ABA Special Committee on Federal Judiciary and ABA Standing Committee on Federal Judiciary; and Cooper nomination, 22–23; and bipartisanship, 71, 73; and Eisenhower administration, 90, 91; and Republicans, 124; and Democrats, 124–125; and Truman, 125; stand on public issues, 145, 160–161; and truth-in-packaging proposal, 160–

161; and Senate Judiciary Committee, 158; political nature of, 160–161; and Judicial Service Commission, 201; and Morrissey nomination, 222n55
  Board of Governors, 122, 123, 124, 126, 144, 159
  House of Delegates, 28, 48, 58, 70, 121, 126, 159, 160, 161: on bipartisanship, 73, 131; relation with ABA Committee on Federal Judiciary, 121–131 *passim*
American Bar Association Journal, 70
ABA Special Committee on Civil Rights and Racial Unrest, 160
ABA Special Committee on Federal Judiciary: history of, 20, 121–124; power to promote nominations, 121, 122–123; and Senate Judiciary Committee, 122; interest in establishing law to set qualifications for judgeships, 123, 125. *See also* ABA Standing Committee on Federal Judiciary
ABA Special Committee on Non-Partisan Selection of the Federal Judiciary, 73
ABA Standing Committee on Federal Judiciary: on bipartisanship, 13, 73, 75, 131–132; relation with ABA, 20, 121–131 *passim*, 146, 159; origin of, 20, 124; and Senate Judiciary Com-

227

Miller, Ben R.: on Eisenhower and Truman administrations, 91, 215–216n3; on partisan nature of appointments, 195–196; on prior experience of judges, 198; concern over role of Justice Department, 199; on Herbert Brownell, Jr., 215n3
Miller, William E., 217n32
Milwaukee Sentinel, 166
Minority group representation on bench: as selection consideration, 33; and Kennedy administration, 78–80, 215n25; and Eisenhower administration, 93
Missouri Plan, 200–204 *passim*
Mitchell, John N., 146, 180–181
Mitchell, William D., 11–12, 220n18
Mize, Sidney C., 217n22
Mondale, Walter F., 172
Moore, Leonard, 39
Morgan, Lewis R., 162, 217n26
Morris, Earl, 145
Morris, Newbold, 126
Morrissey, Francis X., 85, 145, 147, 149, 158, 169, 221–222n55: connection with Kennedy family, 17, 173; and Johnson administration, 138, 170, 177; and Meserve, 152, 153; and ABA Committee on Federal Judiciary, 174–176 *passim*; Senate Judiciary Committee hearings on, 174–177 *passim*; residency in Georgia, 175–176; FBI report on, 176, 177
Morse, Wayne, 172, 220n16
Motley, Constance B., 163
Moynahan, Bernard T., 83

Nation, 125–126
NAACP, 21, 81
National College of State Trial Judges, 139–140
National Conference of Bar Association Presidents, 149
Negroes: among Kennedy appointments, 21, 78, 79; and Kennedy administration, 80, 81, 82, 117, 118; and Eisenhower administration, 93, 117, 118
Nelson, Gaylord, 172
Neuberger, Maurine, 172
New York Herald Tribune, 174
New York State Bar Association, 123
New York Times: on Eisenhower administration, 13; on Kennedy administration, 88; on Rogers, 96; profile of Coleman, 170–171; on Johnson, 180; on Johnson's appointment of Katzenbach, 182–183
Niebuhr, Reinhold, 204
Nixon, Richard, 180: and bipartisanship, 74, 132; and Rogers, 96; on withdrawal of Johnson's end of term nominations, 181
Nixon administration: and ABA Committee on Federal Judiciary, 146
Nuremberg Court, 12

O'Brien, Lawrence F.: role in appointment process, 52–54 *passim*; and Kennedy campaign, 54
O'Daniel, Wilbert, 8
O'Donnell, Kenneth: role in appointment process, 53; and Kennedy campaign, 54
Orrick, William H., 65–66

Packaging: as presidential strategy, 33–34; and Kennedy administration, 49, 82–83, 85–86
Partisanship, 26–29, 30–31: history of in appointments, 71, 195–196. *See also* Bipartisanship; Party affiliation
Party affiliation: issue of and Kennedy administration, 71–78; of Harding, Coolidge, Hoover, F. Roosevelt, Truman, and Eisenhower appointees compared, 72; of Truman, Eisenhower, and Kennedy appointees compared, 112; of judges during Eisenhower administration, 132; of ABA committee members, 150–151; of Eisenhower, Kennedy, and Johnson appointees compared, 179
Patterson, Robert, 12
Peck, John W., 162
Peltason, John: study of southern federal judges and school desegregation, 115–117
Perry, Samuel, 30
Personal Data Questionnaire, 142
Persons, Wilton, 102
Political Foundations of International Law, The, 56
Political philosophy of judicial candidates: Kennedy administration interest in, 80–82; Eisenhower administration interest in, 102, 104–105,

State tradition: as selection factor,
32–33

Stennis, John: on standards for appointment to courts of appeals, 198;
concern over role of Justice Department, 199

Stevenson, Adlai E., 72

Story, Joseph: interpretation of Constitution, 4–5

Symington, Stuart, 39, 100

Taft, Robert A., 98, 99, 100: and
Eisenhower nomination fight, 72,
96

Taft, William H., 213n49

Tamm, Edward Allen, 162

Tate, S. Shephard, 167

Tavares, C. Nils, 76, 78, 83

Templar, George, 76, 78, 83

Tennessee Bar Association, 167

Tenney, Charles H., 220n1

Tenure of office: Eisenhower on federal judges, 95, 194; Rogers on
federal judges, 103; of ABA committee chairman, 133; of ABA committee
members, 151, 152; and ages of sitting judges, 189, 191; judicial retirement proposals, 194; Earl Warren on federal judges, 194

Thornberry, Homer, 165, 220n1: ABA
rating of, 162, 163

Thomas, Daniel H., 217n23

Treasury Department: and recess appointments, 15, 212n30; and Tax
Court judgeships, 49

Truman, Harry S., 10, 145: controversy with Douglas over appointments, 10, 11; and public opinion,
91, 215n3; and ABA, 125; and resignation of McGrath, 126

Truman administration: number of
court vacancies during compared to
Eisenhower and Kennedy administrations, 48; and bipartisanship,
112; and delay tactic, 115; charges
against Justice Department, 125–
126; and ABA Committee on Federal
Judiciary, 127; and partisan appointments, 195

Appointees: party affiliation of,
72; prior experience of, 110, 111;
age of, 113; civil rights record of,
117; ABA committee ratings of compared to Eisenhower appointees,
215–216n3

Truth-in-Packaging Bill, 160–161

Tuttle, Elbert P., 118, 217n27, 217n33

Tydings, Joseph D.: and Coleman
nomination, 172; and Morrissey
nomination, 175, 176; on impeachment of judges, 191–192; and hearings on disability of judges, 192,
193, 194

Tydings committee: hearings on disability of judges, 192, 193, 194

Tyler, Harold R., 76, 78, 83

Udall committee: on congressional
and judicial salaries, 150

United Auto Workers, 166

U.S. circuit courts, see U.S. courts of
appeals

U.S. Congress, see Congress; House of
Representatives; House committees;
Senate; Senate committees

U.S. Constitution, see Constitution

U.S. Court of Claims: description of,
viii; number of judges, ix; and "inferior" or "other" officers controversy, 5; and appointment process,
45–46; ages of sitting judges, 189

U.S. Court of Customs and Patent
Appeals: description of, viii–ix;
number of judges, ix; and appointment process, 45–46; ages of sitting
judges, 189

U.S. Courts Administrative Office,
146

U.S. courts of appeals, 12, 13, 20, 31,
34, 68, 169: description of, viii;
number of judges, ix; for District
of Columbia, 12, 45–46; of Second
Circuit and decision on recess appointments, 15; and appointment
process, 43–45; vacancies in during
Kennedy administration, 49, 50;
comparison of prior experience of
Truman, Eisenhower, and Kennedy
appointees to, 110, 111; comparison
of ages of Truman, Eisenhower, and
Kennedy appointees to, 113; analysis of Fifth Circuit judicial performance in civil rights, 117; ABA
ratings of Johnson nominations to,
162; comparison of prior experience
of Eisenhower, Kennedy, and Johnson appointees to, 179; comparison
of ages of Eisenhower, Kennedy,
and Johnson appointees to, 179;